THE FRAGRANT GARDEN

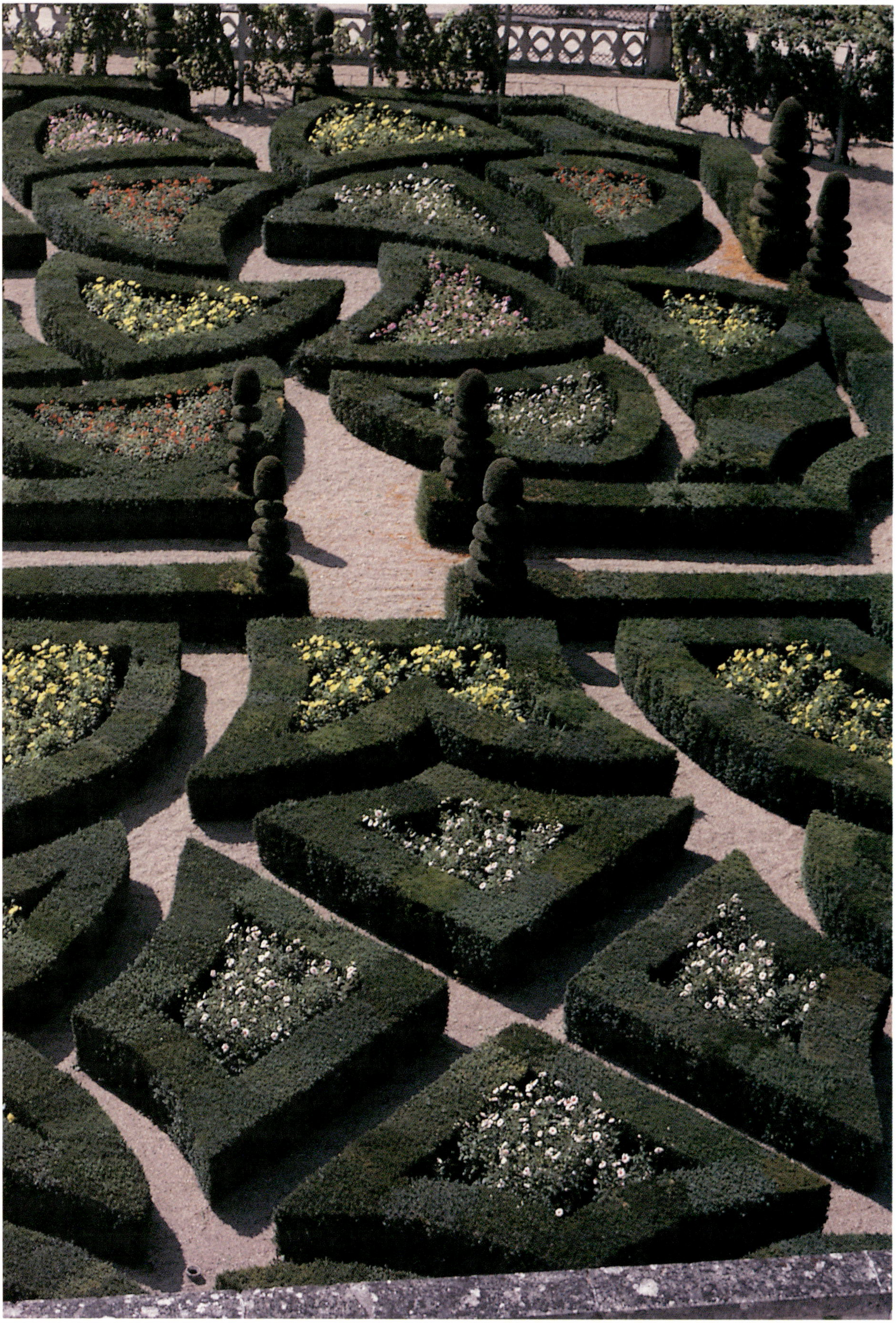

THE FRAGRANT GARDEN

JOHN AND ROSEMARY HEMPHILL

Angus&Robertson
An imprint of HarperCollins*Publishers*

AN ANGUS & ROBERTSON BOOK
An imprint of HarperCollinsPublishers

First published in Australia in 1991 by
CollinsAngus&Robertson Publishers Pty Limited (ACN 009 913 517)
A division of HarperCollinsPublishers (Australia) Pty Limited
25-31 Ryde Road, Pymble
NSW 2073, Australia

HarperCollinsPublishers (New Zealand) Limited
31 View Road, Glenfield, Auckland 10, New Zealand

HarperCollinsPublishers Limited
77-85 Fulham Palace Road, London W6 8JB, United Kingdom

Distributed in the United States of America by
HarperCollinsPublishers
10 East 53rd Street, New York NY 1002

National Library of Austraia
Cataloguing-in-Publication data

Hemphill, Rosemary
The Fragrant Garden

Includes index
Bibliography

ISBN 0207 166684

1. Garden, Fragrant. 2. Aromatic plants
3. Herb gardening. I. Hemphill, John.
635.968

Frontispiece: A formal garden at the Château de Villandry, France
Dedication page: A collection of plants in pots
Opposite Foreword: Herb border in the Culpeper Garden, Leeds castle, Kent
Contents Page: Winter Savory

Cover Heather Angel
Typeset by Adtype Graphics
Printed in Hong Kong

5 4 3 2 1
95 94 93 92 91

Dedication

To Richard and Elizabeth, Ian and Elizabeth;
Thomas, Julia and Samual, Catherine, Margaret and Sophie

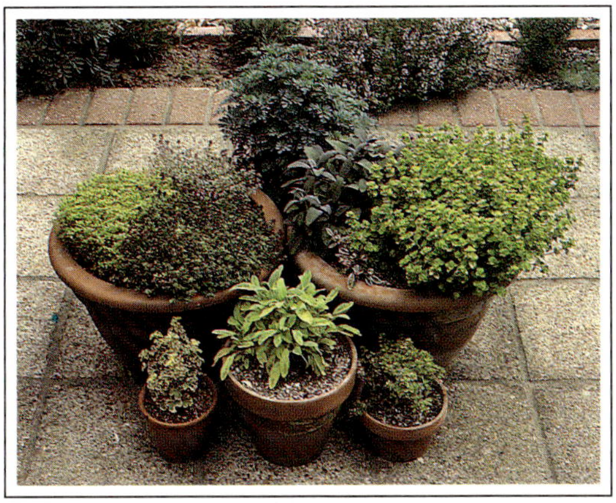

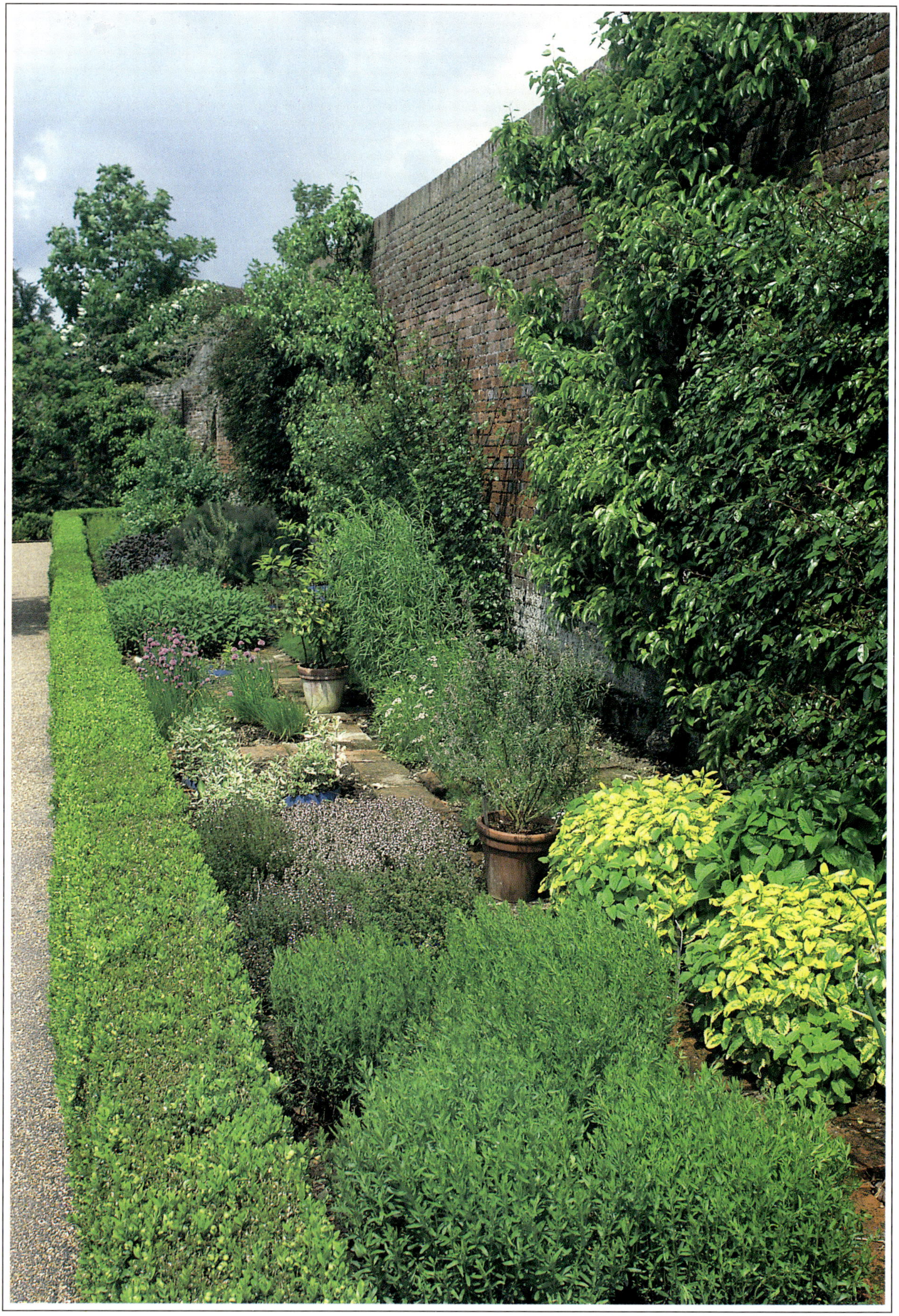

Foreword

This book was written with several purposes in mind: one was that it be a general outline of how gardens began, from prehistory and onwards through the recorded centuries. We gained enlightenment on these eras by reading and investigating erudite books, and by our own informed conjecture. We used much research and cross-referencing to ensure that the book's contents were reliable. The photography has been undertaken with equal care.

The emphasis in the *Fragrant Garden* is on herbs and old loved flowers — most of the latter having previously been classed as herbs — on early garden patterns and their special character, and on the introduction of different garden and landscape styles along with the famous women and men who instigated them. There is also a focus on the influence of these styles on today's garden designs. A recurring theme is undoubtedly romance: a nostalgia for times past and the fascinating people who lived there. This book contains fantasies, and a desire to recreate in a garden an atmosphere of harmony between people and nature. Certain gardens in England and France are living reminders of long ago, and we describe them as faithfully as possible.

It is appropriate here to answer the oft-asked question 'what is the difference between herbs and weeds?' It is generally accepted that a plant which is useful in some way is a herb; other plants which grow anywhere, and are unchecked and unwanted, are called weeds until they are discovered to have a value of some kind . . . then they graduate to the status of herbs. In *The Fragrant Garden*, we concentrate on herbs as well as on flowers and garden forms.

We have avoided the continued use of a plant's Latin classification in brackets as it interrupts the flow of reading. We have only used the Latin name if the plant is particularly unusual.

*Acknowledgments*

Our sincere appreciation goes to friends who have kindly and unhesitatingly answered questions in specialised areas during research for this book. Warm thanks to the late Brian Dobson BA MA, and his wife Nancy ATCL ABDA, for illuminating the Dark and Middle (Mediaeval) Ages, those centuries of the dim past. Grateful thanks also to Robert Purves BA LLB, who outlined the manifold epochs of recorded history to the present, clarifying the sometimes slightly conflicting and therefore confusing designations in Encyclopedias with his pages of handwritten notes. Our particular thanks go to our friend and relative Elizabeth Davis MAIH — for giving her time to lengthy discussions so readily, and for the loan of valuable reading matter on specific garden styles, their classification and their introduction into different cultures. Our very real appreciation goes to Kim Anderson, publisher, and Kathryn Evans, editor, of Collins/Angus & Robertson, for their sympathetic encouragement of this work from beginning to end.

CONTENTS

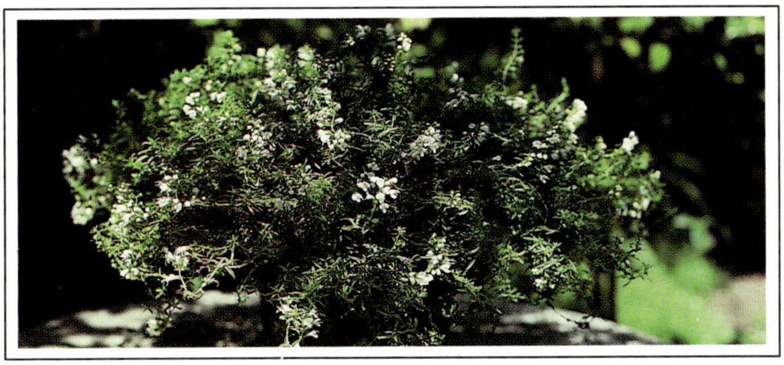

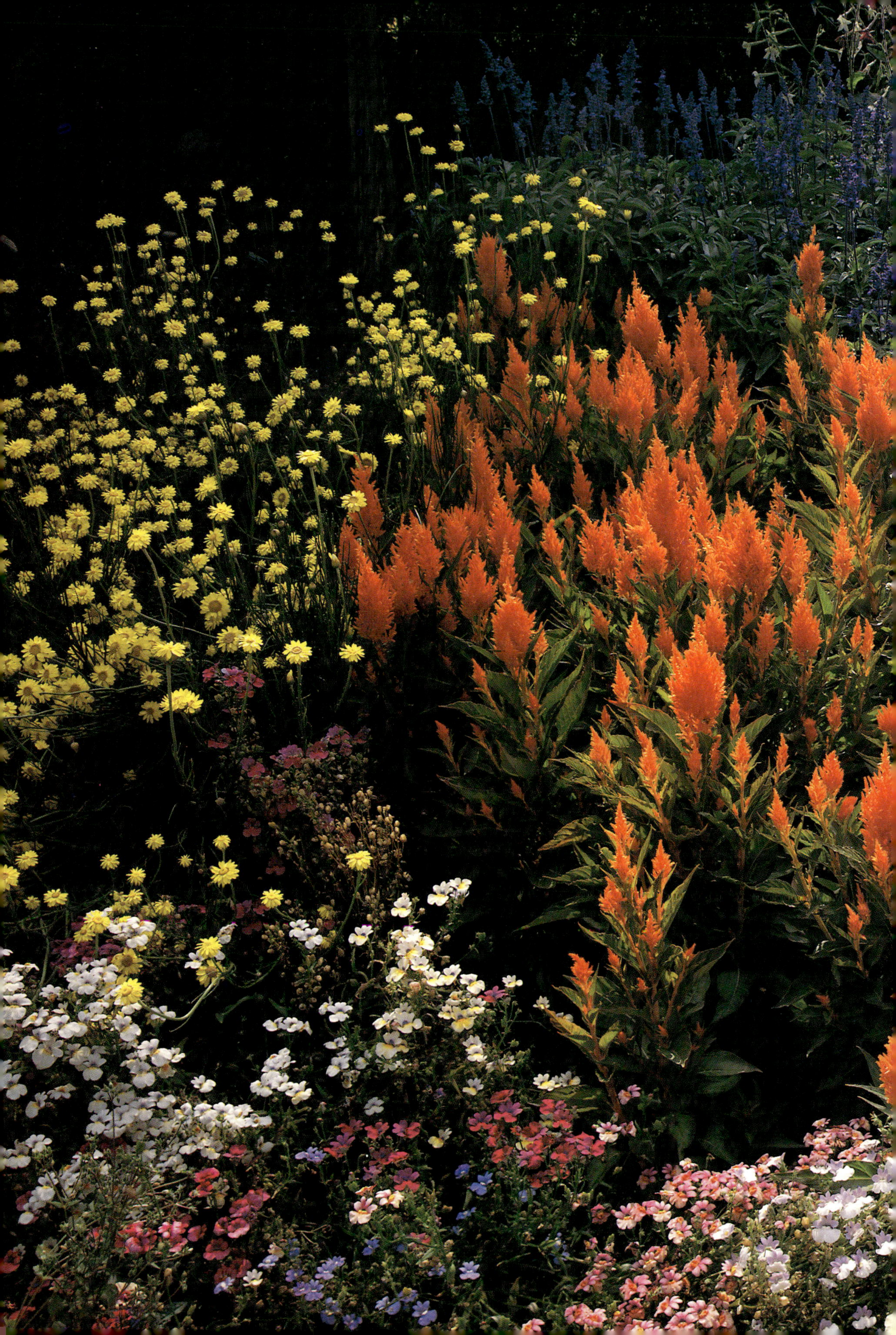

PART ONE

History and the Garden

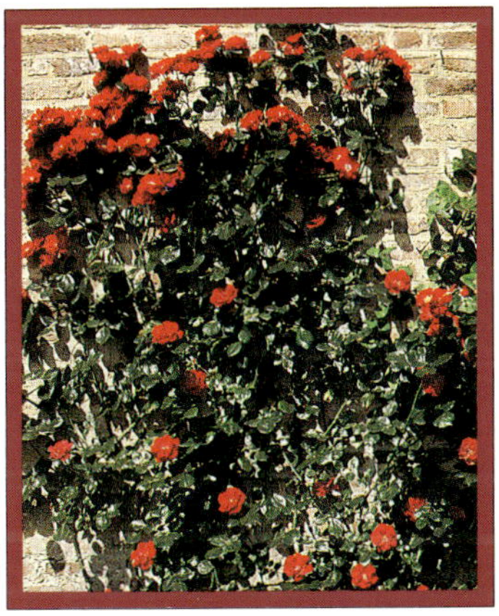

Beginnings

One day, while sitting in our sunny herb garden surrounded by grey-leaved bushes of purple lavender pungent on the noon air, observing the symmetry of miniature box hedges that enclosed beds of many scented herbs, the plots divided by neat stone paths, we wondered how, when, and where did the growing and use of herbs begin? Thoughts came to mind of mediaeval herb gardens and 'still

PREVIOUS PAGES: *Gardens have a long history of both practical and aesthetic uses. This flower border in Surrey explores richness in colour and texture.* INSET: *Red Geraniums at Sissinghurst.*

rooms', and of monks busy in their cloister allotments growing herbs for the dispensary. We recalled the works of the Anglo-Saxon herbals, such as the *Leech Book of Bald* and the *Lacnunga*, carefully preserved in museums. Earlier still were the herb gardens pleasingly designed by the Romans of Britain, uncovered during excavations. Records show that the ancient Egyptians and Greeks were familiar with the art of using herbs, and the Old Testament refers many times to herbs and spices. In fact, the very beginning of plant-life, we are told in the Bible, happened on the third day of Creation: God said 'Let the Earth bring forth grass, herbs, and fruit trees, and it was so'. On the sixth day male and female 'created he them' in his *own* image. Since then mankind has walked planet Earth, not an easy place to survive in since banishment from the Garden of Eden.

Deep within our collective unconscious perhaps we have been striving for a return to Eden. The peace and pleasure found in gardens is a glimmer of what was once in our long history, a perfect experience.

Very old are we men;
Our dreams are tales
Told in dim Eden
By Eve's nightingales;
We wake and whisper awhile,
But, the day gone by,
Silence and sleep like fields
Of amaranth lie.

WALTER DE LA MARE (1873–1956)

In the remote, shadowy past, Europeans were forced to adapt to their harsh environment in the best way possible to remain alive. After the last Great Ice age ended about 7500 BC the Earth slowly warmed, and conditions for survival improved. Humanity had endured other ice ages, when large parts of the world were covered with glacial white, and their fossil bones have been found with the mammoth and reindeer. The island of Atlantis, which would have existed aeons before these periods is, on the other hand, in the realm of mythology, according to writers, while they add that Plato, the distinguished Athenian philosopher-seer-poet of ancient Greece, conceded that Atlantis was 'populous and flourishing' before it disappeared in a cataclysmic upheaval of oceans and lands.

As the planet recovered once more after ice-locked centuries, the evolving European was able to emerge from protecting caves and enjoy the sunlight shining on a green Earth. Other life-forms which had lain dormant were again flourishing in a friendlier climate. Few animals were able to live in the freezing weather of an ice age, except for some, as proved by the discovery of primitive and delicate line drawings on cave walls.

Now that people could hunt again, catch fish, dig for roots and gather vegetation, a previously limited diet became increasingly varied. Herbs, with their individual and potent qualities, grew uncultivated for them to select.

They plucked those that would enhance this crude diet, and others through instinct and lore handed down by forbears were needed to assuage their various ills. Early people were observant as they roamed the land.

Progressing from cave-life to making basic shelters, they became busy outside the dwelling. The first gardens were planted for necessity and, one imagines, with a feeling of satisfaction too. Instead of searching long stretches of countryside for his wants, there came a time when it was obviously more convenient to grow the herbs, pot-herbs (fore-runners of many modern vegetables) and fruit-bearing trees nearby. By carefully uprooting young seedlings and collecting seeds to replant and sow, this aspect of life became easier. So began the domestication of plants and certain animals.

Some centuries later, a powerful sect called the Druids emerged. They were a group of priests and law-givers among Celtic peoples, especially those of Britain and Gaul (roughly the area of modern-day France). Among their members were nobles and men of dignity. They were learned in the natural sciences and astrology, and were soothsayers and bards as well. Pliny, the Roman historian, wrote that they were also sorcerers and masters of medical knowledge. They worshipped in woods and groves, their sacred tree being the oak. The oak-grown mistletoe also played a special part in their rites — the Druids considered the plant to have magical powers, as well as curative qualities, and among its uses was a treatment for nervous disorders. Mistletoe is a vital plant used in the specialist areas of natural and homoeopathic medicine. When the Romans came to Britain, they tried to eliminate Druidism but the Druids bitterly opposed them and the conquerors were only partially successful.

There have long been certain men and women with a gift for healing the sick, who possess a

OVERLEAF: *Wallflowers, ranunculas and irises at Sissinghurst.*

BELOW: *Herbs played an important part in druidic culture, and were used in ritual and medicine.*

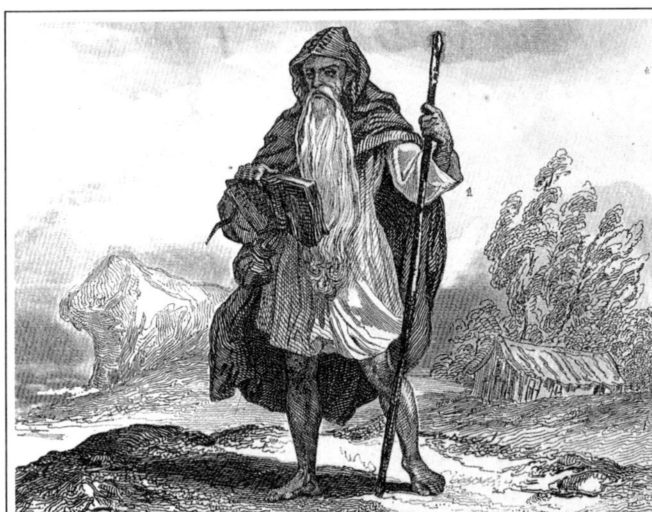

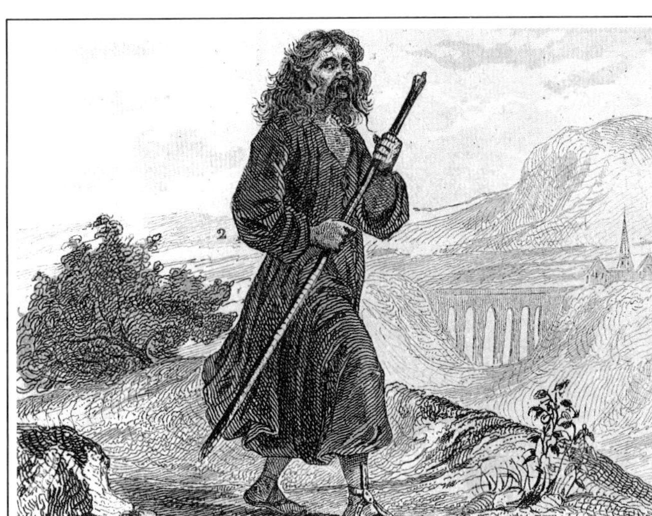

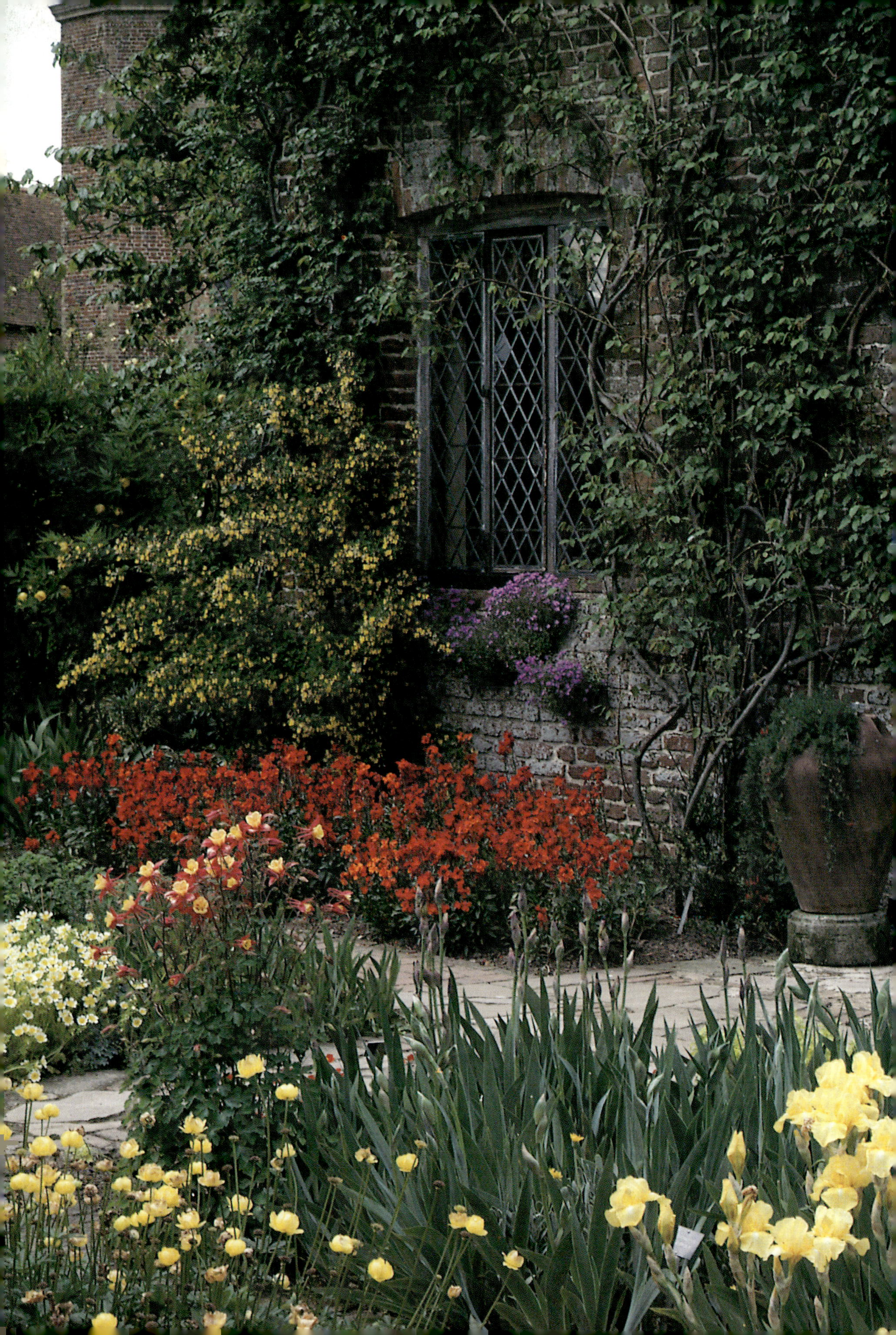

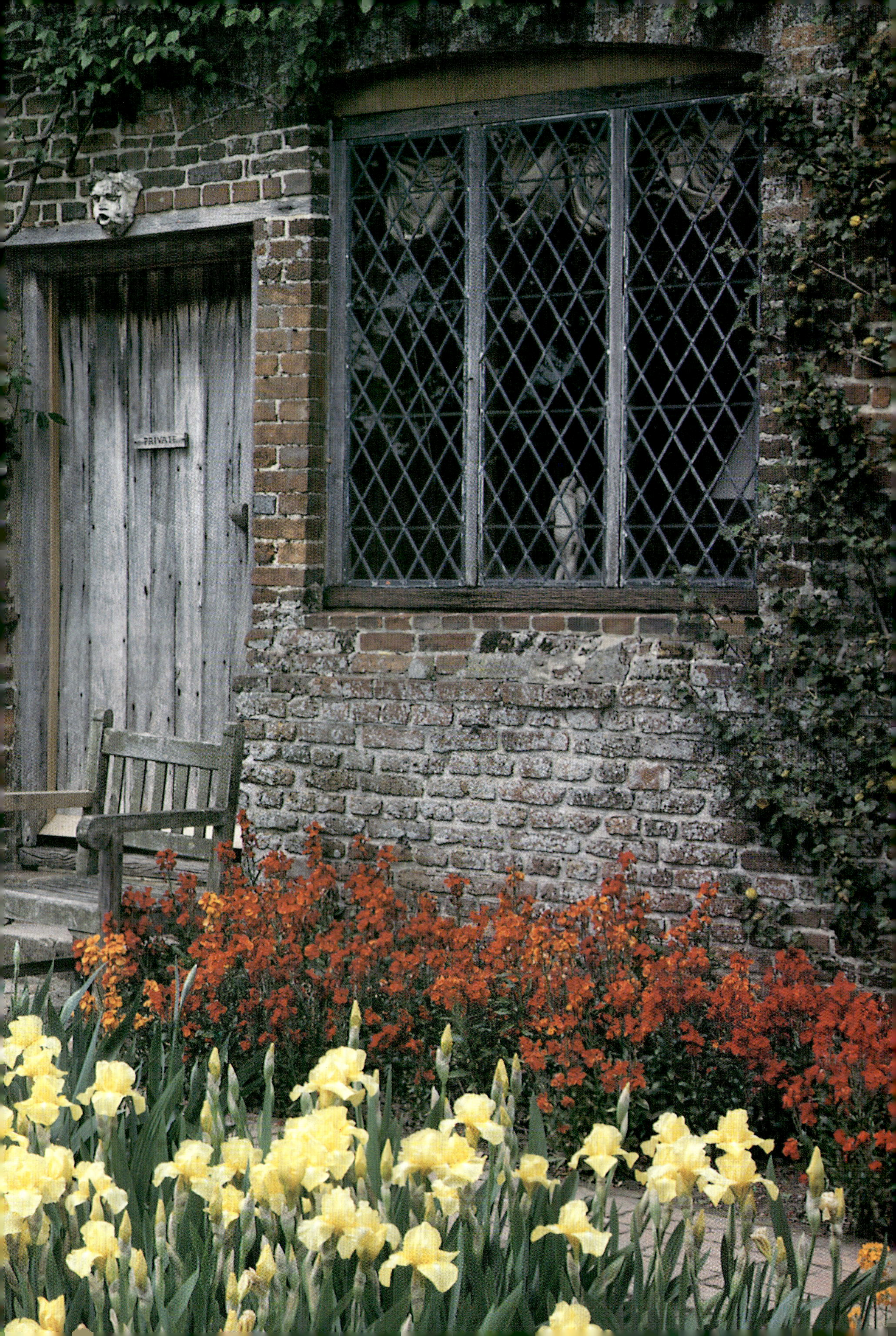
PRIVATE

deep understanding of natural remedies. Some of these wise persons were known as seers and were also genuine faith-healers. They collected appropriate herbs, flowers, berries, roots, bark, and often parts of insects, animals or other creatures, which they then prepared and combined into decoctions to dispense to their patients. For external first aid, selected herbs were bound together as an antidote against diseases, and worn as amulets for protection against the unseen powers of evil and infection, 'the flying venom'. Bunches of favourable herbs were also hung in doorways to guard those within.

PREVIOUS PAGES: *The pleasure found in vibrant gardens — like this one at Sissinghurst — perhaps reflects a perfect experience within our long history.*

Unbeknown to Europeans, races in distant lands across the seas were already enjoying advanced culture. Ancient civilisations believed that their wide comprehension of medicine, architecture and other achievements were first imparted to them by the gods. In Mesopotamia and Egypt Imhotep was revered as a god for his knowledge of medicine, although Homer spoke of him as a mortal. It is said that his healing art enabled him not only to restore health, but to bring the dead back to life. Hippocrates followed the work of Aesculapius (Imhotep's equivalent) whose symbol was a staff with a serpent twisted round it that is still the emblem of medical practitioners.

Imhotep's Egypt had become refined in countless ways, and the Egyptians' understanding of the human body, the construction of buildings, and the garden landscape were of supreme importance to their living standards. But standing in the sphere of health, the Egyptians of antiquity were discerning in their diagnosis of sickness and its treatment. Among their expert armory of restoratives were a multitude of freshly picked or dried herbs, particular spices, essences and oils.

The ancient Greeks continued the study of diseases and their cures, natural remedies being central to their knowledge of healing. Their observations brought the medicine of those days to a pinnacle of achievement. The foremost individual of that time was Hippocrates (460–377 BC), still known as the Father of Modern Medicine, a genius priest-physician who ranks high in the clinical history of medicine and surgery.

The Arab world too drew much of its cultural education from the Greeks and carried it further. They developed botanic medicine, the art of gardening in its many forms, and other areas of enlightenment. The mighty Arab empire, through its expansion, flowed over North Africa into Spain and France, Syria, Persia, Baghdad and India.

In time, the accumulated intellectual learning of the Arabian world had its impact on other civilisations.

Indeed although oceans, vast tracts of land and archaic modes of transport made communication difficult between nations, cultures were in touch, while strange and wondrous merchandise found its way to distant shores.

Quinquireme of Ninevah from distant Ophir
Rowing home to haven in sunny Palestine
With a cargo of ivory,
And apes and peacocks,
Sandalwood, Cedarwood, and sweet white wine.

(A quinquireme was an ancient vessel with five banks of oars, one on top of the other.)

In Europe, ancient Rome had unfolded into a powerful nation, its scholars having attained great skills in politics, philosophy, art and gardening. A number of these abilities were gleaned from the Greeks, who in turn had learned from western Asia and Egypt. The Romans, in expanding their territory, were inspired in the art of landscape and design by various Mediterranean countries. In their domination of other nations, Rome's vigorous legions conquered Britain in 70 AD, and colonised it in due course. The new residents applied their elevated understanding of technology in many ways, such as in the making of roads and in architecture of singular grace and symmetry . . . still appreciated today and seen, for example, in the excavations of Roman spas at Bath. Familiar necessities of life were important to the colonisers, including herbs and other plants that they knew were valuable in their diet. They also knew that they were essential for healing as well as for sweetening the air, or for discouraging vermin. In general herbs helped to enhance gardens, making them havens of visual and fragrant pleasure. There were indigenous herbs, which the Britons had always used, and these were combined with those that were introduced.

Living standards changed under the Romans. Basic houses were transformed as new ones were built to elegant and artistic Roman standards, especially among privileged groups. Gardens were planned to fulfil several requirements while retaining a pleasing balance of design. Varieties of herbs not seen before were introduced, and information about them was gradually acquired. These plants originated in the Mediterranean region and were grown wherever the conquerors made their homes. Most of the plants adapted well to new climates and different soils. Eventually, they multiplied in great numbers, helped by nature. Ripe seed was flying far and wide on the wind, or fell into running streams to be washed onto earthy banks, while birds and animals carried them too. Seeds were brought intentionally by people to new settlements, or they clung to earth on footwear and wheels.

In England today there is a Roman Palace and Museum at Fishbourne, Sussex. Diggings have revealed traces of a garden constructed during the Roman occupation. Some of the garden has

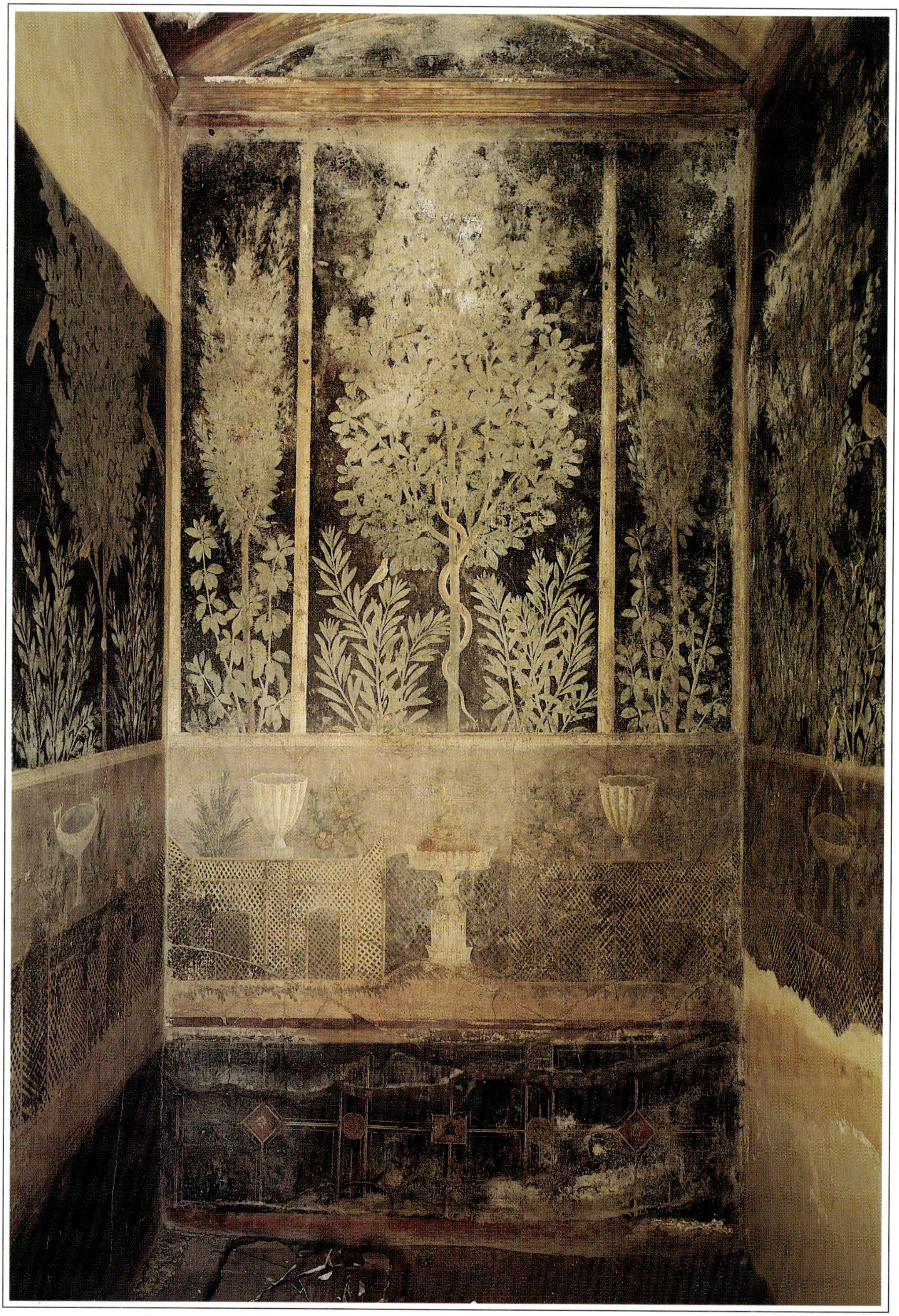

been replanted, and visitors can stroll along pathways edged with clipped box, while contemplating how centuries ago this able race knew so much about fine garden planning. The museum provides information about the herbs, flowers and varieties of plants that the Romans would have imported from Italy, such as box, basil, coriander, oregano, savory, thyme, dill, bay and rosemary, as well as lilies, violets, myrtle, some varieties of roses not native to Britain, and the stately acanthus, with its long spires of clustered, slightly open blooms, in shades varying from amethyst to alabaster (the graceful shape of acanthus leaves has long inspired decorations on classical columns and in art).

A Roman garden would have high hedges: alcoves built into the hedge would house statues or seats. Such a garden would be considered an outside 'room' with ornaments, sparkling fountains and shady places to sit where learned conversation on various topics could take place.

Roman influence on garden style was immense. Their modes and patterns continued to impress others throughout the ages. A seventeenth-century admirer wrote:

The Italians in the time of their Ancient Glory thought no Palace nor habitation complete without its Garden . . . Which gardens they have from Age to Age so improved that it is itself with other Sciences into these Northern Climates, so hath the Art of Gardening been handled along with it, as though the former were imperfect without the latter.

There is also a fascinating Roman cookbook by Apicius (*de re Conquinaria*, literally 'on cooking') called *Cooking and Dining in Imperial Rome* written in Latin early in the first century AD. Joseph Dommers Vehling, a renowned professional chef, edited and translated the original into English in the 1930s. Apicius' work is said to be the oldest known cookbook in existence. Numerous herbs and spices are among the ingredients in

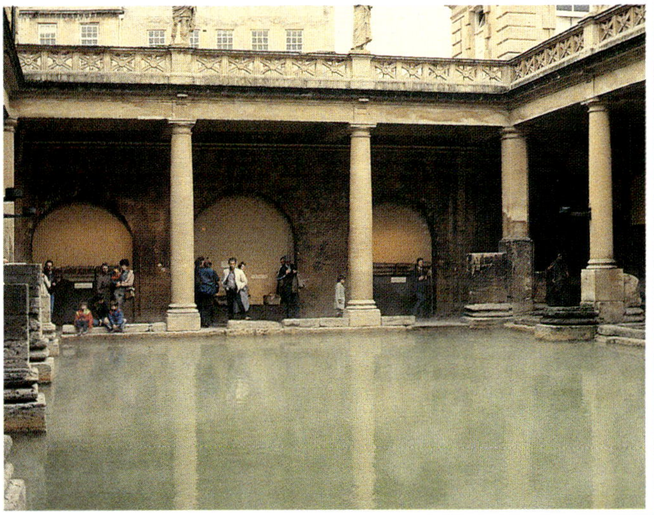

recipes that have not dated. One for boiled lobster with cumin sauce lists cumin (seed), pepper, lovage, parsley and 'dry' mint. Among other delightful headings are Elderberry Custard or Pie, Rose Pie and Rose Custard or Pudding. The ancient flower recipes are especially captivating to read with the reawakened interest in preparing edible flowers for delicious, healthful and enchanting dishes.

After the Romans left Britain in 270 AD Barbarian invasions became frequent. The origins of these raiders comprised several

ABOVE: *In Britain, too, the influence of ancient Roman design can be seen, as at these Roman baths at Bath.*

OPPOSITE: *Wall paintings such as this from the Roman colony of Pompeii give us a sense of garden structures from the past.*

OPPOSITE: *Herb gardens have existed in a variety of forms through time: as medicinal/magical places, as a natural part of an ordinary garden, or as part of a grand design, as here at Knebworth House.*

BELOW: *Witches, devils and sorcery have long been themes which link women, knowledge and herb lore.*

warrior tribes, mostly described as Germanic-pagan. They intermixed with the local inhabitants — the end result being the Anglo-Saxon race.

When the Barbarians came to Britain, several hundred years of split kingdoms with different sovereigns began. This period of chaos is usually classified as the Dark Ages beginning in the fifth century, although some historians make no division between the Dark Ages and the Middle (Mediaeval) Ages, preferring to regard the Middle Ages as having two periods, the first being the Dark Ages (from the fifth century), and the second the Age of Chivalry (from the eleventh century), ending before the Renaissance in the fifteenth century.

Witchcraft

THE RIDE-BY-NIGHTS

Up on their brooms the Witches stream,
Crooked and black in the crescent's gleam;
One foot high, and one foot low,
Bearded, cloaked and cowled, they go.
'Neath Charlie's Wain they twitter and tweet,
And away they swarm 'neath the Dragon's feet,
With a whoop and a flutter they swing and sway,
And surge pell-mell down the Milky Way.
Betwixt the legs of the glittering Chair
They hover and squeak in the empty air.
Then round they swoop past the glimmering Lion
To where Sirius barks behind huge Orion;
Up, then, and over to wheel amain,
Under the silver, and home again.

WALTER DE LA MARE

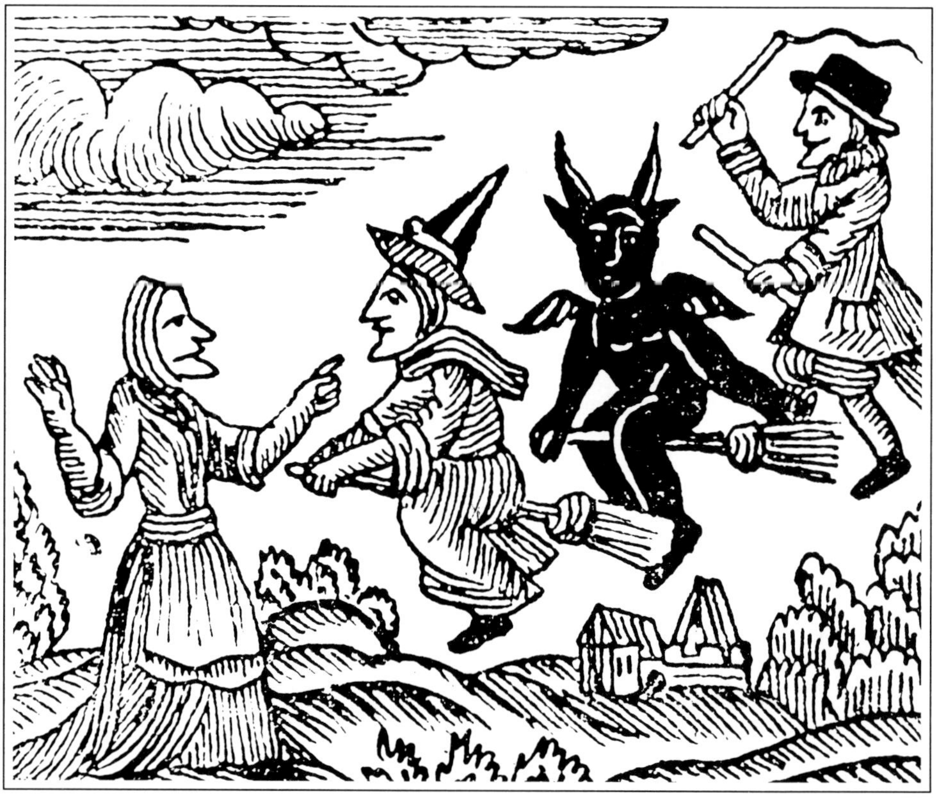

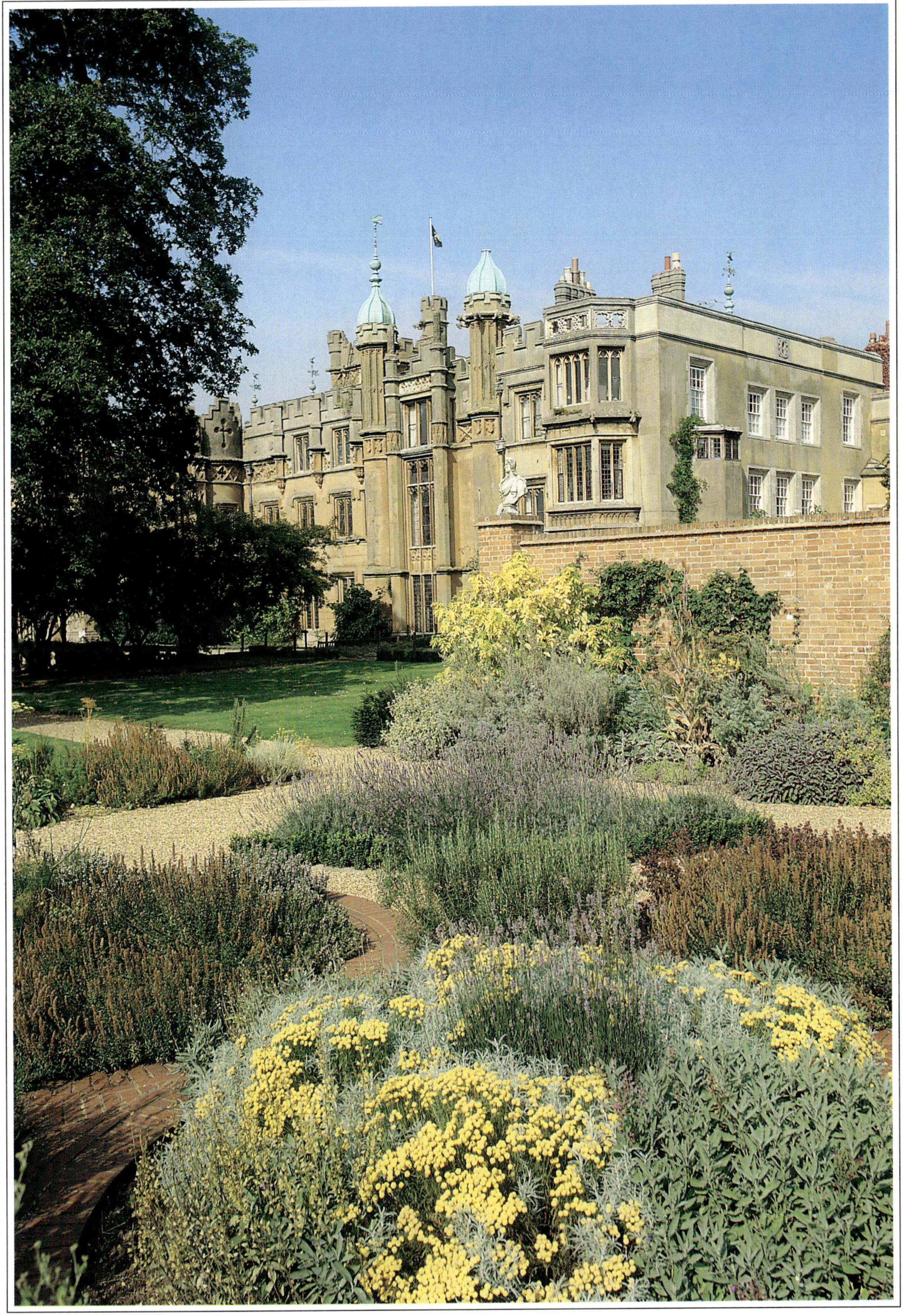

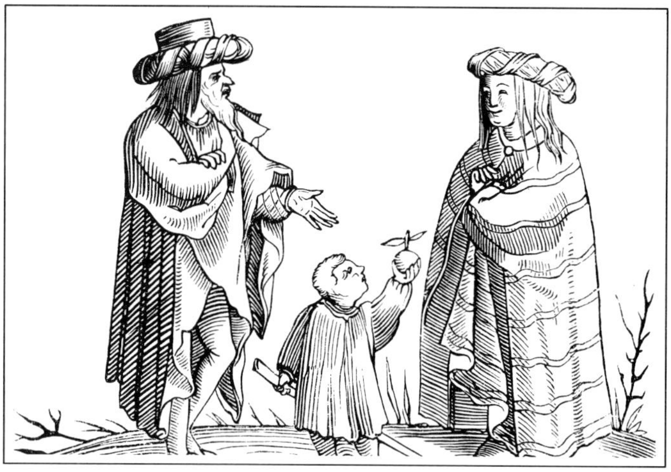

ABOVE: *A sixteenth century representation of gypsies.*

Roaming gypsies had a reputation and a perception for cures, performing rituals with herbs (together with other ingredients) learned from their ancestors and from their life of dependence on an ever-changing environment, their only shelter from the elements being their moveable horse-drawn wagons. They, like the wild animals of the forests, could forecast any shift in the fluctuating weather, and they scrutinised the landscape for food and medicinal plants wherever they camped. They studied the heavenly firmament, and noted the waxing and waning of the moon and the position of the sun during the changing seasons. The ingredients needed for making potions were gathered at an auspicious time of day, evening, or night, when the planets were favourable for the plant's utmost effectiveness. Romanies were also said to have second sight and much wisdom in astrology.

Since before the Dark Ages, a firm belief has persisted in magic, the chanting of spells, and the mixing of all kinds of herbal blends for specific purposes. Especially favoured were draughts for love, for revenge, or to cause death. The practitioners involved in these pursuits were generally women who were feared as black witches (as opposed to white witches) and were said to travel on broomsticks, and to turn themselves into animals. The three witches in Shakespeare's *Macbeth* met in a murky cavern to utter malevolent charms over a bubbling cauldron, while throwing into their 'hell-broth' offerings such as 'eye of newt', 'toe of frog' and 'root of hemlock digg'd i' the dark'.

In the Arthurian Legends, King Arthur's half sister Morgan Le Fay was trained in the fine arts of herbal craft and the making of magic spells. She was fostered on the enchanted Isle of Avalon by the Lady of the Lake, her mother's half sister. From her she learned skills, and the ways of the original 'Old People' of Britain whose second sight was said to be inborn, as was their awareness of the earth's sub-world of elves and 'faerie', which was very real to them. The conviction that some have always been born with these gifts, especially among Welsh, Irish and Scottish people, is acknowledged in our own age.

According to folklore, some of the herbs in a witch's collection were mandrake, henbane, thornapple, deadly nightshade, vervain and hemlock, the latter being the fatal herb that killed Socrates in 399 BC. These herbs also have medicinal uses when correctly prepared, and are not necessarily connected with sorcery.

Witchcraft has not completely disappeared. Modern society regards it with curiosity, although not entirely with disbelief. Confidence in extra sensory perception (ESP), faith-healing, and in the helpful power of crystals, for example, is not witchcraft. Most of us have experienced inexplicable events at some time. Legends about witches continue in stories, plays, poems, and in the celebration of Halloween and fancy dress.

There were men too who delved into alchemy. Their main interests, apart from magic, seem to have been in astrology, chemistry and in assisting significant individuals, as did Merlin the Magician, King Arthur's guide and mentor. Some unscrupulous rogues were held in superstitious awe as 'black' magicians, wizards, warlocks or sorcerers, and were eventually disposed of if not too elusive. In some groups 'witchcraft' still exists as part of the culture, in particular in medicine. A 'Medicine Man' possesses the same skills as a herbalist, and to his people is both physician and psychiatrist.

Folklore in the Western world is full of conviction in supernatural beings. Elves, fairies, water sprites and mermaids are mostly enchanting and as bright as Shakespeare's Ariel, or have an unearthly beauty described 'sheen as an elf'. Goblins, dwarfs and pixies are mischievous; gnomes industrious and benign; dragons, giants, ogres and demons described as malevolent. Cultures of the ancient world, both East and West, had their own mystic creatures, which persist within the psyche of different races today, such as ghosts, banshees or leprechauns.

Essential to the beliefs of the people of Old Greece, Rome and Egypt were their gods and goddesses with their attendants and acolytes — for example, the centaurs, satyrs, nymphs and dryads of ancient Greece and Rome, or the priest and priestesses who consulted the oracles and the sybils who predicted future destinies.

Many people have experienced the reality of nature spirits. Because our ancestors absorbed their natural surroundings fully into themselves, it is not surprising that they felt and 'saw' the actual existence of some entities invisible to those with unobservant eyes and ears.

King Arthur of the Round Table

In old dayes of the King Artour
Of which that Bretons speken gret honour,
All was this land fulfilled of faeries;
The elf-quene with hire jolie company
Daunced full of te in many a grene mede;
This was the old opinion as I rede,
I speke of many hundred yeres agoe,
But now can no man see non elves mo.

GEOFFREY CHAUCER

The legendary King Arthur of the Round Table is said to have lived during the turbulent years of the sixth century and not in the Age of Chivalry, which came later. The term though is rightly his, as chivalry and King Arthur are synonymous, forever shining in a dark, confused time. The Arthurian Legends have held people's fascination for centuries, perhaps even more so today than before. A number of books continue to be written about Britain's most famous monarch. The great poets Geoffrey Chaucer, John Masefield and Alfred (Lord) Tennyson are just a few of the noted men of letters whose words on this subject fire the imagination.

Arthur's life is in the hinterland of history, merging into myth and romance, although there is some proof of his actual existence. In the twelfth century it was recorded that Arthur's grave was found in Glastonbury with the inscription 'Here lies Arthur King of the Britons buried on the island of Avalon'. In those days, Glastonbury was surrounded by watery marshes hung with mists and is said to have been part of the Isle of Avalon. There are still some who say that this mystic island, where the Lady of the Lake lived, existed in another dimension. It was certainly thought so in Arthur's day and before, the access only known to initiates.

BELOW: *Arthur and Guinevere's last meeting: love, tragedy, and the judgments of time.*

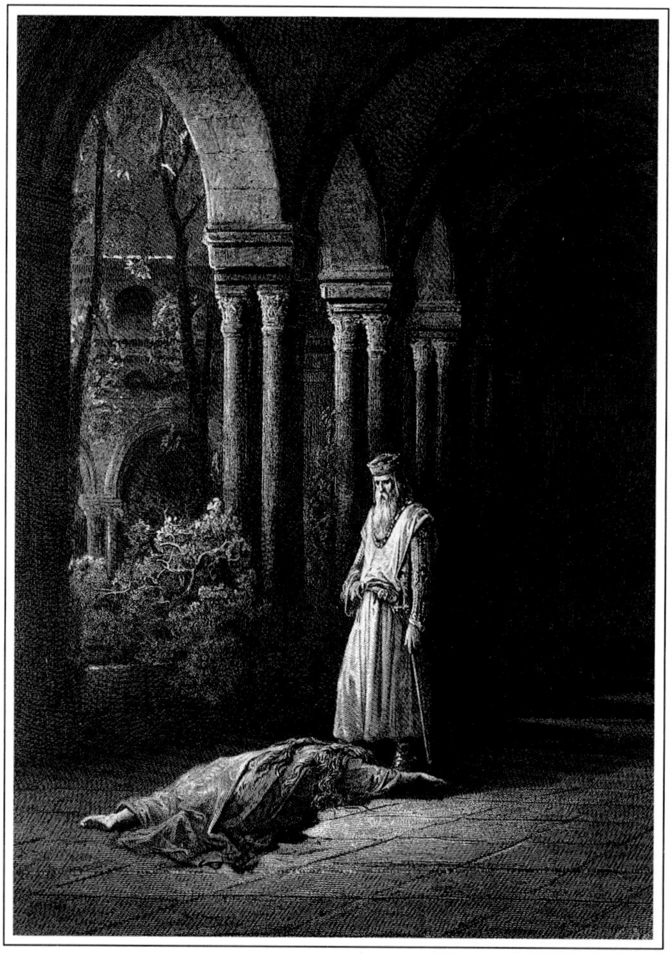

In *The Mists of Avalon*, Marion Bradley says:

> *Here, in fact, the inland sea was receding, year-by-year giving way to dry lands: one day this would all be rich farmland . . . but not Avalon. Avalon now lay eternally surrounded in the mists, hidden from all but the faithful, and when men came and went in pilgrimage to the monastery which the Christian monks called Glass Town, the Temple of the Sun was invisible to them, lying in some strange otherworld.*

Morgan Le Fay, King Arthur's half sister, was a high priestess of Avalon, trained to inherit the title of 'Lady of the Lake'. She was versed in the secrets of weaving spells and invocations and the mixing of potions made from herbs to ensure their effectiveness. From time to time, she left Avalon and lived in the real world before returning there for good.

It is said in folk lore that Morgan Le Fay — or 'Morgan of the Fairies' — plotted the downfall

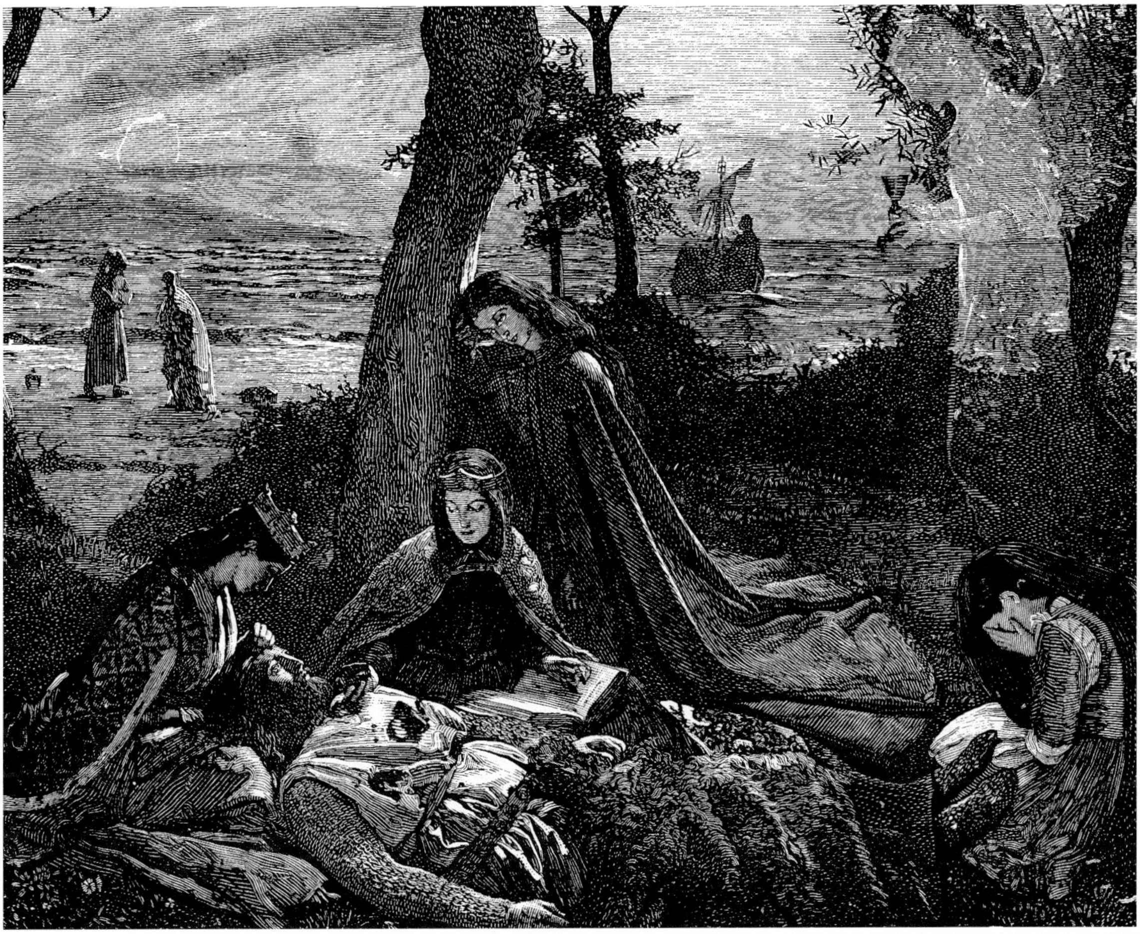

But now farewell. I am going a long way
With these thou seest — if indeed I go—
(For all my mind is clouded with a doubt)
To the island-valley of Avilion

ALFRED (LORD) TENNYSON
Morte D'Arthur

of Arthur because he had become the leader of Christianity, forsaking the old pagan doctrine of Avalon and the people of early Britain. In these intrigues she ruthlessly used her supernatural knowledge and powers of second sight, and ritually cast spells reinforced by the use of special herbs such as henbane, mandrake, yarrow, elder and betony, which were said to have magic powers. Some Arthurian legends say that Morgan Le Fay altered the course of several peoples' lives, in the belief that she was fulfilling the will of the goddess she worshipped — as well as scheming for her own ends.

King Arthur was said to be highly idealistic and valiant, and not selfish or intent on material gain. His destiny was to be a leader of Christendom: to defeat the countless, internal warring kings, protected by Excalibur his magical sword, and to bring about a peaceful regime. At the zenith of his reign he was the 'hole' king of

'Ingelond, Curnuayle, Walys, Scotlonde and Irelonde', and many other realms where various kings ruled. All the kings were willingly under obeisance to Arthur, for they respected him as the greatest of all warriors and rulers. King Arthur fell in battle, ending his kingdom. He was mortally wounded by his jealous kinsman, Modred, who was said to be either his son or nephew. It has been a long-held belief that after his death, King Arthur would return, when needed, to help his countrymen.

So Arthur passed, but country-folk believe
He will return, to triumph, and achieve;
Men watch for him on each Midsummer Eve.

King Arthur and his band of honourable knights in 'many-tower'd Camelot' strived for spiritual attainment in their quest for the Holy Grail. The brotherhood of 'fayre' and gallant young men on pacing steeds, their squires flying colourful banners behind them, went forth together on many occasions. 'All in the blue unclouded weather, the knights rode two by two' on their way to accomplish heroic deeds. The creed they lived by was one of chivalry and courage, setting a standard of manly conduct that has lasted to this day. Today, Arthur's name recalls a romantic and wistful moment in time, and a brief Golden Age.

Inextricably woven into the legend of King Arthur is one of literature's great love-stories — the unyielding romance between Sir Lancelot, the most handsome and brave of the Round Table knights, and Arthur's beautiful wife, Queen Guinivere (Gwenivere or Gwenhwyfar).

Guinivere was a daughter of one of the many kings of that age. She was the epitome of grace and beauty, and married Arthur because he would have no other. Merlin, the all-knowing wise man of Britain, forewarned Arthur that Guinivere and Lancelot were destined to love one another, which would lead to circumstances that eventually would cause the kingdom to fall. But Arthur would not listen to his mentor. Guinivere loved and admired her husband, but not with the passion she and Sir Lancelot felt for one another. Their love was a tragedy in which Guinivere and Lancelot were fated to part forever in this world.

After King Arthur's death, his noble band of men dispersed and his regime disintegrated. Guinivere fled to a convent, where she became the Abbess, and did penance for her enduring love of Lancelot. She changed her 'ermines for a goat-hair stole, But love remained a flame within [her] soul'. Sir Lancelot, overcome by his betrayal of the King, joined some of his fellow knights in a monastery, where he lived for the rest of his life. On his death-bed he longed to be with Guinivere, and Bors of Gannis told the Queen. She rode at once to Lancelot, but it was too late, he had died.

For flowers for him dead, my king of men.
I wandered up the brooklet, up the glen;
A robin watched me and a water-hen.

There I picked honeysuckles, many a bine
Of golden trumpets budding red as wine,
With dark green leaves, each with a yellow spine.

We buried him by Hector, covered close
With these, and elder-flower, and wild rose.
His friends are gone thence now; no other goes.

And beyond her own death she foresaw that 'surely my love will burn within me still . . . Death cannot make so great a fire drowse . . .' as stated so poetically by John Masefield in his poem 'Guinevere Tells'.

The Vikings and the Norse

From the eighth to the tenth centuries Vikings of Scandinavia began to raid the tantalising, obscure island of Britain in open boats. After repeatedly plundering, and forcibly abducting people that could be of use to them, some of these fierce warriors decided to settle in Britain, becoming powerful despots within communities in different parts of the country. Gradually they merged with the Britons. Like the Romans and Barbarians before them, the Vikings brought with them, from their northern regions, their own familiar essentials. In particular they introduced herbs that adjusted to their new surroundings and eventually grew wild, like those introduced from the Mediterranean. One essential herb already known to and used by the invaders was dill, the common name of which stems from the Norse word *dilla*, meaning to lull. Dill water, a decoction made from the seeds, was given to babies to soothe them, just as it is today. A native of southern Europe, dill found its way many centuries ago, as did numerous other herbs, to cooler regions.

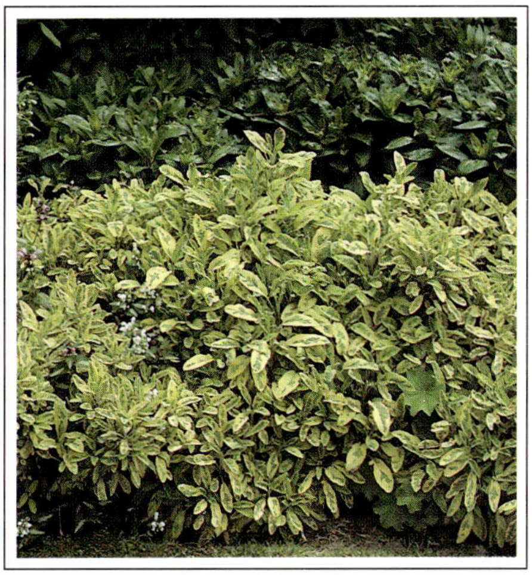

LEFT: *Sage is a perennial Mediterranean herb that can be traced back to ancient times. Its name is linked to both Old French and Latin, and refers to 'good health'.*

As in other cultures, there were highly esteemed healer-apothecaries, who were brilliant in the art of diagnosis and herbal treatment. The most eminent were sought after by kings, noblemen and the members of other important families, for employment as resident physicians in these illustrious establishments. There were also respected consultants within a community, who were visited by rich and poor seeking advice for curing the ills of body and mind.

OVERLEAF: *Religious communities have long built gardens, as places of learning, healing, and beauty, as at Fossanova Abbey.*

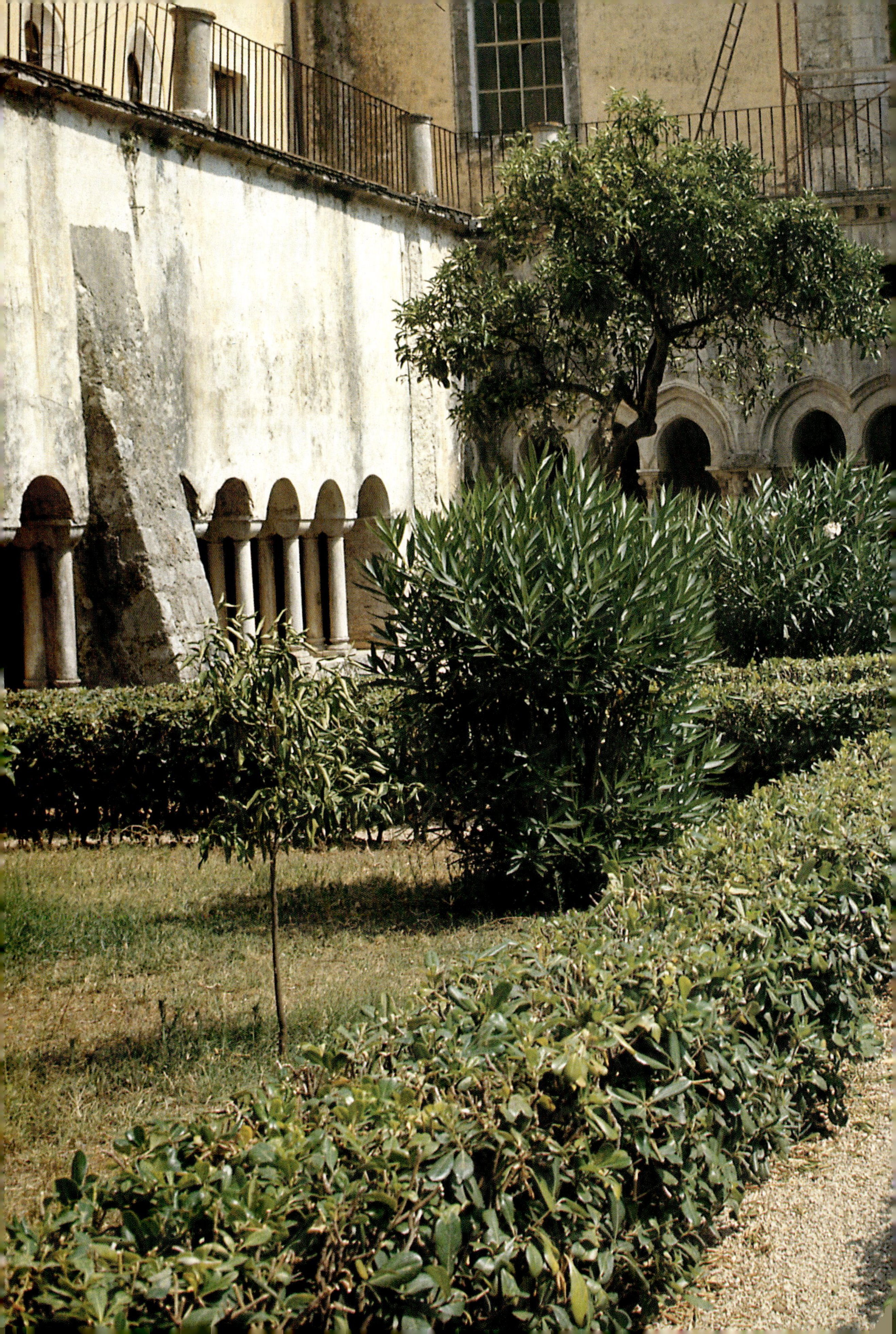

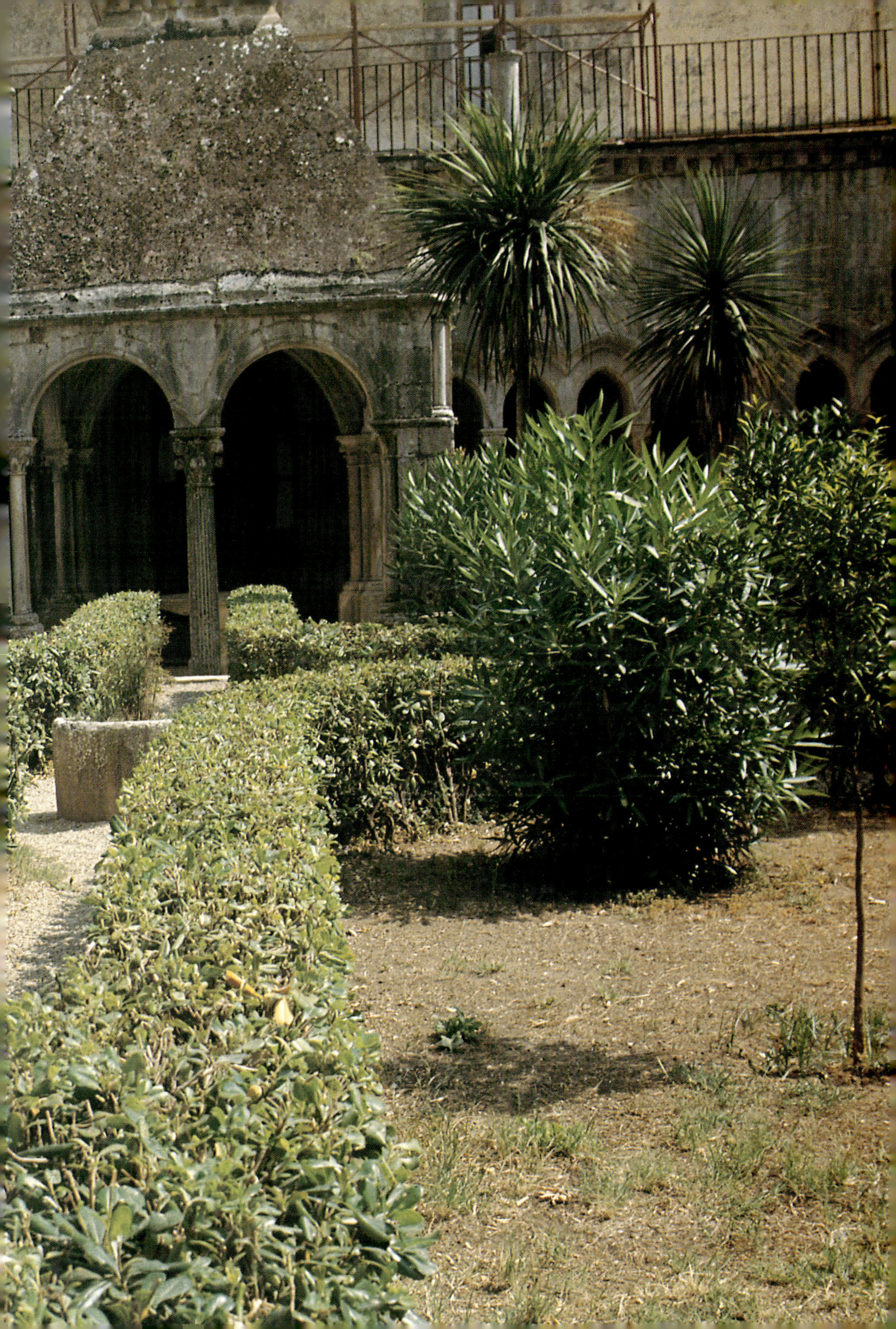

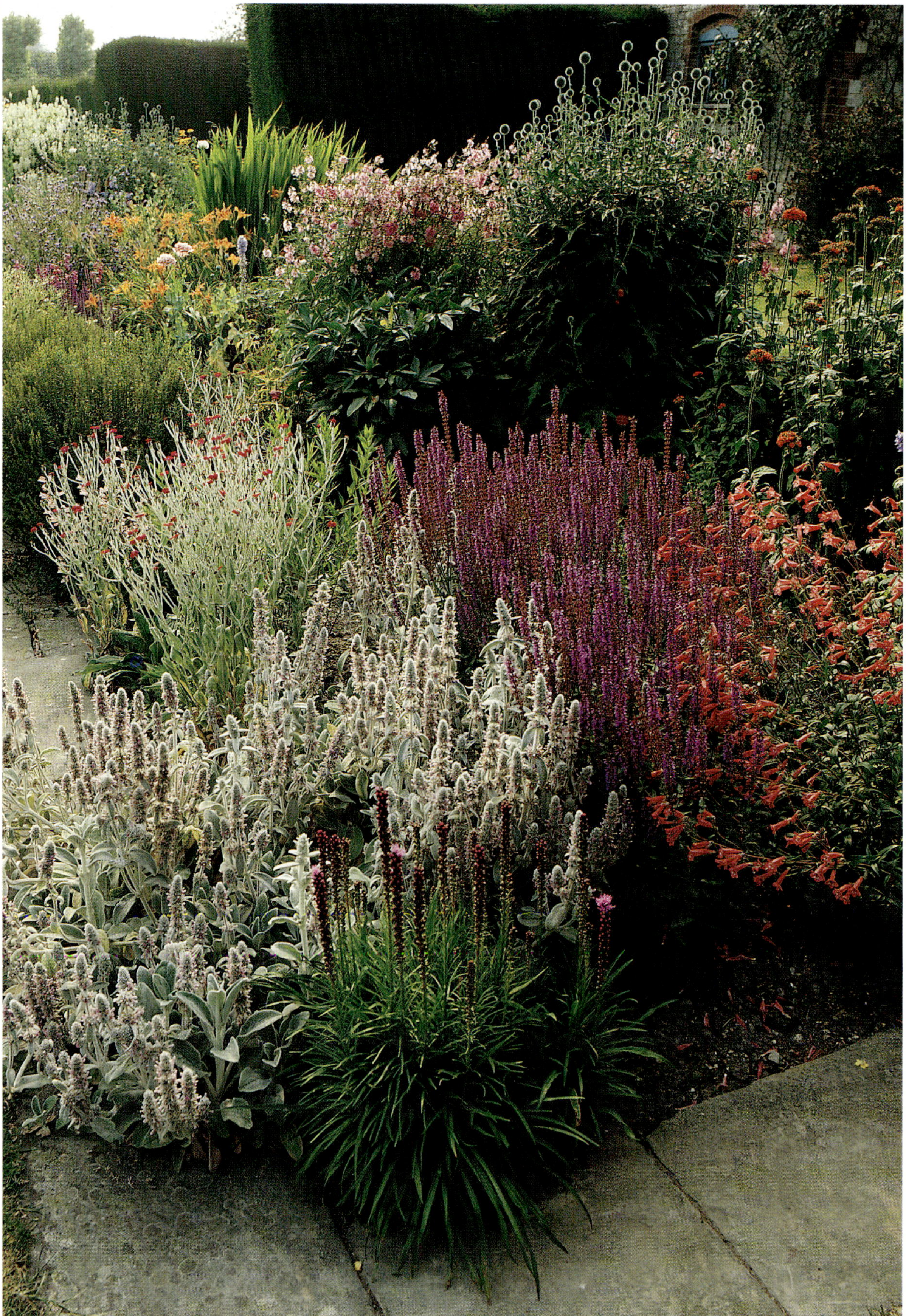

Monasteries were well-known as healing centres. Monks attended to the growth and preparation of plants gathered for treating the sick. Liqueurs are said to have started in this way, for curative blends were given in small cups or glasses . . . the forerunners of liqueur glasses. One does not begrudge the good monks for testing and tasting the warming liquid, especially in freezing weather, when they would possibly have a little more than usual. Several popular liqueurs are still being made in monasteries and are for sale in commercial outlets.

Gardens were essential for the survival of the residents within monastic enclosures. Documents describing cloister gardens in detail go back to the ninth century and are preserved in libraries and museums. The oldest plan of a monastery (from about 816–20 AD) is in the Abbey of St Gall in Switzerland. This plan shows a section of the cloister the monks relaxed in. Other sections are for different kinds of gardens or 'garths': a garden for supplying vegetables and herbs for the kitchen, and an infirmary garden providing the herbs for medicines which were prepared by the monk's physician.

The cloister-type herb garden endured in elaborate or simplified forms, with neat geometric beds intersected by pathways for easy maintenance and harvesting. Surviving illustrated manuscripts of this methodical design show that early Eastern garden plans were a continuing guide to orderly planting.

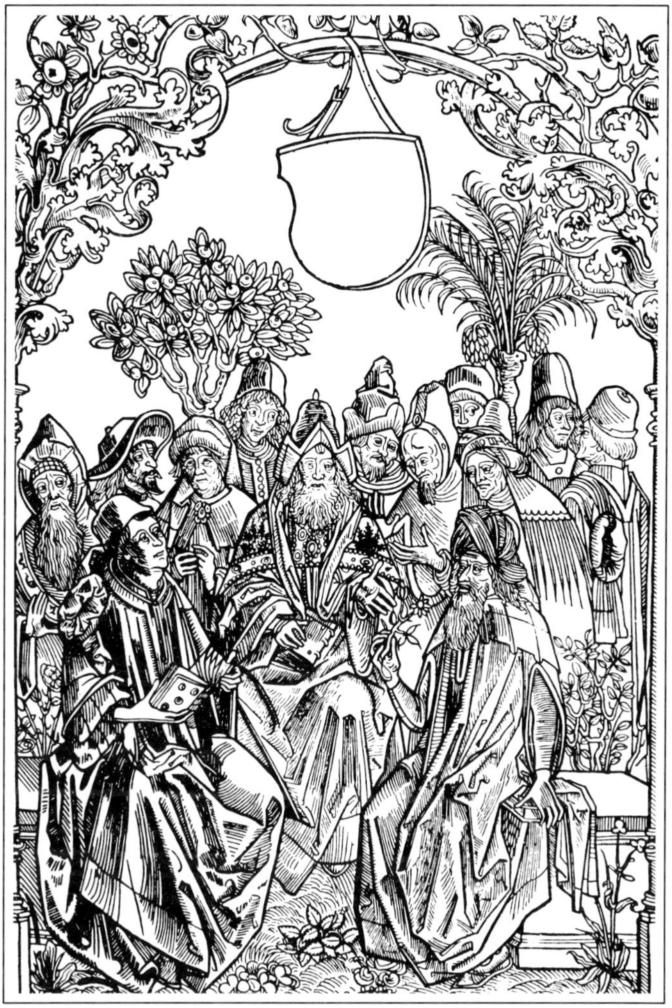

ABOVE: *Gardens, garths or garts: places of relaxation and learning.*

OPPOSITE: *This herbaceous border at Jenkyn Place, Hampshire illustrates how gardens can also be healing places visually.*

A manuscript from the ninth century written by Walafred Strabo, Abbot of Reichenau on Lake Constance, describes the love and joy he experienced in his many-faceted cloister garden:

Amongst my herbs sage holds the place of honour; of good scent it is full of virtue for many ills. Then there is rue, with its blue-green leaves and short-stemmed flowers, so placed that the sun and air can reach all its parts. Great is its power over evil odours . . .

Further on he states 'mint I grow in abundance and in all its varieties. How many they are. I might as well try to count the sparks from Vulcan's furnace beneath Etna.'

Strabo lived during the ninth century in the reign of the French emperor, Charlemagne. He is documented as wanting many plants grown in gardens within his vast domains in central Europe, and he suggested that his people grow fennel and anise outside their dwellings. Alcuin, a learned monk from Ireland, came by royal command to teach the king his profound knowledge of herbs and their uses. Some of Charlemagne's favourites were anise, fennel, costmary and lovage.

Giovanni Boccaccio, the fourteenth-century creator of Italian classic prose and contemporary of England's Geoffrey Chaucer, wrote in *The Decameron* of a cloister garden's beauty:

. . . The sides of these walks were almost closed in with jasmin and red and white roses, so that it was possible to walk in the garden in a perfumed and delicious shade . . .

The Normans

The last great invasion of Britain was undertaken by Norman troops at the Battle of Hastings in 1066. The invasion was led by William, Duke of Normandy (later known as the Conqueror), who subsequently became King William I of England. The Normans were effected by Latin order and discipline, and so exercised methodical regulation in lands under their control, which included England. Although a new system was introduced, it did not destroy all traces of English law and customs.

Lifestyles of the invaded people were altered once again, for example the language was enriched, absorbing fresh words. In the household realm there were no new ideas for uses of herbs in food or medicine as the Normans were not as experienced in the knowledge of herbs, so it is said.

The Meddygion Myddfai

About one hundred years after the Norman occupation, a group of physicians practised their healing skills at Myddfai, Wales. They belonged to a highly respected traditional school of medicine flourishing in the twelfth and thirteenth centuries, and the interesting story of the 'Meddygion Myddfai' was told in the *British Herbal Review* in the Summer of 1988. Without the benefits of advances in all areas of medical treatment made this century, the remedies provided by this group were gratefully followed by those who sought help, and were undoubtedly therapeutic, practical and sound. There are a few surviving Welsh manuscripts recording the Myddfai nostrums which have been translated into

English, and copies can be found at the University of Wales in Aberystwyth, and at Cambridge University. The article points out that much of the physicians' information was derived from earlier sources, such as the writings of Hippocrates, Pliny, Dioscorides and Galen, all famous Greek and Roman recorders of herbal medicine.

Here are a few Myddfai remedies, which the writer says are derived from early manuscripts.

For a Cold: take a pound of garlick, and pound well, adding thereto a quart of good bottled wine, let it macerate well covered, drain under a press and drink lukewarm. If the cold affects a joint, warm the remains of the garlick and apply to the part as warm as it can be borne. It is proven.

For sensible eating: when you et, do not eat away all your appetite but let some desire for food remain . . .

Hemp agrimony is suggested for coughs, red roses for toothache, and sage both for sore throats and as a toothpaste.

Explorers and Travellers

In mediaeval times there were a number of intrepid explorers of strange lands and navigators of uncharted seas, such as the thirteenth-century Venetian Marco Polo, who journeyed across the Gobi desert to China and its great emperor Kublai Kahn. After

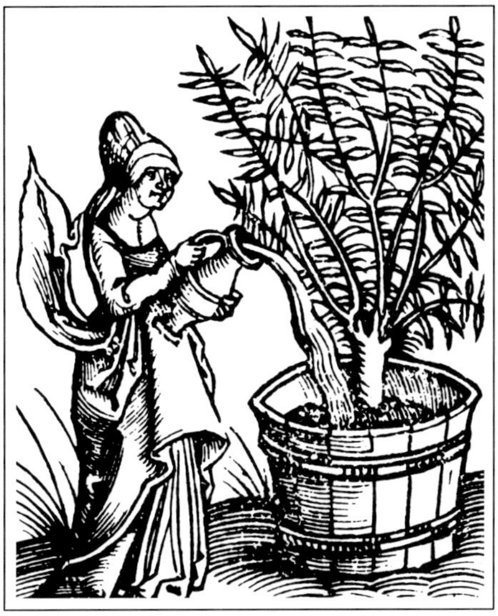

LEFT: *Rosemary was held to have a number of uses: ritually, for remembrance, culinarily, for appetite, and cosmetically, to whiten the face.*

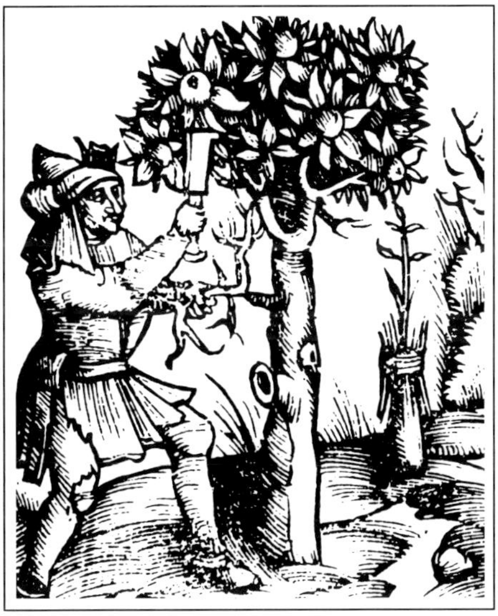

LEFT: *Travel, with its variety of purpose, spread plants and methods around the world. The pomegranate, as pictured here, moved from Africa to Europe, growing with mixed success.*

spending some decades in China, Polo returned to Venice and revealed his discoveries of the many spheres of Chinese accomplishments, including garden planning, food and the arts. There are many who say that he introduced pasta in its diverse forms — already used in Chinese cooking — to the Italians, who then adopted it (there are also those who believe that it was the other way around, that Marco Polo

OPPOSITE: *This picture illustrates many facets of fourteenth-century gardens, from minstrels entertaining to water spirits and revelry, all within a structured environment.*

brought the idea of making pasta to the Chinese).

In the fourteenth and fifteenth centuries, when the Renaissance was in its full flowering, other enterprising men set out to search for 'unknown' countries and seas, one of whom was Vasco de Gama, who mapped a sea route to India in 1446, while another was Christopher Columbus who discovered central America in 1492. The 'golden road' to the court of Tamerlain, king of Samarkand, was taken in the fourteenth century by a Castillian representative, a diplomat who wrote vivid reports of the gardens he saw, there and nearby.

Once these lands, and others, became known to Europeans, plants, food, flavourings and ideas of all kinds were found to be new and stimulating when brought back to the countries from which the travellers had ventured forth. For instance, the potato and tomato are not of European origin, rather the Spaniards introduced them from America; rhododendrons, now so much a part of Western gardens, are native to Nepal, Northern India where they grow vigorously. Friends were able to sit high above the ground surrounded by a cloud of rosy blooms in the strong forked branches of a great rhododendron tree while on a trekking holiday in Nepal.

Travelling minstrels or 'gleemen' strolled through countries singing of mysterious distant lands, of fresh creative ways with gardens, architecture, cuisine and fashions; of important marriages, romance, gossip, exploration, war, and other topics of every sort . . . a gladsome manner of imparting news with song, while gaining careful attention. Such gleemen acted as the media of the day, as is made clear in the tragic romance of Heloise and Abelard, while the term itself comes from the old Saxon (where 'glee' meant music). In this way, the interchange of ideas on many subjects took place between different cultures and influenced them.

Geoffrey Chaucer

An old man in a lodge within a park;
The chamber walls depicted all around
With portraitures of huntsman, hawk, and hound,
And the hurt deer. He listeth to the lark,
Whose song comes with the sunshine through the dark
Of painted glass in leaden lattice bound;
He listeneth and he laugheth at the sound,
He writeth in a book like any clerk.
He is a poet of the dawn, who wrote
The Canterbury Tales, and his old age
Made beautiful with song; and as I read
I hear the crowing cock, I hear the note
Of lark and linnet, and from every page
Rise odours of ploughed field or flowery mead.

JOHN MASEFIELD

During the fourteenth century, when the mediaeval period was ending and the Renaissance was about to begin, to recharge the European world with new and

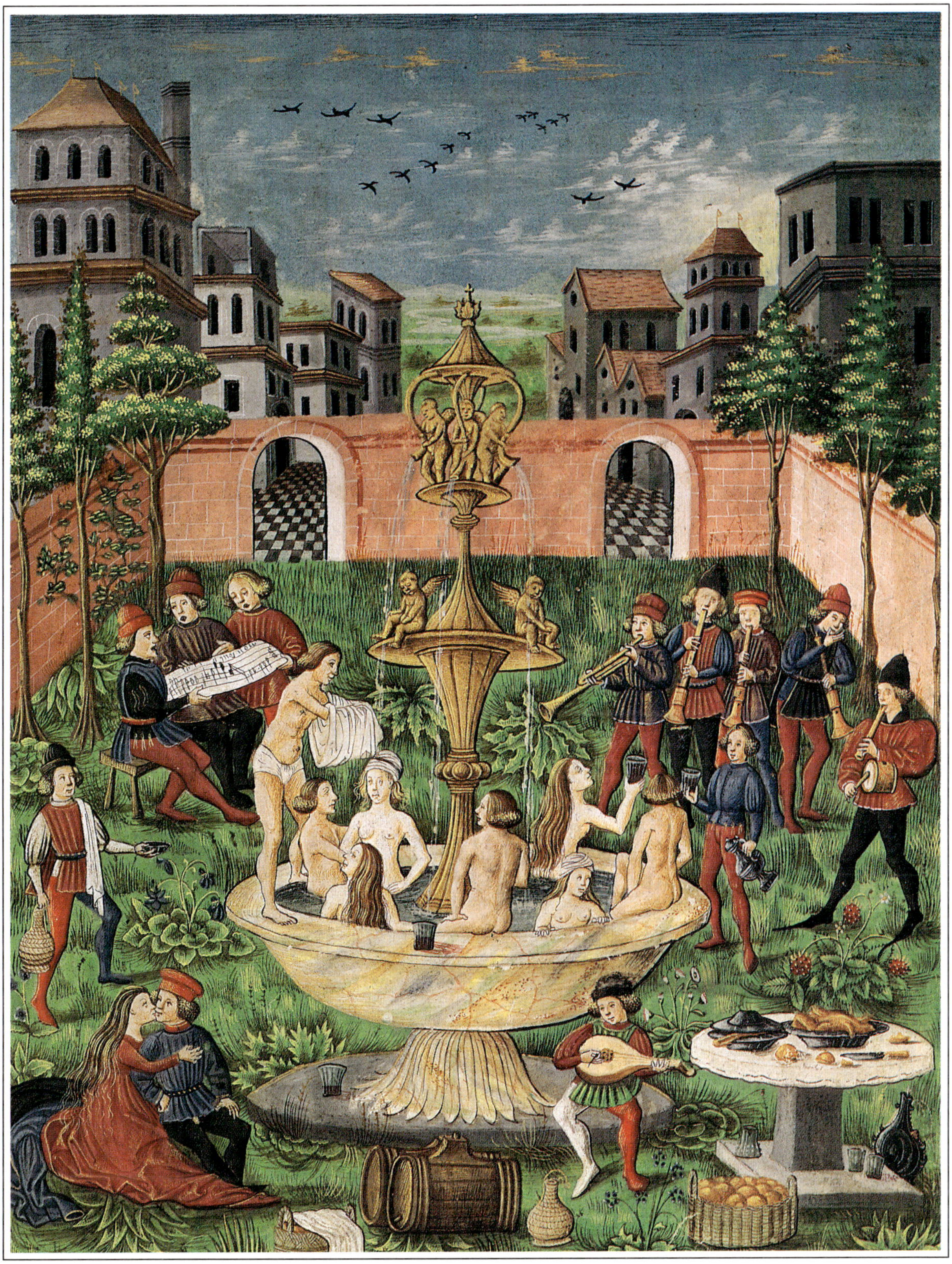

enlightened thinking, Geoffrey Chaucer wrote his lasting works. His Italian contemporary, Boccaccio, was writing poetry tales at the same time, and it is believed that the two met several times. Chaucer also translated from French nearly one third of the lasting verse classic the *Romaunt de la Rose* (The Romance of the Rose) into English. The original poem was begun in 1225 by one poet and completed by another about 1270. This long descriptive poem talks, in part, of personified love searching for beauty (typified by the rose). The poem also throws much light on the life and thought of the thirteenth century. The work had great influence in France, Italy and England.

Fulgay was al the ground, and quaint,
And powdered, as men had it paint,
With many a fressh and soundry flowr,
That casten up ful good savour.

FROM *THE ROMANCE OF THE ROSE*, TRANSLATED BY GEOFFREY CHAUCER.

Chaucer's acknowledged greatest work is his *Canterbury Tales*, which vividly portrays a section of life in his day. His fellow travellers '. . . on pilgrimage . . . to Caunterbury' were going there to pay homage to the holy martyr St Thomas Becket, twelfth-century Archbishop of Canterbury, who had helped them, and healed their ills through prayer. The pilgrims are clearly seen through Chaucer's perceptive descriptions. Each tale is told to enliven the long journey on horseback. Aware, as always, of the herbs and flowers seen on the way in early spring, he says:

When the sweet showers of April follow March,
Piercing its drought down to the roots that parch,
Bathing each vein in such a flow of power
That a new strength's engendered in the flower . . .

He notes that among the diverse company was a chivalrous crusader-knight, attended by his son, a comely young squire:

A merry blade, a lover full of fire . . .
Embroidered was his clothing, like a mead
Full of fresh flowers, shining white and red . . .

The Goodman of Paris

Le Ménagier de Paris, or *The Goodman of Paris*, is a charming and famous tale told by a fourteenth-century elderly husband, newly married to a young wife. Because she was inexperienced, he wrote a complete book of household management for her, including a chapter on gardening. It contains sound advice on caring for plants, including a caution not to water in the sun's heat, to place cinders underneath cabbage leaves against caterpillars, instruction that dead branches of sage be removed in winter, and that you should not grow marjoram in the shade. Lavender and mint, as well as other herbs for everyday seasonings in those days included hyssop, tansy, parsley, garlic, borage, rue, and rosemary, to name but a few.

Tania Bayard in her *Sweet Herbs and Sundry Flowers* notes that *The Goodman of Paris* was translated and introduced by Eileen Power, London, Routledge, 1922. We believe it is still available.

The Renaissance

We hear of a remarkable 'Golden Age', which may have actually existed. It is a time in classical mythology when Saturn, the Roman god of agriculture, reigned as king in Latium, a central district of ancient Italy, where he taught agriculture and the arts of civilisation to his people. During his rule everyone experienced peace, happiness and prosperity, and accordingly this period became known as the Golden Age. Another era described as a Golden Age is the Renaissance.

Accounts of world developments tend to trace movements starting from the end of the last Ice Age, covering periods spanning in sequence vast epochs, in what is widely recognised by academic garden writers as the gradual emergence of gardens as we know them today. The eras begin with the primitive age; this was followed by the stone, bronze, and iron ages (the last being the Tanian culture in central and western Europe, which overlapped in Britain the late-Celtic) passing into Romano-Britain and Anglo Saxon civilisations. The next ages to come

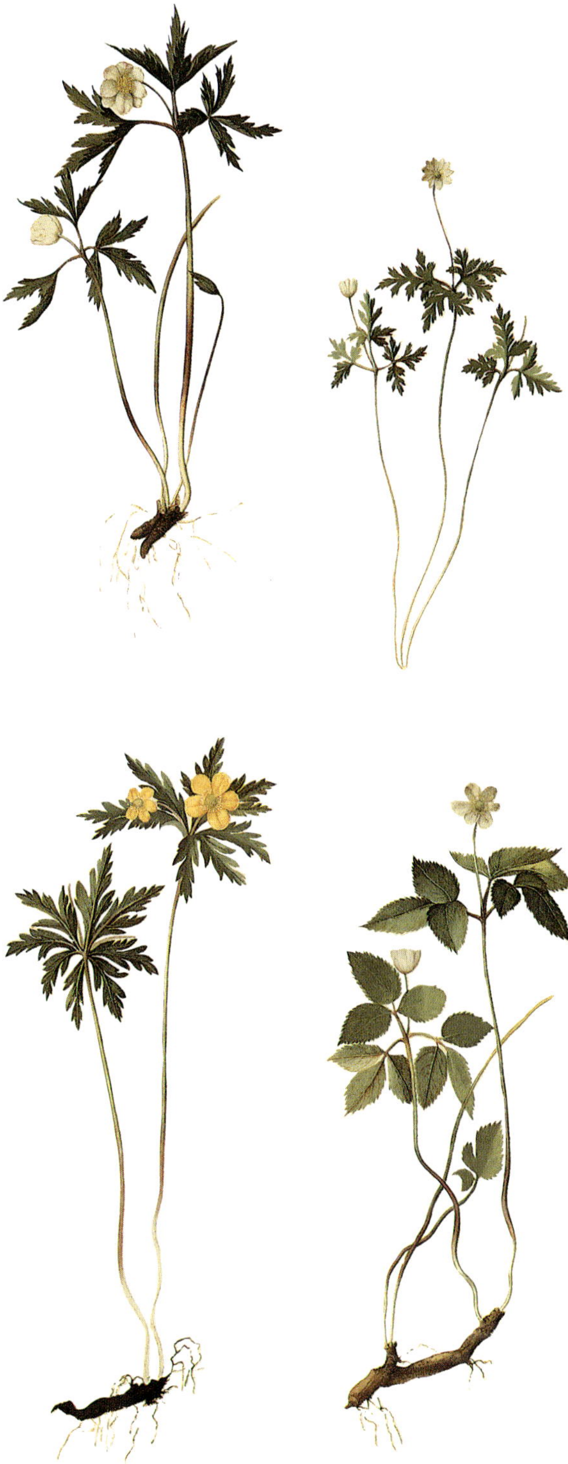

A scientific, analytic approach to plants is evident in these sixteenth-century drawings.

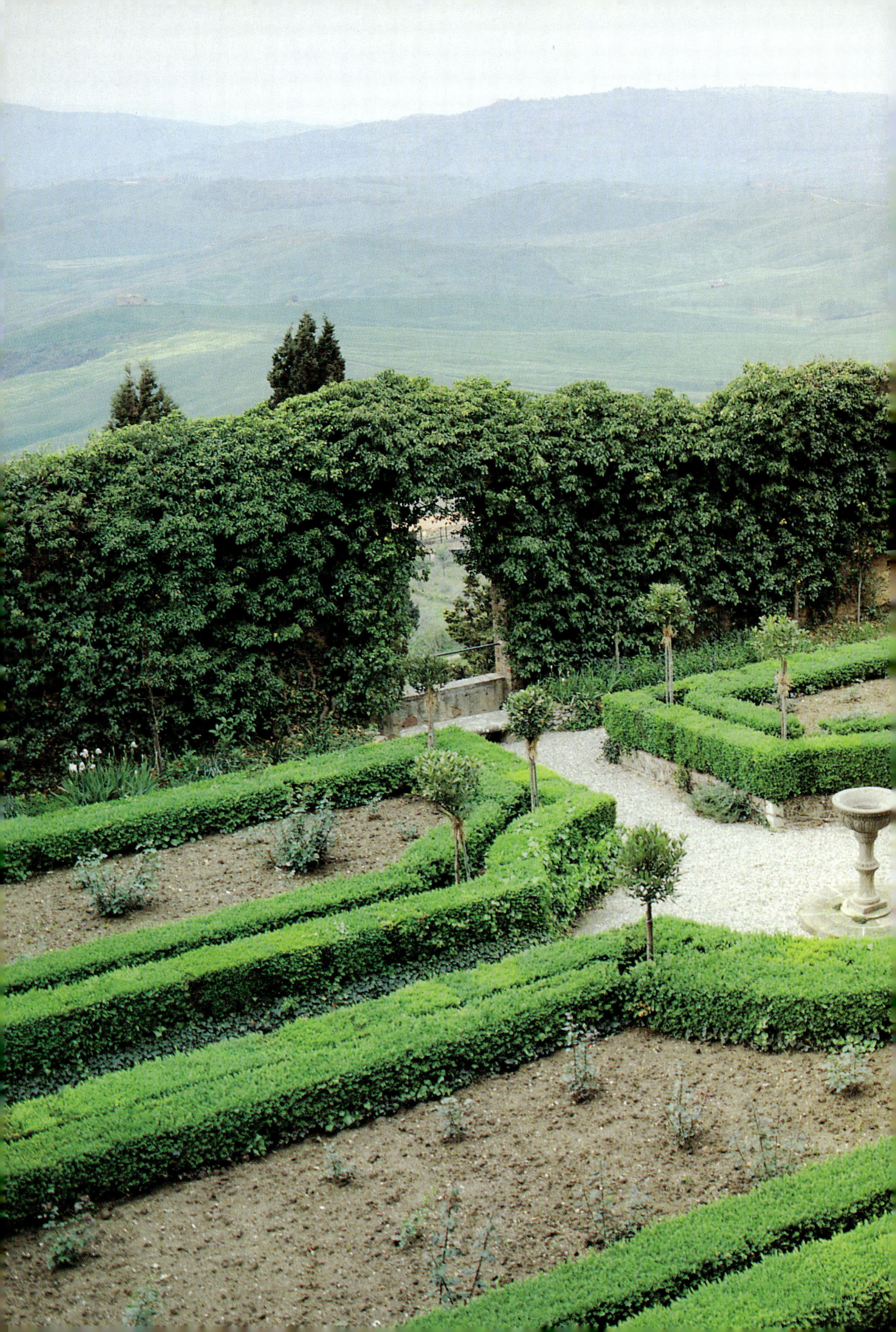

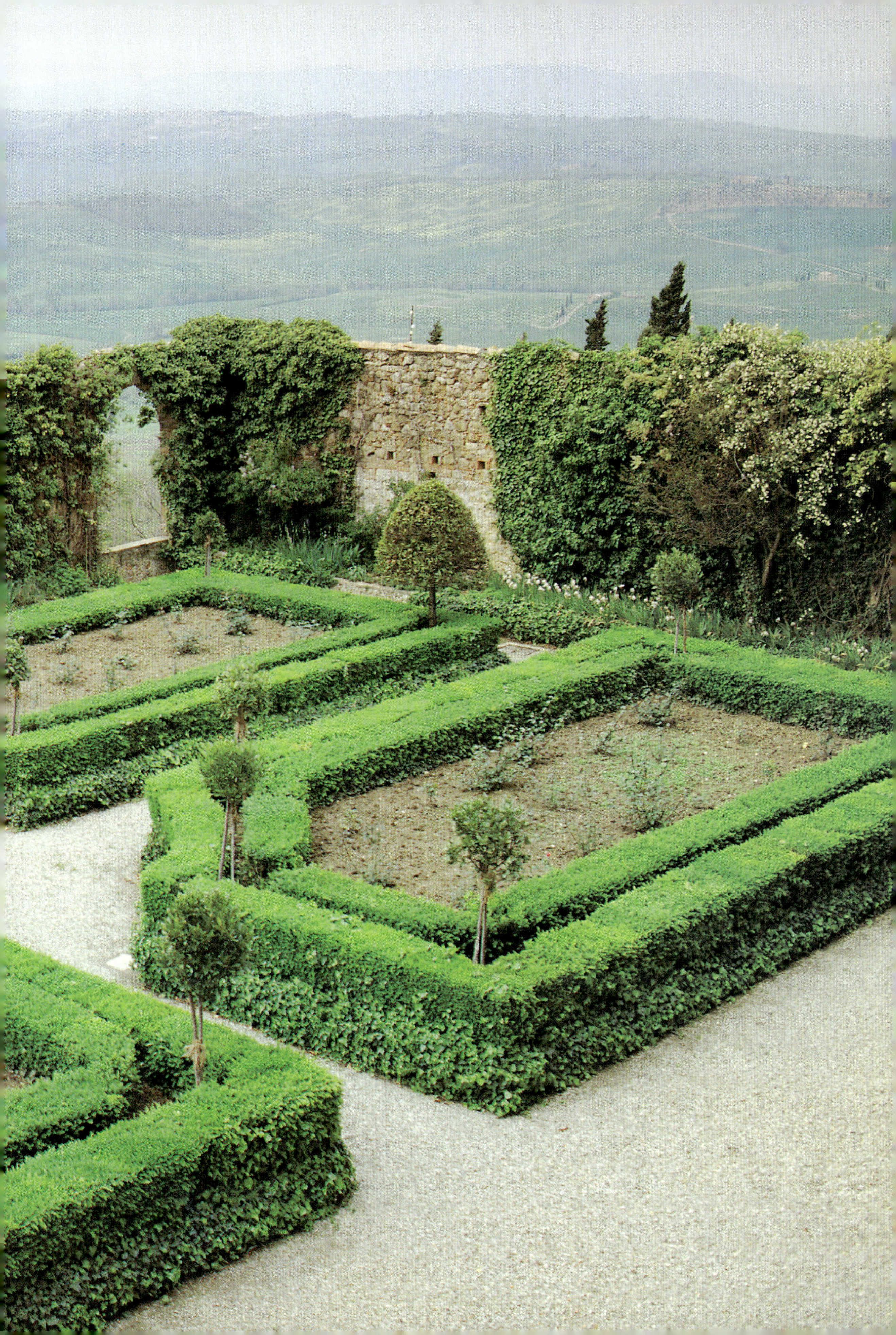

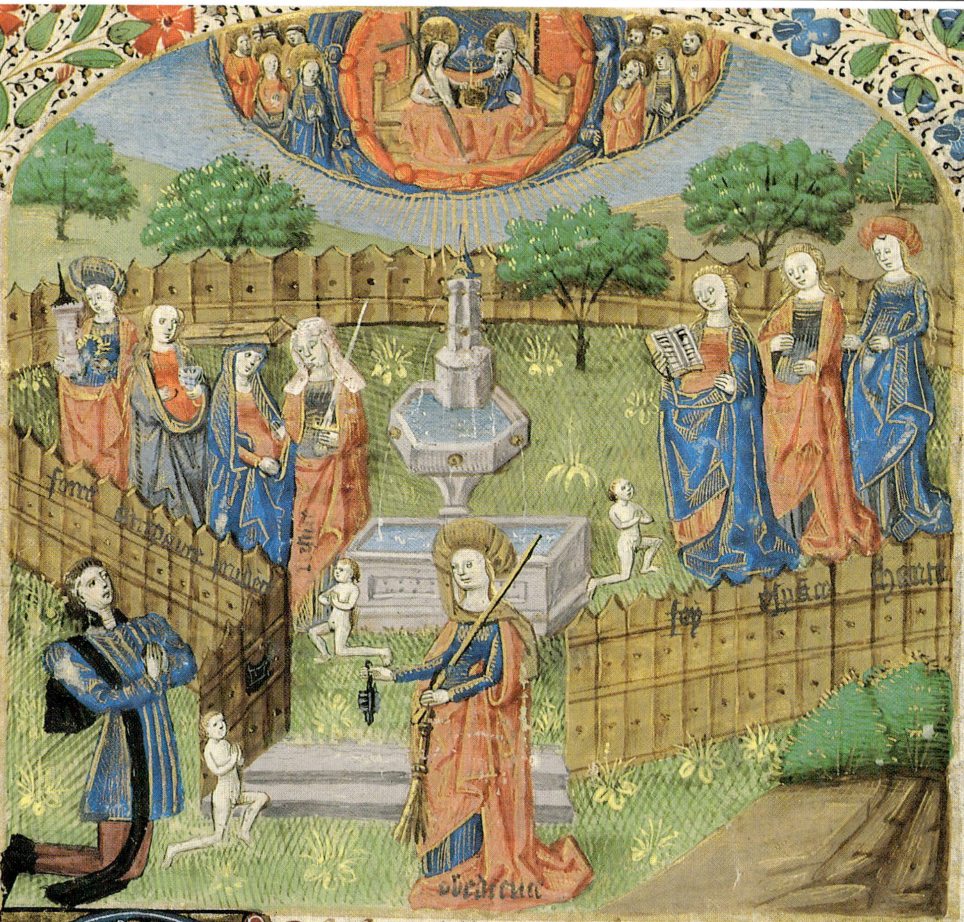

En labitte de devote religion fondee en ce mon
de un desert cest le iardin de vertueuse conso
lation. ou le vray dieu damans habite. Cest
le iardin gracieux ou habite le doulx ihe
sus et ou quel il appelle samie quant il dist ou
livre de chanconnetes amoureuses vien dit il en mon iardin
ma doulce seur ma chiere espouse. Ceste doulce voix ceste
chanconnete chante melodieusement doulcement ihesucrist
le loyal amant en appellant a soy la saincte ame qui est de
lui enamouree par consanguinite et son espouse par affi
nite de grace. Par semblance de nature humaine quil print
de la vierge marie. Est son espouse pour la lomulte de estre

were in turn the Dark, Middle and Mediaeval Ages leading to the Renaissance.

It is said that the last vestiges of the powerful Roman Empire disappeared because Constantinople was captured by the Islamic empire in 1453. Scholars of the previous regime fled to Italy and were the impetus for the Renaissance. This wonderful time began in Italy, spreading eventually throughout all the 'known' world in the fifteenth century. It was a transition in Europe from mediaeval thinking, a freeing of minds from sterile dogmas of the past; it was a revival of learning, of fresh ideas, of higher culture in every form. Garden design too was approached on a more complex level during the Renaissance, an outstanding example of which was achieved with great success by Diane de Poitiers, the beloved mistress of Henri II of France at her home the Chateau d'Anet.

From the Renaissance onwards, a momentum towards greater achievements developed in all areas. The Reformation is the name given to the great religious reconstruction of Western Christendom which took place during the sixteenth century. It also had an impact on thinking, styles, and of course influenced developments in garden planning.

While on the subject of the great movements that affected gardening, and in this case the use and application of herbs as popular, necessary plants, the Age of Reason confronted reality via the use of scientific method; herbal remedies, which worked in a way not *then* amenable to scientific analysis, were dismissed as sorcery and witchcraft. The Industrial Age, which began in the mid-eighteenth century, made the process of manufacturing garden implements (among others) more efficient, and led inevitably to the need for less manual labour.

PREVIOUS PAGES: *Remnants and influences of the Renaissance exist in art and philosophy, and in gardens like this one at Pienza, Italy, with its box-edged beds.*

OPPOSITE: *The garden could be both an enclosure and a place of freedom for women, and served as a motif in illustrated manuscripts.*

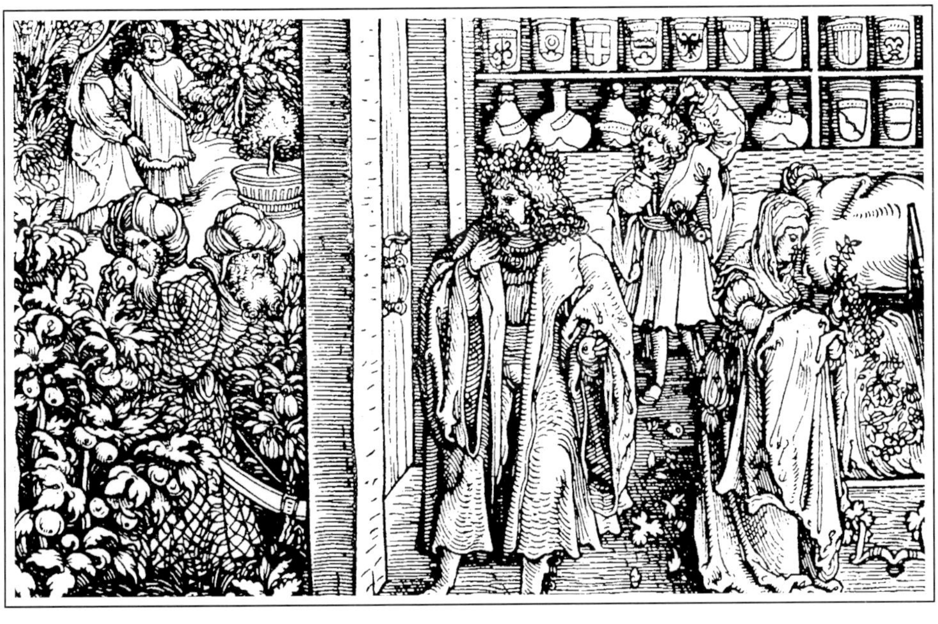

LEFT: *This sixteenth-century image draws attention to the links between the garden and the still room, in a time when reality was being confronted by scientific method, and age-old remedies continued to be drawn upon.*

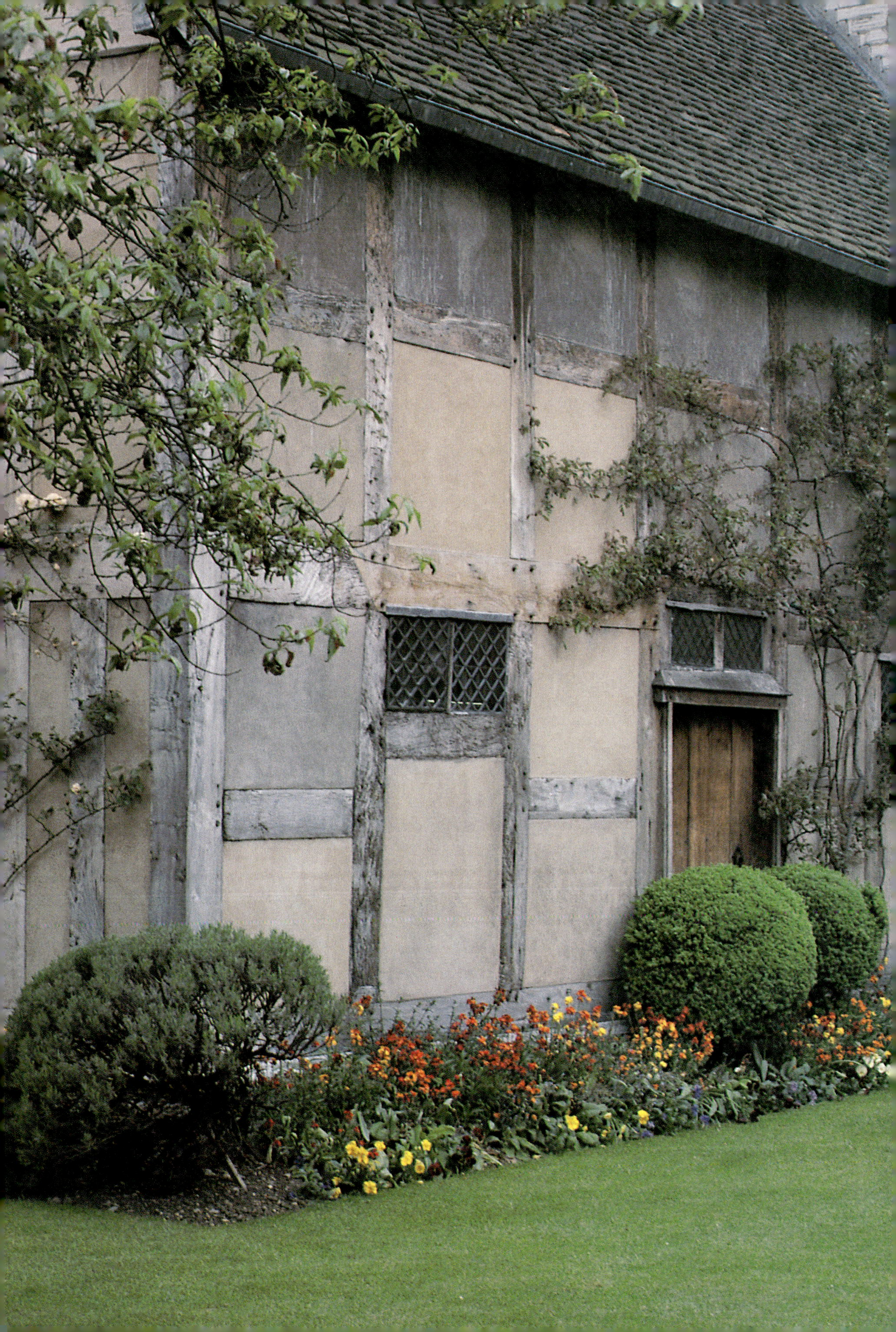

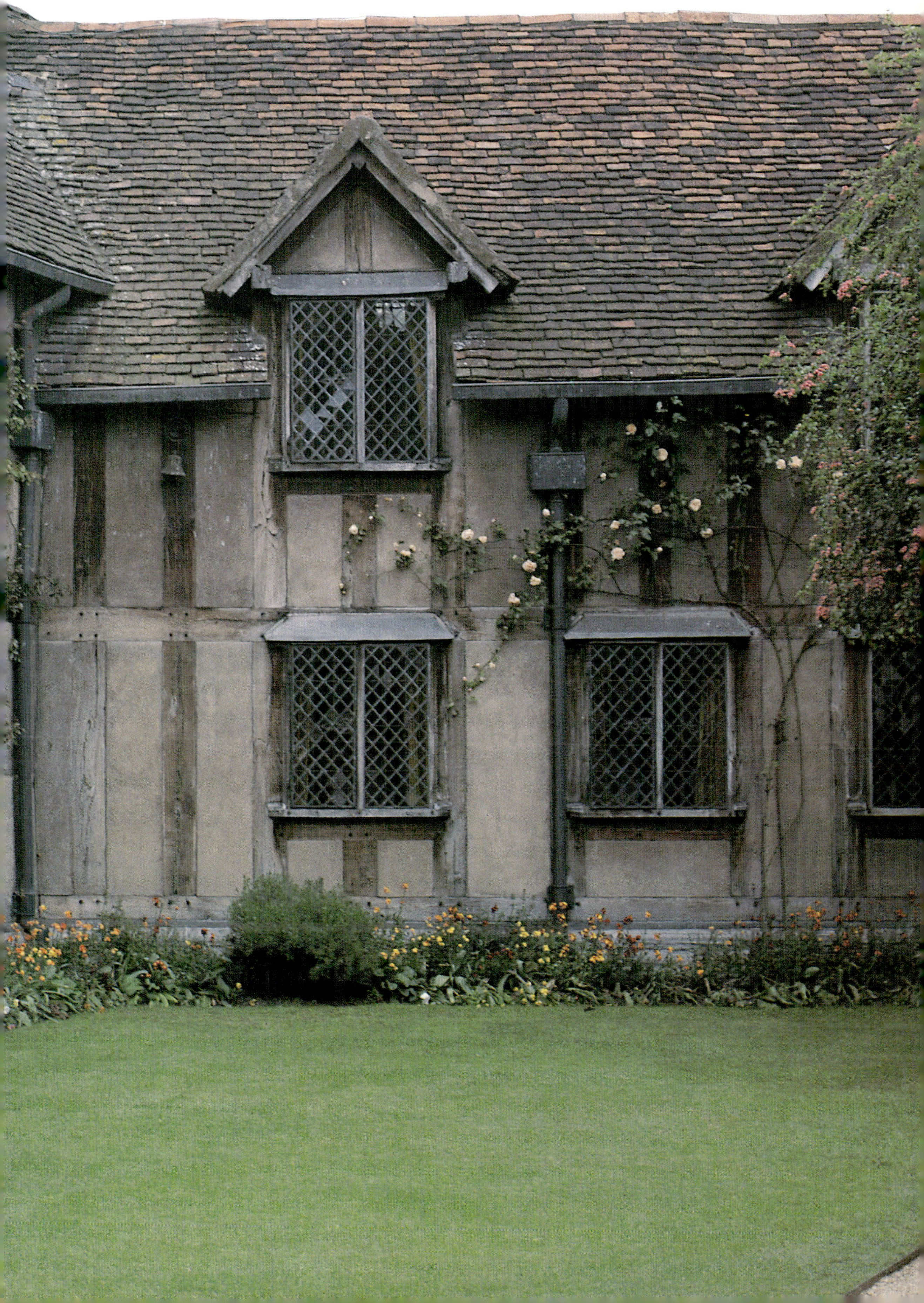

PREVIOUS PAGES: *Shakespeare's birthplace at Stratford-on-Avon.*

OPPOSITE: *New Place Stratford: a tribute to the richness of words, flowers, imagery and lushness.*

William Shakespeare

But flowers distill'd, though they with
winter meet,
Lease but their show; their substance still
lives sweet.

WILLIAM SHAKESPEARE

Two hundred years after Chaucer lived, the immortal Elizabethan Bard William Shakespeare was born in the sixteenth century. He was baptised in the parish church of Stratford-on-Avon, Warwickshire, on 26 April 1564, and lived until 23 April 1616.

Shakespeare is acknowledged as the greatest playwright and poet in English literature. He was the son of Mary Arden and John Shakespeare of Stratford, a prosperous dealer in agricultural produce, who later became mayor. William was well educated at the local grammar school. Growing up in the country, his works reveal that he was a lover and expert chronicler of nature, often writing of herbs and flowers, their charm, appeal and their special meanings:

Ophelia: There's rosemary, that's for remembrance; pray you, love, remember. And there is pansies, that's for thoughts . . . There's fennel for you, and columbines. There's rue for you; and here's some for me. We may call it herb of grace o' Sundays. O! you must wear your rue with a difference. There's a daisy. I would give you some violets, but they wither'd all when my father died . . .

(HAMLET, ACT IV, SCENE V.)

It was quite natural with Shakespeare's pastoral background, comprehending eye, and sensitivity of soul, that he wrote expressively and often of elves, fairies, sprites, and witches. These beings appear in many poems and plays:

Ariel: (an airy spirit)
Where the bee sucks, there suck I
In a cowslip's bell I lie;
There I couch when owls do cry.
On the bat's back I do fly
After summer merrily:
Merrily, merrily shall I live now
Under the blossom that hangs on the bough.

(THE TEMPEST, ACT V, SCENE I.)

We were in London when the much loved and distinguished actor, Sir Laurence Olivier, died. On Saturday, 15 July 1989, the *London Daily Express* wrote movingly of his funeral: 'One floral tribute summed up the feelings for Lord Olivier who will forever be remembered for his Shakespearean triumphs on stage and screen. It borrowed Horatio's words to the dead Hamlet . . . "Goodnight Sweet Prince; and flights of angels sing thee to thy rest." '

In the oak casket were the family's 2 foot floral crown in a bed of mixed herbs and flowers: 'All the flowers had connections with the works of Shakespeare — lavender, savory, mint, marjoram, marigold, violets, daffodils, oxslips, lilies, rosemary, pansies, fennel, columbine, ruc and daisies.'

In England there are nostalgic Shakespearian gardens at Stratford-

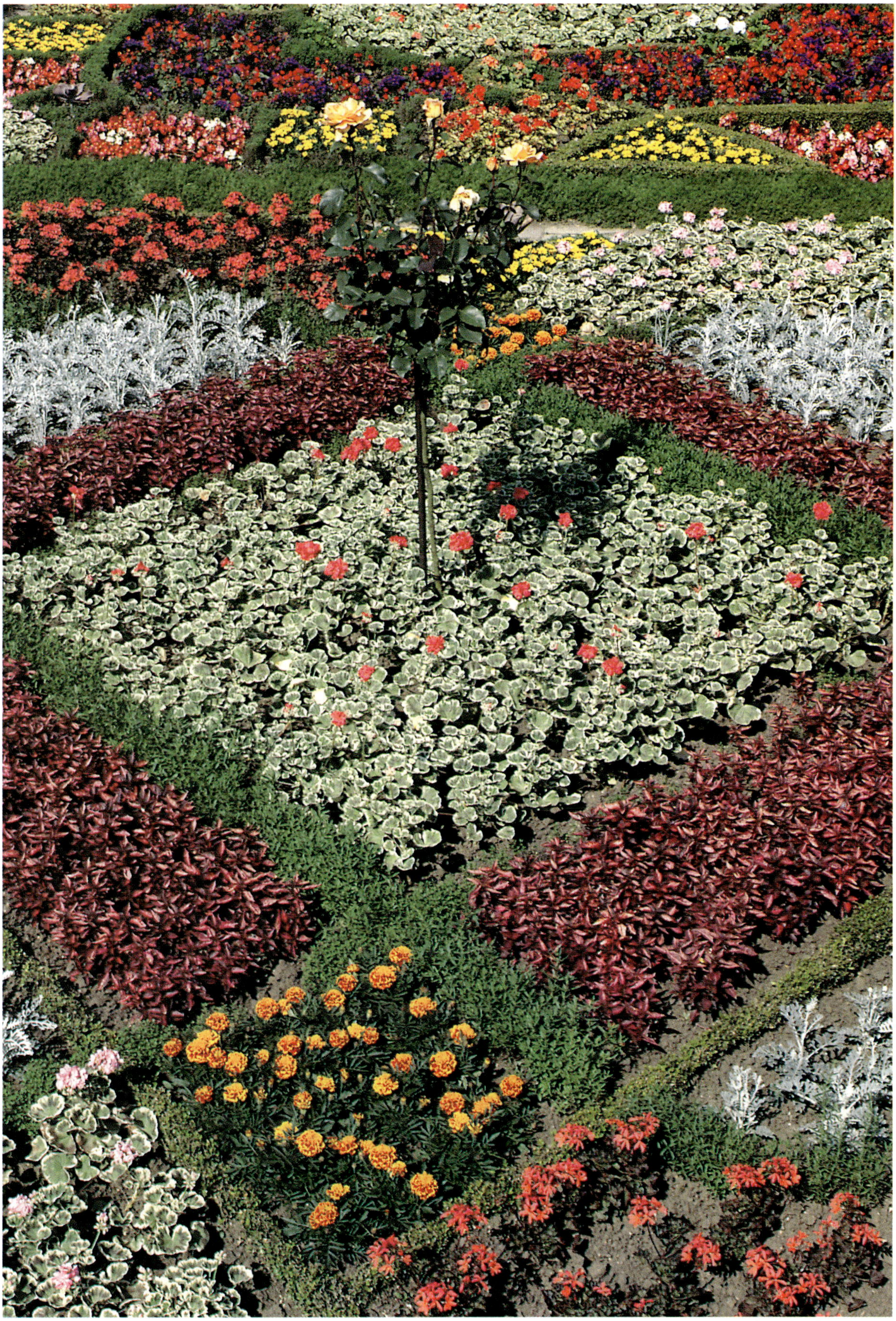

on-Avon. Shakespeare's birthplace was purchased and restored in 1877, the Trustees replanting with herbs, flowers and trees in memory of the poet, and the original layout remained unchanged. There is a dedicated Shakespeare Birthplace Trust, with a Director; the institution has the responsibility of maintaining the Shakespearian properties.

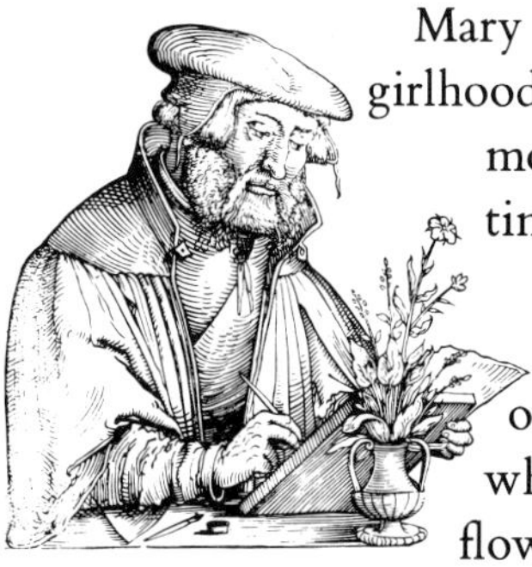

Mary Arden's House, the girlhood home of Shakespeare's mother, is a fine, half-timbered Tudor Farmstead at Wilmacote. Old-fashioned red and white roses climb over the front of the house, while among the herbs and flowers are quaint, shaped hedges of box, obviously very old.

Anne Hathaway's cottage belonged to Shakespeare's wife, and Levi Fox in his charming booklet *The Shakespearian Gardens* describes it as 'the picturesque thatched farmhouse where Shakespeare's wife lived before her marriage is famous the world over, famous because with its infinite variety of colour, the fragrance of its flowers and herbs, and the restful beauty of its orchard in blossom, it affords an almost perfect setting for this gem of early domestic architecture.'

When Shakespeare retired from his busy theatre life, he lived at New Place, a handsome estate in Stratford. It is also planted with the flowers, herbs, trees and shrubs that he loved and wrote into his works. The intricate Elizabethan knot gardens were once defined as 'one of the most enchanting sights of Warwickshire'.

The Shakespeare Birthplace Trust is responsible for all people the world over to see, and remember the poet's inspirational power with words, best described by Levi Fox when he says:

Of Shakespeare's own love and knowledge of flowers and plants and of his delight in the natural scenery of his native Warwickshire there is ample evidence in his plays and sonnets as with his profound understanding of human character, so with his knowledge of the processes of nature; the poet's power of observation and sympathy were matched with the genius not only to describe what he saw, but to convey in happy phrase and touching epithet something of the inner meaning and mystery of their loveliness.

Shakespeare is responsible for having enthusiastically furthered, together with a long chain of men and women throughout the ages, the awareness and the history of the potent forces and simple beauty of our inheritance of herbs and flowers.

The Old Herbals

Various countries have old hand written manuscript-herbals in safe-keeping. Two tenth-century Anglo-Saxon treatises are the *Leech Book of Bald* and the *Lacnunga* as already mentioned, and there is also the Saxon translations of the *Herbarium of Apuleius*. In the thirteenth century, Bartholomew the Englishman wrote an advanced, simply written book on herbs which was popular with Parisian scholars, and was read for three centuries afterwards. This renowned professor of theology was born in England, studied in Paris and lived the greater part of his life in France. William Caxton's press enabled writers to have their works printed, and the first English herbal appeared in print in 1525, published by Richard Banckes. The work was taken from old manuscripts and called *Banckes's Herbal*. Herbalists, especially monks, also wrote, and later there was John Gerard (fifteenth century), John Parkinson (seventeenth century), Nicholas Culpeper (seventeenth century) and William Coles (seventeenth century).

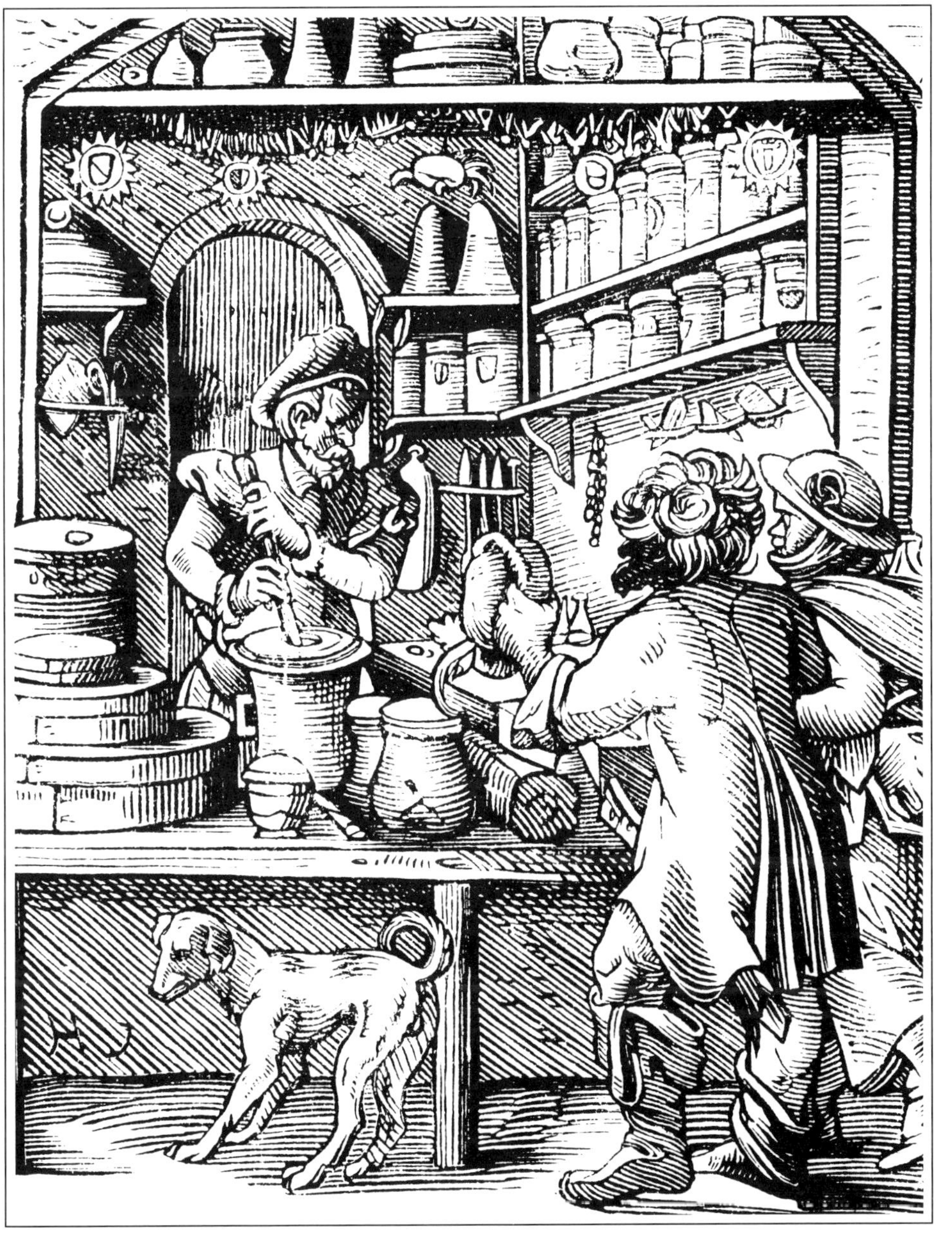

LEFT: *Herbals, herbs and folklore all have their place in any consideration of natural medicine and health in history. This sixteenth-century picture of a druggist helps us imagine the day-to-day application of such knowledge.*

The Doctrine of Signatures

In the sixteenth century, the Swiss Paracelsus was advancing a new theory about herbalism which became known as the *Doctrine of Signatures*. It was based on the belief that Nature had shown by the appearance and scent of each

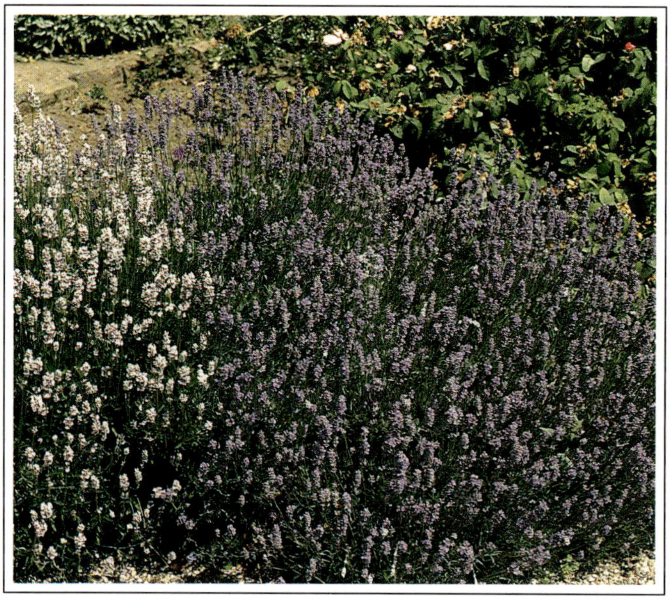

ABOVE: *Physic gardens were, and still are, a place for organised knowledge and growth. This mauve and white lavender is growing at Chelsea Physic Garden.*

plant their healing properties, for those who observed carefully. Many of the old herbalists followed this doctrine, but not all: there are practitioners today who feel there is truth in the *Doctrine of Signatures*.

It was also held that the plants of each country cured the ills of the individuals living there, which included those herbs naturalised in different lands over hundreds of years. Some modern specialists in herbal medicine think this theory is still apt, and a clever European homoeopathic doctor who came to Australia to live, and who was our family physician until he died, was making a study of Australian plants for this purpose: he cured my cystitis in 24 hours with homoeopathic drops he had prepared himself from the native 'trigger plant'.

Gardens and Still-Rooms

When people began to live in dwellings, whether in groups of houses (later called a village), singly, or in the larger domains of families of substance living in small manors and farm-houses, every plant that was grown — herbs, certain trees and shrubs, or 'cottage garden' flowers — were of use to the mistress of the house. Roses, violets, honeysuckle, lavender, poppies and periwinkles are but a selection of blooms that comprised a useful garden. They, along with fragrant herbs, were needed for flavouring food, strewing on floors, preparing for medicines or laying in closets to repel insects, and all in their own way were a necessity for the members of the household. Only the very wealthy, even in Tudor times, had separate gardens for pleasure.

Our ancestors were resourceful, and knew how to make the most of what nature had given them. For instance, in mediaeval times and before, ash twigs were tied together and used as egg whisks, horsetail made brushes, and the wood from elder trees was cut and polished into meat skewers, shoemaker's pegs, and needles for weaving nets. Combs and musical instruments were also made from elder wood, while the pretty pink-flowering herb soapwort (*Saponaria officinalis*), often called 'Bouncing Bet', was made into a gentle lather for cleaning old and delicate fabrics, and for washing white kid gloves. Nowadays, this herb is known as the most effective, non-harmful cleaner for washing antique tapestries, bringing back the original bright colours dulled by centuries of dust.

From Tudor times onwards, the flower garden and the beginning of complicated plantings, like knot gardens, were separated from herb gardens. Some gardens were very large, having owners who were rich and powerful, while the smaller gardens of poorer folk, in villages and on minor farms, were smaller holdings crammed with scented herbs and colourful flowers, all growing happily together.

Most households, from the grandest employing a head housekeeper to the average cottage with its thrifty owner, possessed a still-room where medicines and potions of all kinds were concocted from herbs and certain flowers from their gardens. The shelves would contain healing unguents, beauty creams and lotions, wash-balls, healing decoctions, perfumed waters, preserves, crystallised flowers, elixirs and syrups, perfumed oils, infusing vinegars, scented candles, and many other compounds copied from old family 'receipts' obtained by or exchanged with friends, or gathered from the early 'herbals'. There was also a multitude of delightful and practical recipes in manuscripts with fascinating titles such as *The Good Housewife's Jewel and Rare Conceits in Cookery* by T. Dawson (1585), *The Queen's Closet Opened* by W. M. (Cook to Queen Henrietta Maria) (1685), *The Compleat Gardener* by John Evelyn (1699), and *Leechdome,*

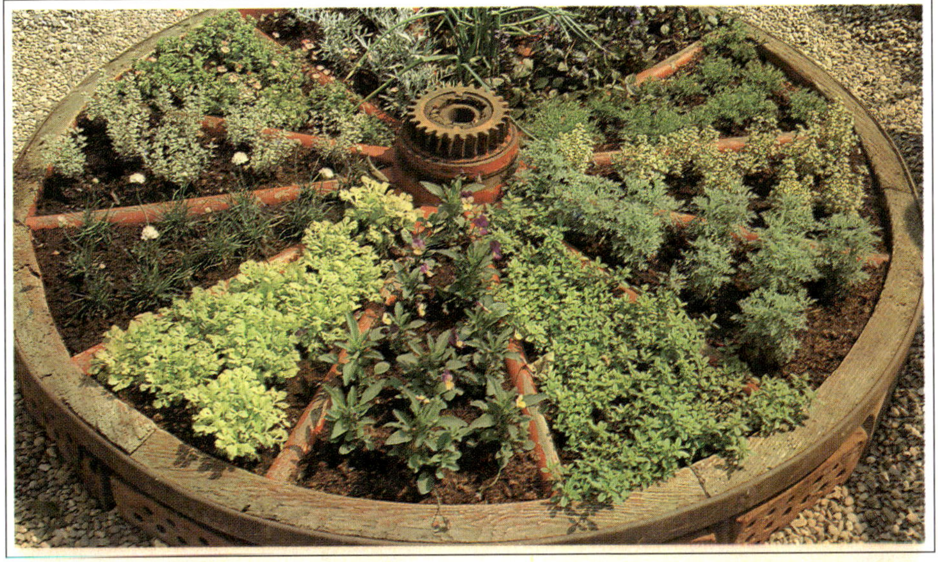

LEFT: *Herbs can be grown in a variety of forms for ease of access, from huge estates and gardens in institutions, to individual pots, or a simple but attractive herb wheel.*

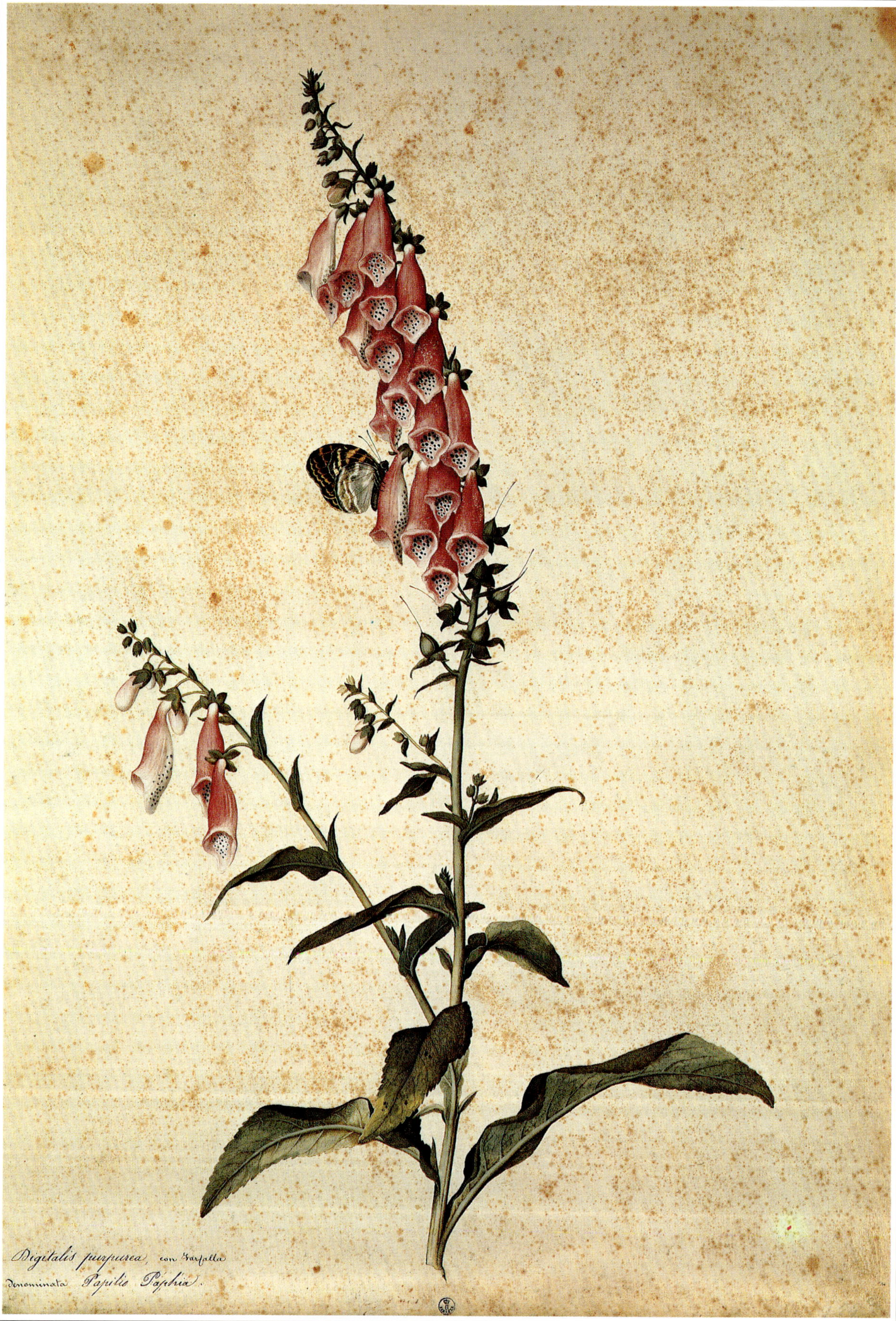
Digitalis purpurea, con farfalla
denominata Papilio Paphia.

Wortcunning and Starcraft by D. Cockayne (1865).

These titles evoke another more leisurely age, an era that believed in the real power of certain plants, and of veiled mysteries, which today arouse the mind to muse on the scent of old roses, the textures of fine silk and old lace, and the elusive waft of flower-permeated beeswax candles, for:

Scents are the souls of flowers; they may be even perceptible in the land of shadows. The tulip is a flower without a soul, but the rose and the lily seem to have one.

JOUBERT

Carl Linnaeus (1707–78)

In the eighteenth century, Carl Linnaeus was born. He is an outstanding person in garden history, renowned as the first individual to classify plants into scientific botanical orders. Latin names were given to every plant, the first being the name of the plant *family*, and the second a separate name, thus setting each one apart within the same structural group.

Linnaeus was born in Sweden; the son of a clergyman, he first researched theology and then botany, which led to a study of medicine. His knowledge of plants impressed his professor so much that the teacher handed over his own botanical work to Linnaeus. Linnaeus wrote the *Bibliotheca Botanica* in 1736, and other works followed. He graduated as an MD at Leiden, and on his return to Sweden practised as a physician. Because of his scholarship and attainment in the science of plants — a comprehension which went hand in hand with medicine then as it had in the past — he was eventually appointed professor of Botany at the University in Upsala.

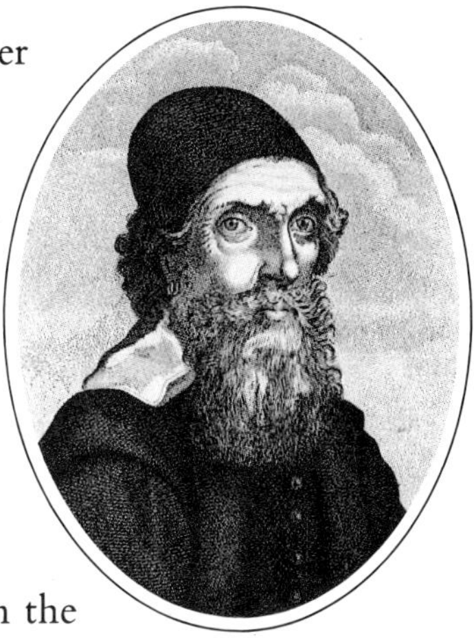

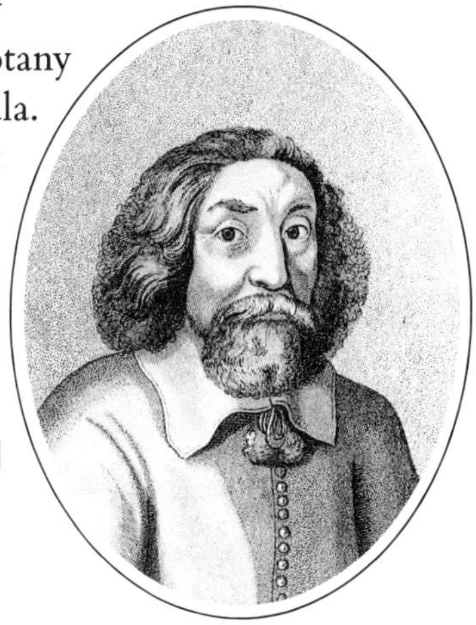

Linnaeus's arrangement of plants into groups formed the basis for a more exact botanical system and placed plant research on a new path . . . his basic method is still in use today.

Some Important Garden Makers

In Europe from the sixteenth century a change in the character of garden styles and various modes of landscaping made an exciting appearance. There were talented men, and later women, who had profound effects on garden fashions in their own homelands, and the results, when admired, were copied by other countries.

It is worth recalling that long before this the construction of manifold features in the art of landscaping, including the use of water, had been achieved as far

ABOVE TOP: *John Tradescant Senior (d. 1637)*
ABOVE: *John Tradescant Junior (1608–1662)*

OPPOSITE: *Digitalis purpurea* by Ligozzi Jacopo (1547–1632).

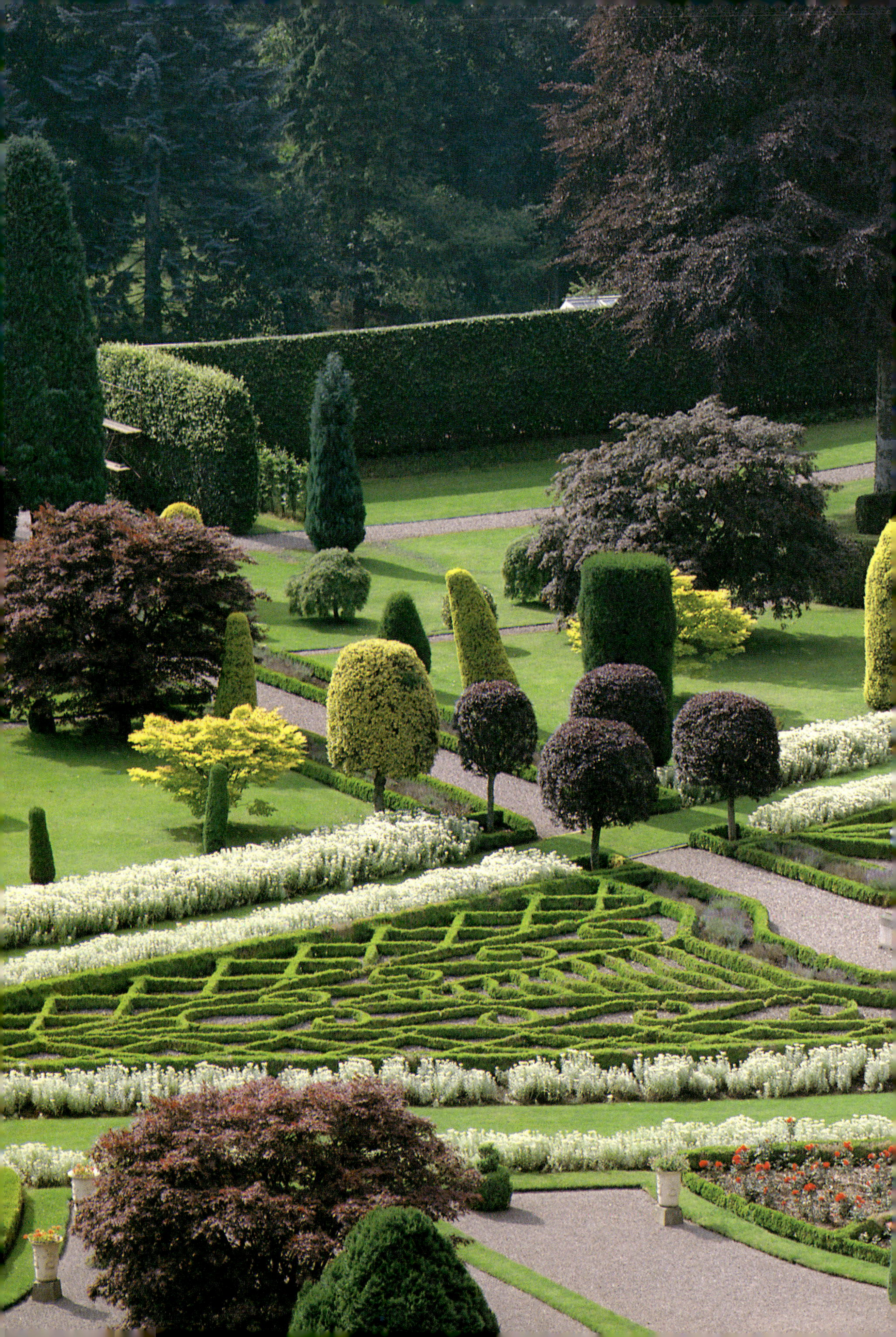

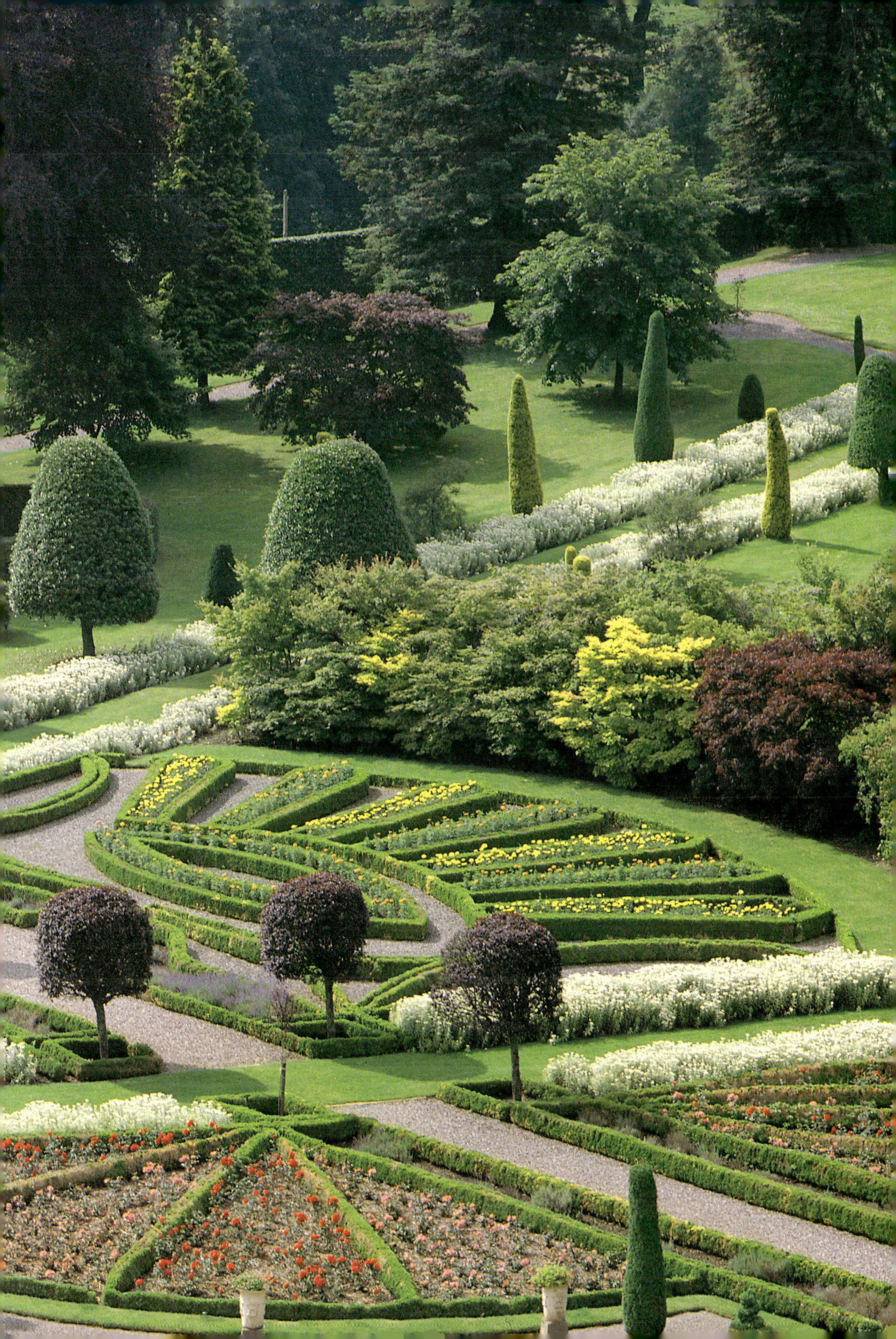

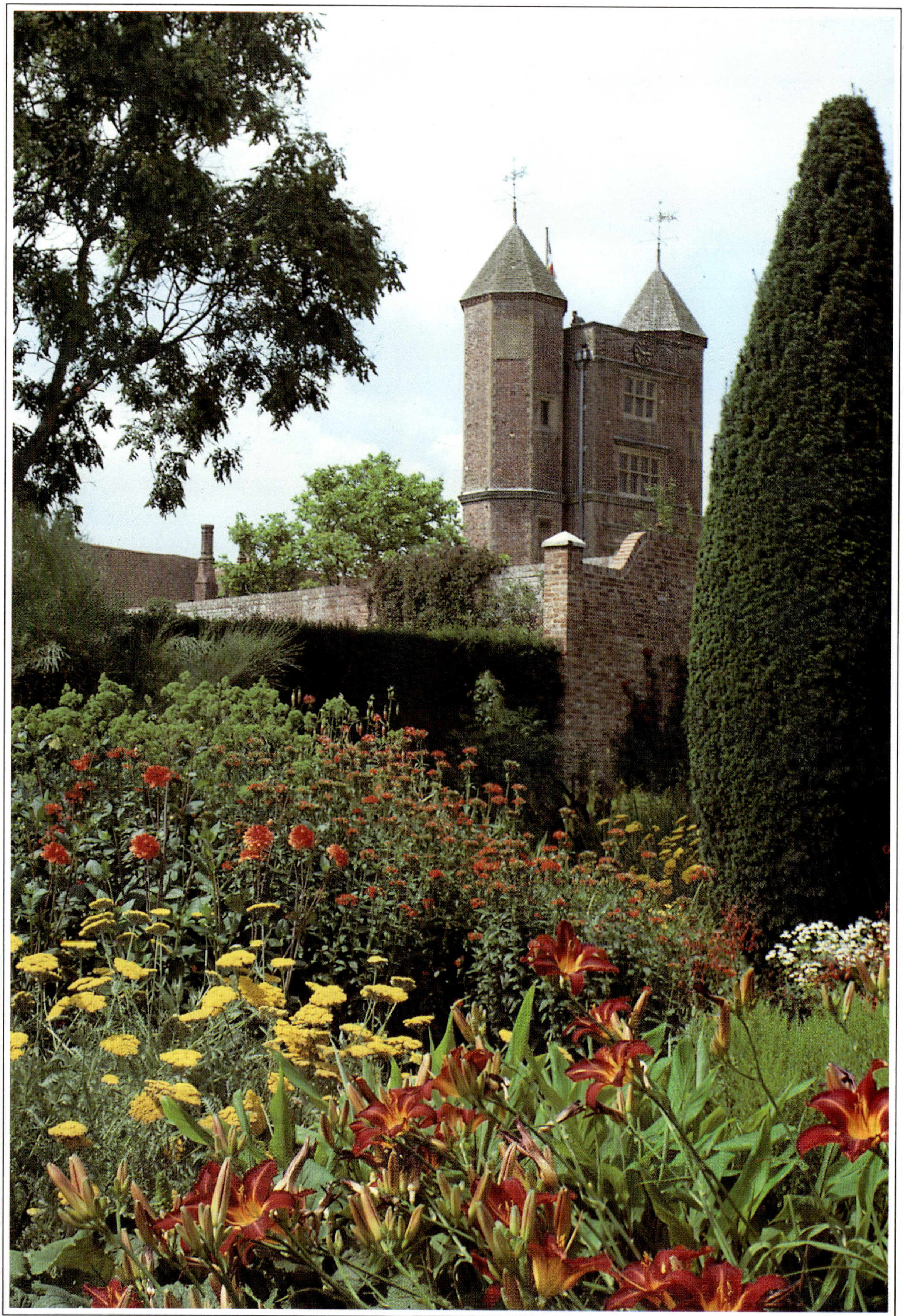

back as ancient times. Some amazingly complex designs in the creation of landscapes have influenced garden patterns throughout the ages and in the present includes the symmetry of old-fashioned-type herb gardens.

In England in the sixteenth and seventeenth centuries there were several great gardening men, and some inspired aristocratic amateurs. Outstanding among them are the distinguished Tradescant family, father and son; they were keen plant collectors too and travelled widely to find new specimens. John, the elder, was head gardener to Charles I and John the Younger also became a Royal gardener. William Kent is remembered as the first recognised professional English landscaper, and he had a man working for him called Lancelot 'Capability' Brown. Brown eventually became Kent's illustrious successor. Capability Brown refashioned many large estates without diminishing their size, styling them into beautiful landscapes with lakes and tree plantings opening out into vistas. His work can still be seen at several great and historic properties, such as Blenheim Palace.

Among other notable garden professionals are Alexander Pope, Humphrey Repton, Sir William Chambers, and Charles Bridgeman. Well-known garden planners in the twentieth century are Lawrence Johnston, Christopher Lloyd and Sir Edwin Lutyens. Lutyens was an architect and designer who frequently worked in creating gardens with Gertrude Jekyll, who still shines forth as an inspired garden designer. Other famous gardening women are Beth Chatto, Margery Fish, Anne Scott-James, Edna Walling of Australia, and Victoria (Vita) Sackville-West. Vita Sackville-West and her husband, Sir Harold Nicholson, were both gifted writers and creators of beautiful gardens, including their especially lovely and final one at Sissinghurst Castle, which you can still visit and which is, indeed, an enchanting experience (see 'Sissinghurst Castle' p. 109).

The many faceted Constance Spry — cook, artist of social etiquette, and inspiration to many of us — must also be mentioned, not because she was an eminent gardener but because she was an originator, a brilliant perfectionist in everything she turned her hand to, whether it was in the garden

PREVIOUS PAGES: *As garden makers and garden fashions developed, formations as stylised as this parterre at Drummond Castle, Perthshire, emerged.*

OPPOSITE: *The gardens at Sissinghurst castle provide an enchanting experience, and reflect complexities in garden styles.*

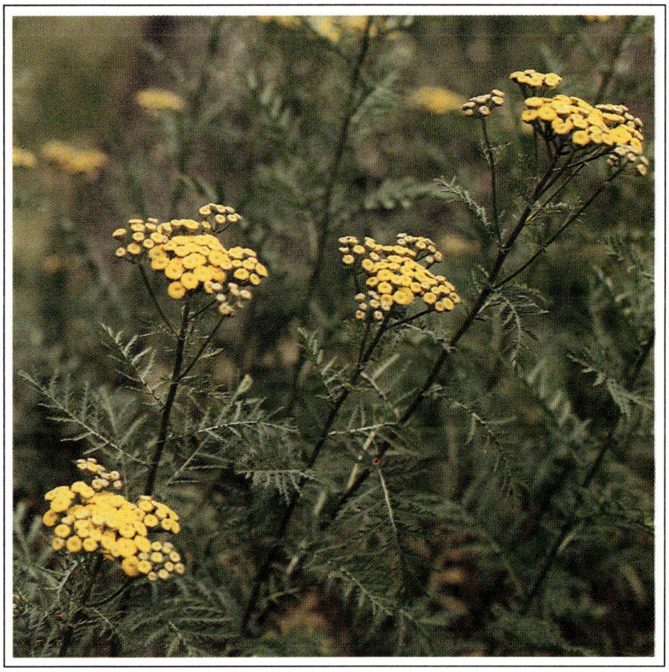

BELOW: *Tansy, photographed in Chelsea Physic Garden.*

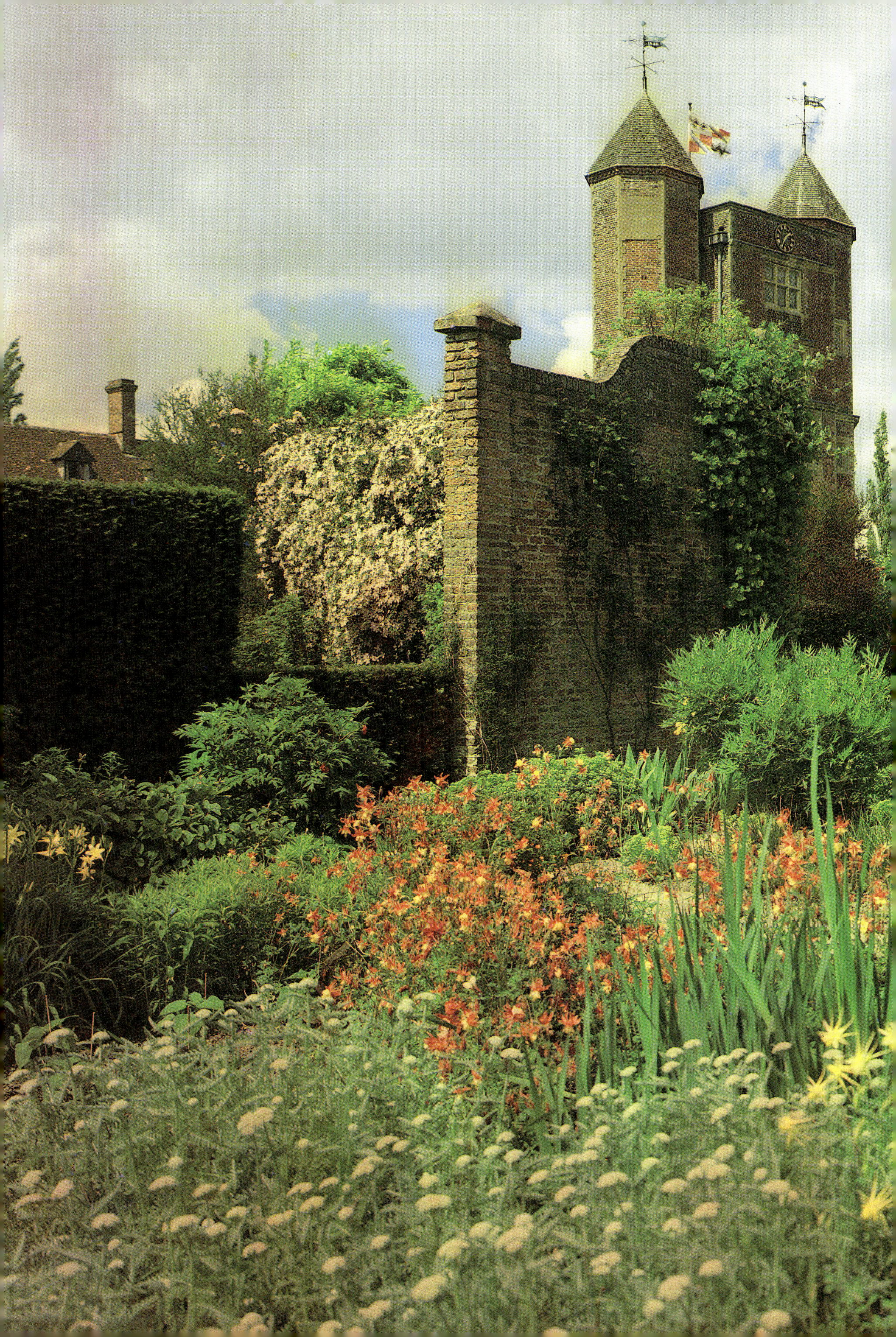

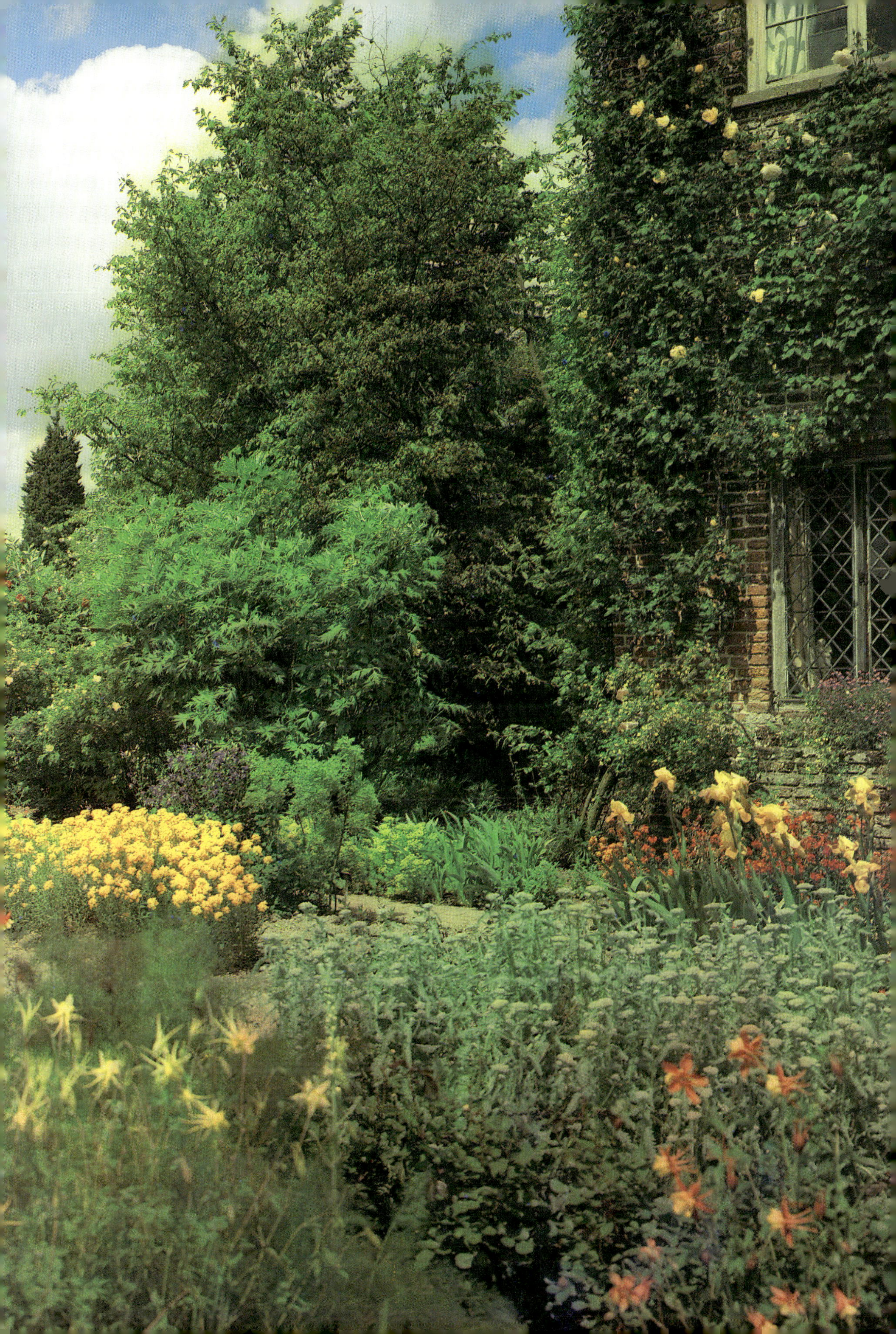

PREVIOUS PAGES: *A formal castle and a lush body of colour show clever considerations of balance and contrast at Sissinghurst Castle gardens.*

BELOW: *Constance Spry, a woman of innovation and inspiration, helped renew appreciation of old roses such as this perfumed variety,* Rosa Reeusa.

growing herbs for her cooking, embroidering a filmy luncheon cloth, or inventively arranging flowers, fruit and (if the occasion was suitable) vegetables and bread. To our minds her special appeal is in her use of different kinds of carefully picked old roses flowing out of unlikely containers normally used in other ways, such as silver teapots, copper samovars, needle-work boxes, or every-day brown pottery jugs and pretty china gravy boats. Possibly because of Mrs Spry's decorative ways with roses, she helped bring back the current appreciation and nostalgia for them; there is certainly a new old-rose called Constance Spry. It was bred by David Austin of Wolverhampton, England from the Gallica 'Belle Isis'; the unfurled blooms have a tender sweet-spice fragrance, with a tightly packed display of clear pink petals. Austin is world-famous to rose-lovers for his work in bringing back the incomparable old scented ones.

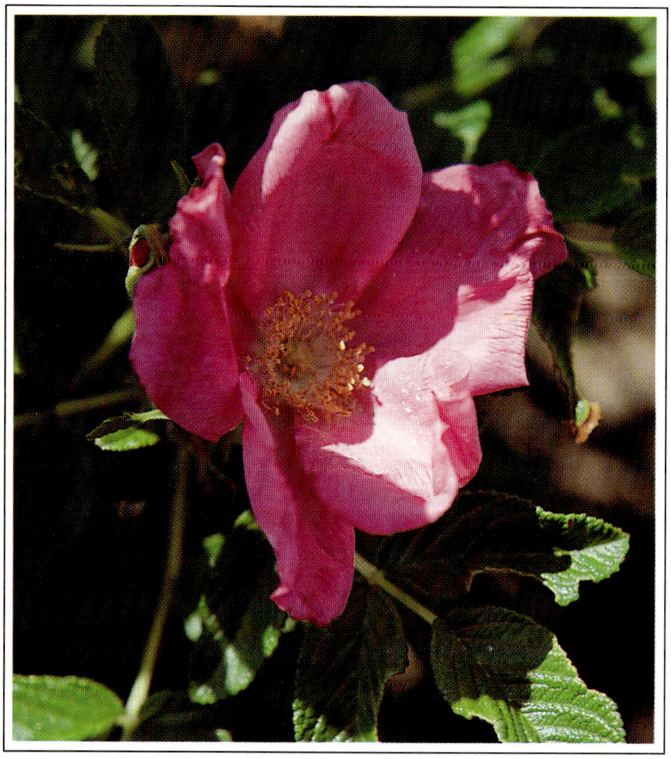

Eleanour Sinclair Rohde has the gratitude of all herb-devotees; she wrote many erudite and enthusiastic books on herbs, scented flowers, old herbals and gardens and what was grown in them, tirelessly researching in libraries for ancient and forgotten works. A deeply perceptive extract from *The Scented Garden* is evocative of the everlasting delight of a true lover of plants:

The melodies of the flowers — the music of fairyland — cannot be heard by mortal ears. Yet throughout the year this lovely music is being played. When the snowdrops appear, do we not feel we are listening to fairy bells, the 'horns of elfland faintly blowing,' telling us of the coming spring, when the golden trumpets of the daffodils will take up the refrain? . . . the scents of the summer flowers are rich and joyous and sweetest of all are scents of the 'old' roses. The scent of the cabbage rose is more than a scent. It is the beauty of life itself, of its sorrows as well as its joys.

Moreover, there are still important garden writers, for example Rosemary Verey, Avilde Lees-Milne and Penelope Hobhouse who have all written about, and created, unique and glorious gardens. We are fortunate that most of their garden genius can be seen today.

It is true to say that garden-making never stands still; there has

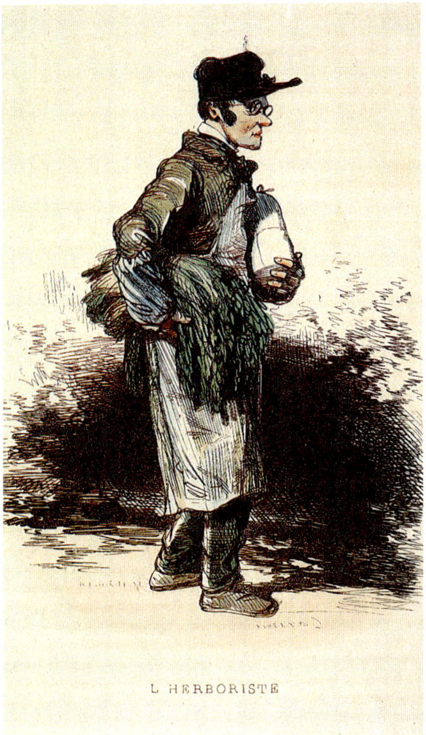

been in the past and the present a living, flowing transition which is forever exciting. Creating a personal environment gives a vibrant sense of achievement, and the result appeals directly to the five senses . . . sight, smell, taste, touch and, finally, sound. There is the thrill of finding a thrusting shoot from fallen seed to begin a new cycle; a delicious waft of scented foliage and flowers; the sweet taste of a plucked bergamot petal, and the astringent tingle on the palate of bitter rue; the velvet-textured greenness of peppermint-geranium silvered with dew; a whispering of breeze-rustled leaves; a resonance of humming bees ecstatic from feasting on nectar; and the music of birds carolling in descant a song of praise for the making of a garden.

Mrs C. F. Leyel and Culpeper House

In the first half of the twentieth century Mrs C. F. Leyel wrote many books on herbs, including *The Truth About Herbs*, *Compassionate Herbs* and *Elixirs of Life*. She also opened a herbalist's shop in Baker Street, London, calling it Culpeper House in memory of the seventeenth-century herbalist, Nicholas Culpeper, and there established the business as the Society of Herbalists Ltd.

The shop was an immediate resounding success.

Mrs Leyel worked hard for the recognition of herbs as a healing art, as this practice had gone out of date since the introduction of modern scientific discoveries. Now there are many branches of Culpeper House, carrying the same types of 'still-room' products that Mrs Leyel introduced in the first shop. Elixirs, lotions, creams, wholesome sweet-scented distillations of plants in the form of medicines, perfumes, lotions, soaps, creams, tisanes, and fresh and dried herbs for cooking. The natural cosmetics are made from such healing flowers as lilies, roses, cowslips, and chamomile, and other herbs used are rosemary, sage, lavender, thyme, balm, mint and saponaria.

Having visited one delightful Culpeper House in London, and another in Cambridge, we were enchanted with the concepts Mrs Leyel had begun and which are obviously still highly popular.

LEFT: *This French herbalist from the mid-nineteenth century reminds us that gardens are made by nameless workers and individuals as well as eminent garden makers.*

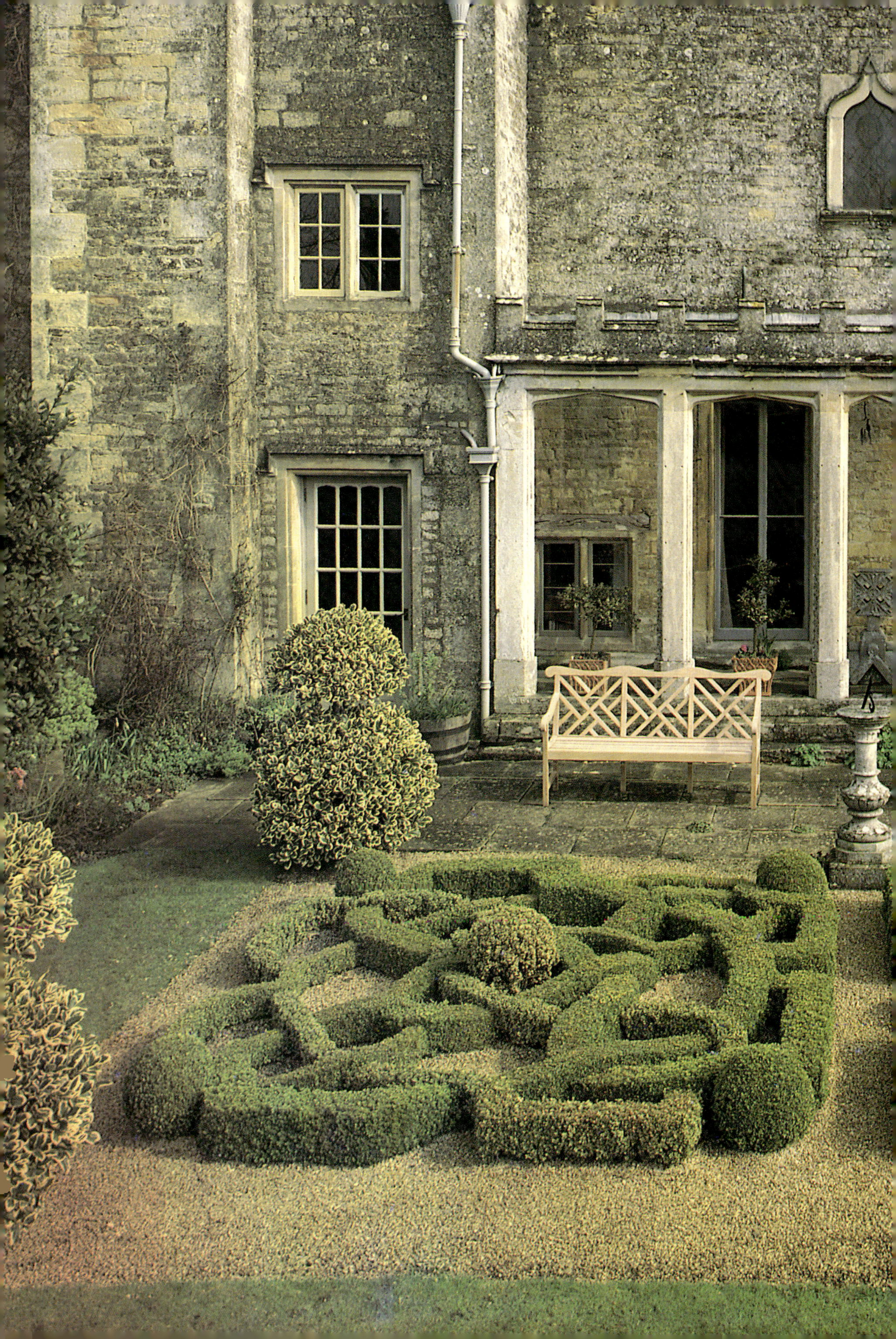

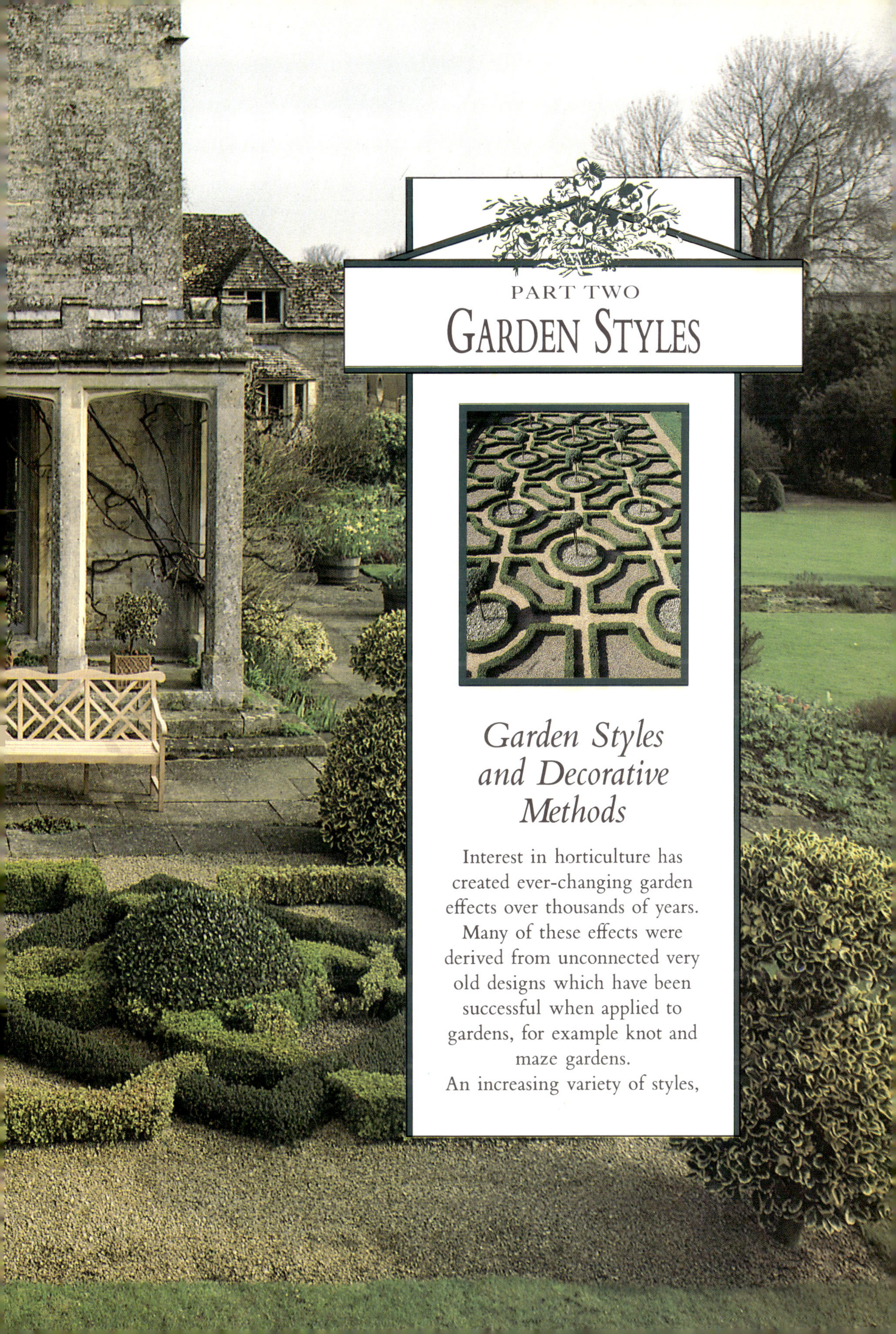

PART TWO

GARDEN STYLES

Garden Styles and Decorative Methods

Interest in horticulture has created ever-changing garden effects over thousands of years. Many of these effects were derived from unconnected very old designs which have been successful when applied to gardens, for example knot and maze gardens.

An increasing variety of styles,

PREVIOUS PAGES: *This knot garden at Barnsley House reflects a whole history of ritual and symbolism, visions of eternity and style in both gardens and culture.* INSET: *A seventeenth-century design for a knot garden, featuring clipped box, gravel infill and standards, at Mosely Old Hall, Wolverhampton.*

RIGHT: *The dignity of formality . . .*

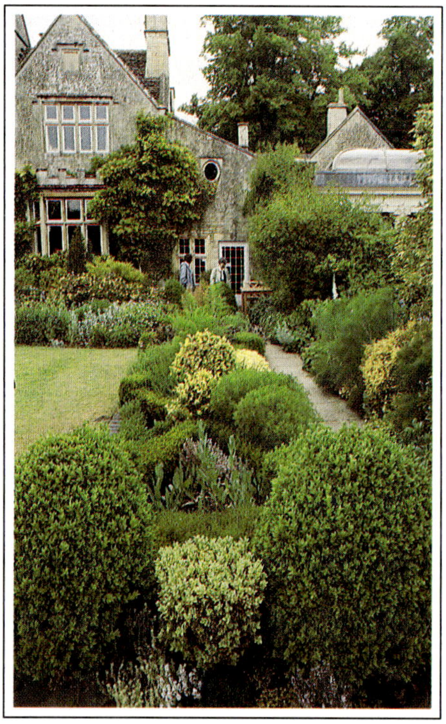

such as the dignity of formality or the spontaneous generosity of informality, were to be admired. Intricately woven knot gardens and bewildering mazes developed, as did sculpted topiary and elaborate parterres. Consider the discipline of interlaced branches on top of the bare lower trunks of several trees, a process called pleaching, or the elegant shaping of standards, graceful and practical espalier-work and the use of separate enclosures for growing herbs and vegetables (and later flowers for the house) where bee-hives too were placed. Some gardens were enhanced further by grottoes, Greek-inspired small 'temples', gazebos, pavilions and summer-houses. Arbours, pergolas, herbaceous borders, ha-has and water gardens of infinite variety also existed.

Experiments were undertaken for a new look with some plants: cross-pollination, grafting, cloning, and other methods were used for a permutation of colour, size, shape, and frequent reproduction of the same species, as in modern cloning. All these procedures have become an art, still being worked upon with dramatic results. Herbs have mainly been left alone, remaining unchanged, except for natural cross-breeding by pollen-carrying insects — mints for instance now have an astonishing range of flavours and scents. Old cottage flowers and almost extinct wild flowers have been saved from oblivion by the heritage-conscious in many parts of the world. Old-fashioned roses have come into their own again, many having been rescued from weedy, overgrown church yards, or found in abandoned, forgotten gardens, and on little-used country road-sides.

Explanations and uses of box hedges, standards, topiary, herbaceous borders, mazes and labyrinths, parterre gardens, knot gardens, potagers, herb gardens, pleaching and plashing, espalier work, ha-has, formal gardens, informal gardens and wildflower meadows will all be illustrated in the following pages.

Box Tree

(*BUXUS SEMPERVIRENS*)

Box trees are constantly referred to in this book, as they are an important element in the making of many gardens.

A small tree native to the

Mediterranean area, 'English' box (*B. sempervirens*), is also a herb and it has been in use since Roman times for making low hedges, for clipping and shaping, and for topiary work. 'Dutch' box (*B. sempervirens suffruticosa*) is another popular variety for planting in great numbers for delineating patterns in knot gardens, and in parterres; it has slightly larger leaves and grows more quickly. 'Japanese' box (*B. microphilla*) is bigger again, its leaves are a little larger and it grows quite rapidly, for box. Box trees make excellent hedges for formalising herb and flower beds designed in simple, geometric forms, or for planting around areas planned to be separate from the rest of the garden, the low, even continuation of the neat, clipped plants give this illusion of division.

Slow-growing box has a hard, woody stem, and closely packed, pungently spicy leaves that are smooth-edged, small and evergreen. As box grows taller, it also becomes wider, eventually touching the branchlets of its neighbours. We plant them 0.3 m/1 ft apart. If propagating the plants yourself, they can be put more closely together. When we owned 'Somerset Cottage' Herb Nursery, we would place box cuttings into glass-houses in the approved manner of plant nurseries. However, we have many friends who have saved much expense propagating new box plants themselves, by trimming off firm cuttings in spring or early autumn from older, established plants, dipping the pruned stems into cutting powder (optional) and putting them straight into the ground, where they remain green while making roots. We were told by a specialist nurseryman that a quick and easy method for the home gardener is to bury three quarters of the box in soil including leafy branches and trunk. After approximately six months, the covered parts will have established roots and can be cut off and planted.

Clipping starts once the plants touch each other and the height is right, 0.6 m/2 ft or more, less if preferred. The first step is to even off the tops. As the box grows and widens, which it does in a surprisingly short time now, clipping begins in earnest. This is not done constantly, only when the hedge looks as if it should be neatened and shaped. If allowed to flower, the tiny, pale yellow blooms appear in spring to early summer.

Box trees can grow taller and shrubbier over a long period if not cut back, and they are sometimes used in gardens for higher hedges,

BELOW: *Growing box for topiary.*

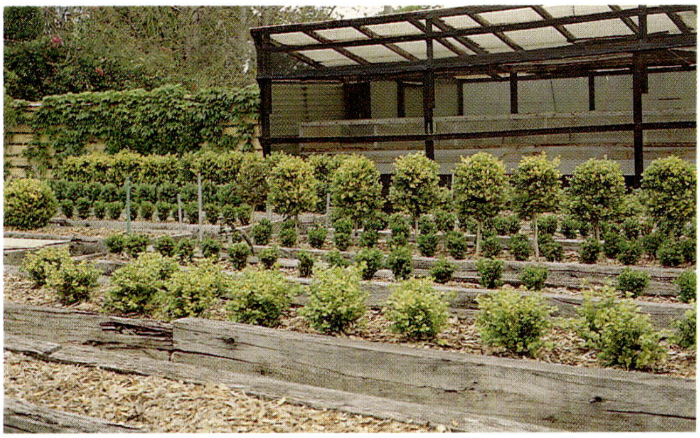

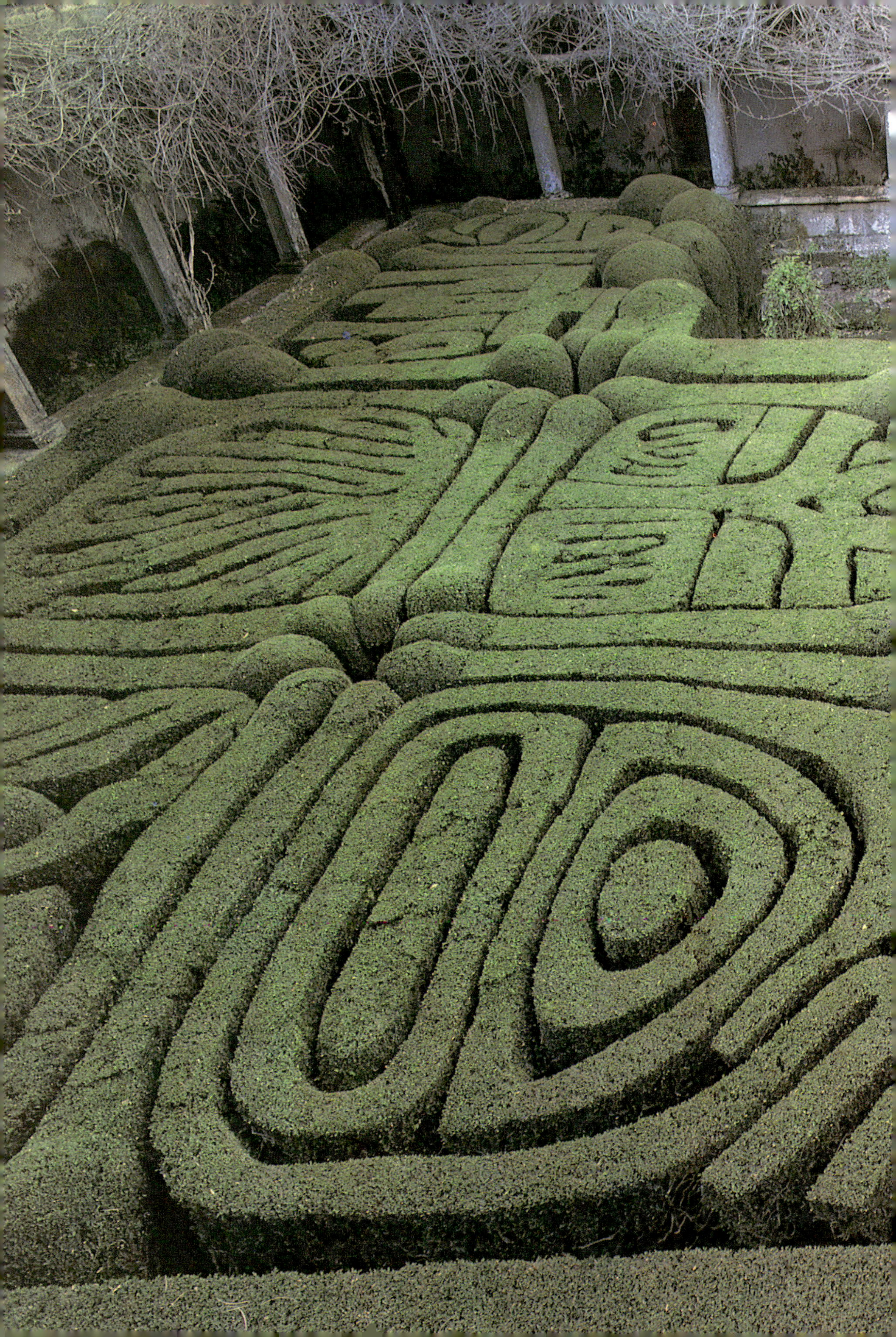

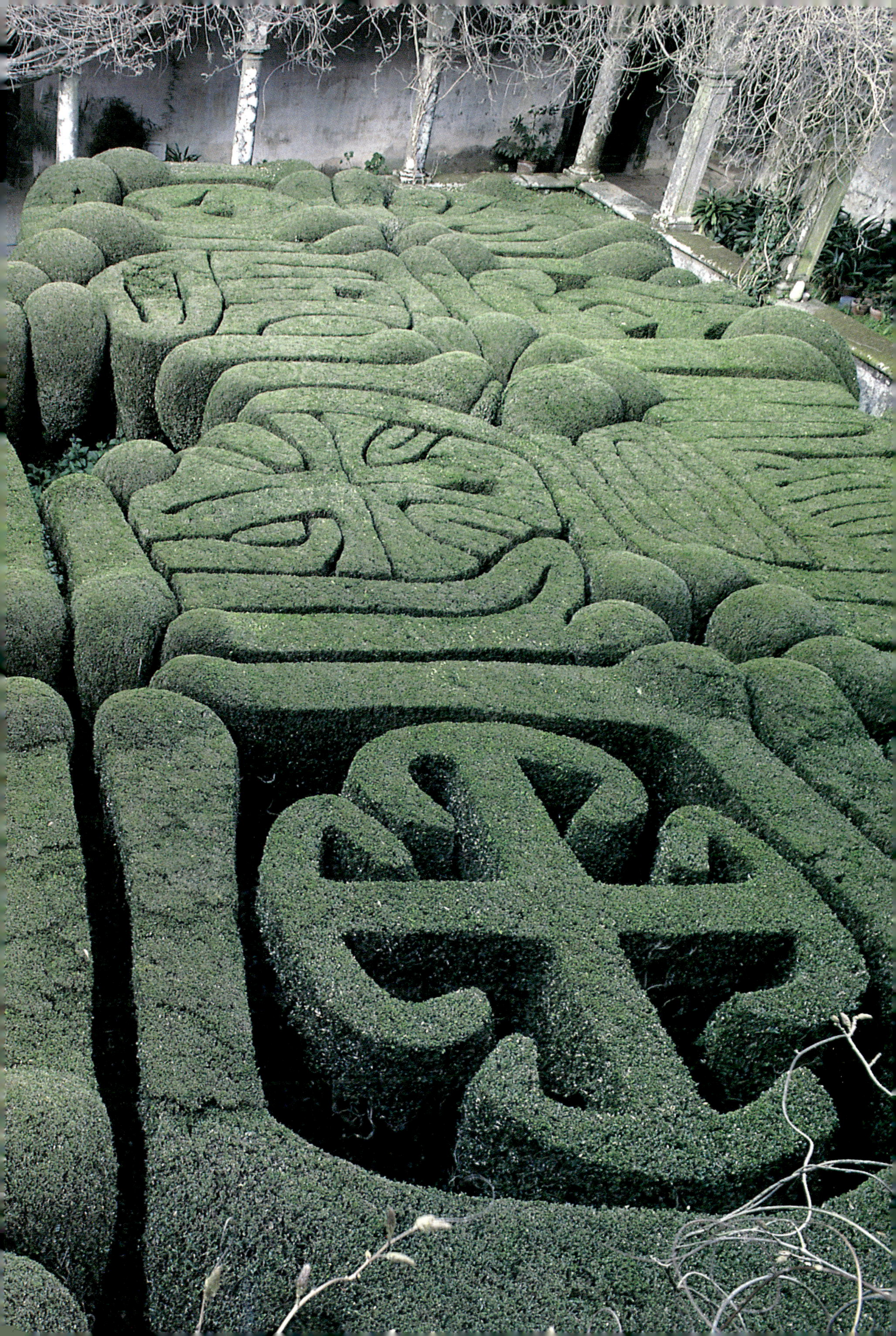

PREVIOUS PAGES: *Not all spectacular gardens exist for individual wealthy families. This garden has symbolic and allegorical significance, and has been maintained since the seventeenth century in the Monasterio de san Lorenzo de Tradonto, Spain.*

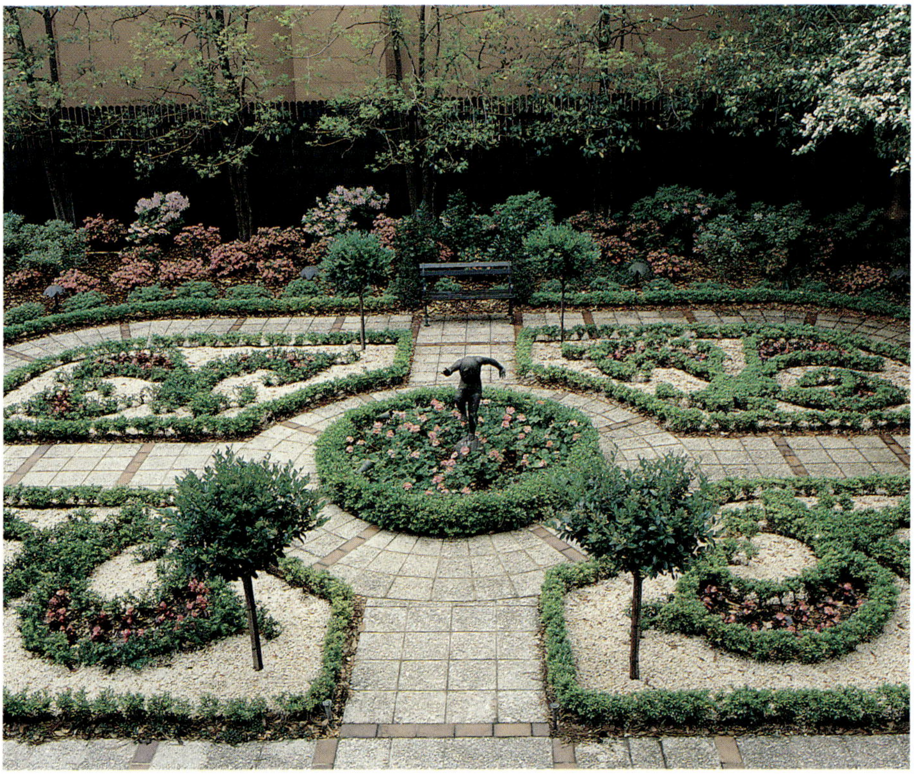

RIGHT: *Expansion and transference of cultures has meant traditional European garden styles have drifted around the world. This formal parterre, with standard* Ligustrum, *infilled with river gravel, is in Georgia, United States.*

and for larger topiary specimens. It was once employed medicinally: the oil extracted from the wood was a treatment for toothache and epilepsy, while a perfume was made from the bark. Chess pieces, turned boxes and manufactured instruments have been made from the timber because of its durability. Once, long ago, the leaves and sawdust were prepared as a dye for turning hair auburn.

Standards

'Standard' is a descriptive name for a plant that has been trained from a single, bare stem into a rounded or helmet-shaped dense head of flowers or leaves, standard roses being a familiar example. (Standards are classed in our botanical dictionary under topiary.) John Evelyn (1620–1705), an English garden writer, designer and translator of gardening books, speaking of his own standards at Sayne Court, Deptford, London writes that 'there are . . . four large round philareas smooth clipped raised on a single stalk from the ground, a fashion now much used'.

Nearly all perennial plants may be trained into a standard, from the very small 0.3 m/1 ft to the tall, 3 m/10 ft. Box, bay, privet, rosemary, lavender, germander, santolina (lavender cotton or cotton lavender) and thyme have all been grown as standards, for a vertical emphasis in parterres or in knot gardens. In America, we saw a large, formal herb garden with 1.8 m/6 ft high bay trees in square, white-painted tubs, placed at regular intervals in orderly pairs. They were standards, with their enormous, leafy heads clipped into helmet forms.

The art of topiary is an ancient one (see Topiary, p. 60) and was prevalent in the first century in Roman gardens. Over the following centuries, the practice lapsed in favour, until a revival for shaping plants took place in early Renaissance Italy, and included 'ring standards'. In this process a large ring is placed at the top of a stake supporting the bare trunk, and the foliage growing from the head is encouraged to weave on to and over the ring, eventually covering it completely in a dense cluster, or allowed to 'weep'.

For training into a standard, a plant with a straight stem is chosen to start with (we will exclude creepers at this stage) and is kept in a pot. If there are any side shoots, they should be pruned off immediately, leaving the top part alone. Patience is now essential as the standard grows. Keep the trunk trimmed and, if necessary, tie it to a support. The top of the 'tree' is allowed to thicken and send out shoots, and if it becomes unruly, the pieces must be trimmed off with secateurs or nipped back constantly with the fingers to encourage compact growth. Bigger standards may need a 'cone' wired on top of the stake, as will be explained for the management of standard creepers. For tall samples, repot into larger containers with fresh soil, and when ready take away the stake if the trunk is strong enough.

Jenny and John Peck of New South Wales are consummate artists in the making of standards, and are willing to experiment with almost any plant. They use several kinds of box: small-leaved English box, the similar Dutch box and the larger-leaved slightly bigger

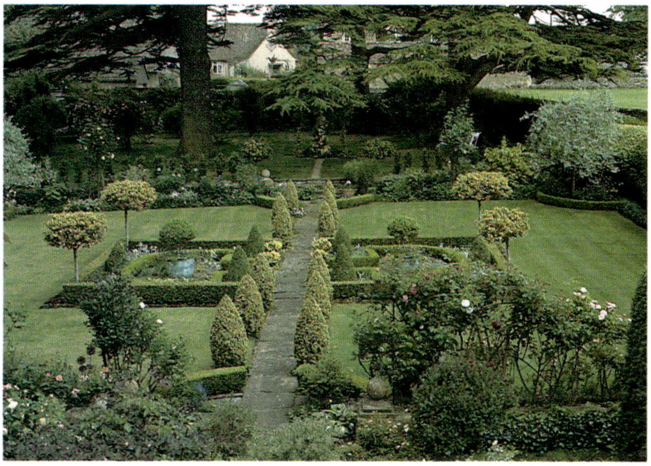

ABOVE: *Standards* in situ, *Essex house.*

OVERLEAF: *Standards, parterre work, water and a gracefully formal garden complement each other at the Villa Gamberaia.*

Japanese box. Among their flowering standards are a beautiful Brunsfelsia also called 'yesterday, today and tomorrow' because of its multi-coloured appearance when in flower, as it opens to violet, fades to pale blue and then turns white on successive days. Other great examples of flowering standards are daisies in every colour and a wide variety of oleanders and fuchsias, and duranta or golden dewdrop — its single pale blue or snow white flowers are followed by trusses of golden berries. Gardenias are exquisite blooms, both *florida* and *magnifica*. Of special interest, and a glorious sight, are Jenny and John's standard creepers, which are first wound around stakes with a

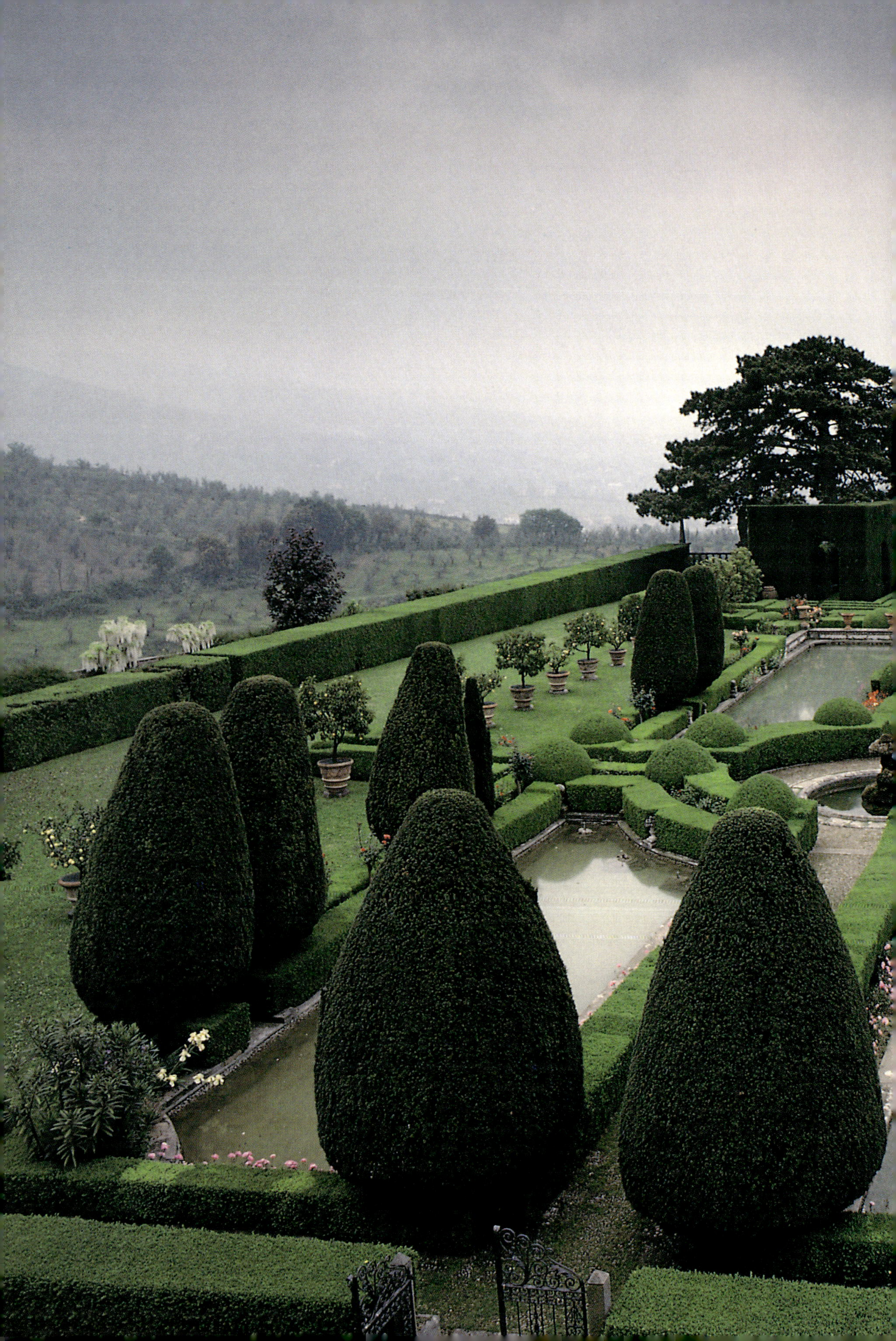

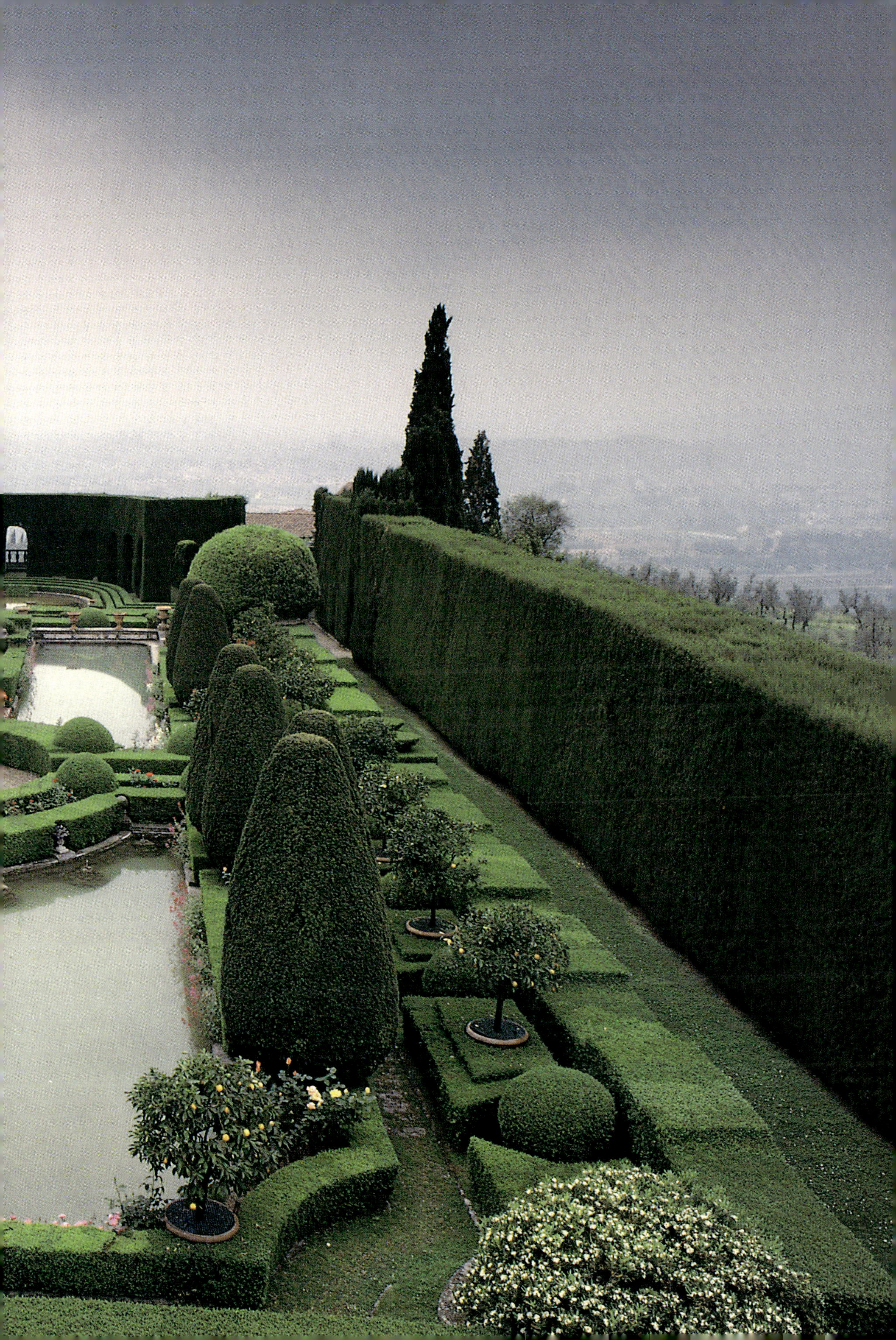

simple wire cone on top (the rings mentioned earlier are used for heavy, exuberantly weeping plants). When training these standards, prune away side shoots as the creeper grows and then train the tops through the cones. When the foliage is thickening it is trimmed ready for the flowering season. Honeysuckle, star jasmine (*Trachelospermum jasminoides*), potato vine (*Solanum*), stephanotis and bougainvilleas in different colours — including a pretty variegated white and green with a pale pink flower — are all excellent performers. Standard honeysuckle is often used for background height in herbaceous borders, and we often saw it planted in English gardens. Climbers were also grown onto tall, shaped wire frames as pyramids, and they look splendid when treated in this way.

The Peck's 3 m/10 ft weeping figs (*Ficus benjaminii*) and upright fig (*F. hillii*) are also spectacular, as are the bay trees with ample round heads of dark green leaves, pungently aromatic.

We notice that a number of people in Sydney are now planting standard glossy-leaved trees in green lawns outside their boundary fences or their nature strips.

Topiary

The craft of shaping trees and shrubs by clipping and training, known as topiary, has been practised at least since the time of Pliny the Elder (first century AD), who described such work as depicting '. . . hunt scenes, fleets of ships and all sorts of images' carved and clipped out of cypress. Trimmed box trees were also used in Roman gardens, sometimes spelling out the name of its owner or planted as an edging to a complex garden design.

During the Middle Ages, plants were still being trained and clipped — although into simplified shapes — often on to tough, flexible twig frames, called 'withy' frames. There are no records indicating particular enthusiasm for this art in those days.

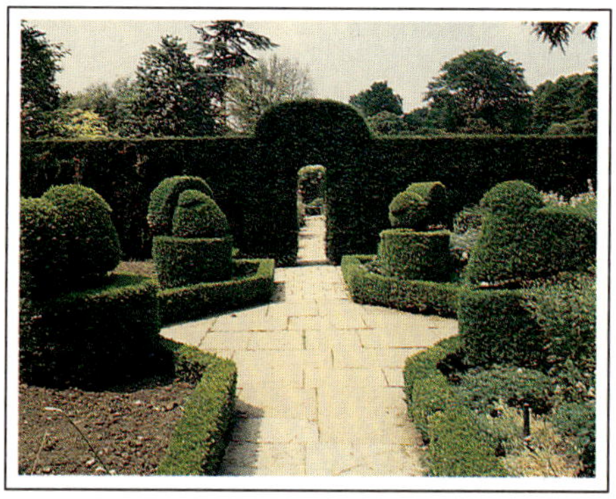

RIGHT: *Topiary — the craft of shaping trees and shrubs by clipping and training — can take many forms, and has been in use at least since the first century AD.*

OPPOSITE: *Yew birds, such as these resting on their box bases at Chenies Manor House, are particularly delightful.*

Topiary work did not disappear altogether, however, and was revived in early Renaissance Italy. A romance published in 1499, written by a Dominican friar, shows woodcut illustrations of elaborate topiary, and flower-beds laid out in intricate, interlacing designs — it is the earliest known chronicle of its kind. It shows simple topiary shapes — spherical, mushroom, and ring standards — as well as involved groups of human figures, urns, and other structured forms. Another example of topiary is at the Recellai garden

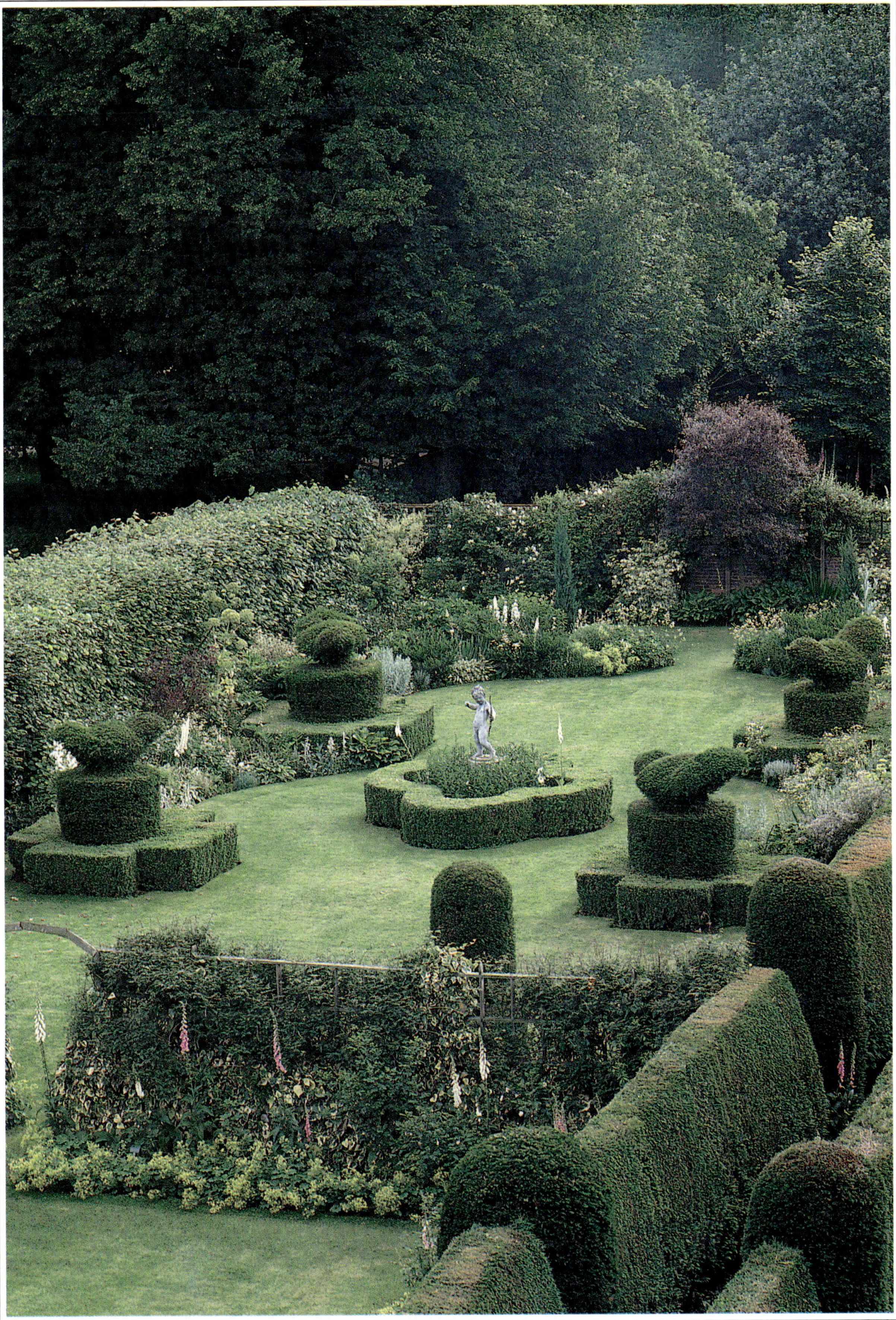

in Florence, which according to *The Oxford Companion to Gardens* was created in the second half of the fifteenth century, and '. . . porticoes, temples, vases, urns, apes, donkeys, oxen, a bear, giants, men, and women' were all formed of various evergreens on bound withy frames. In England, similar work was described at Hampton Court in 1599 by a German visitor.

In the sixteenth and seventeenth centuries there was a zealous devotion for topiary in England. Rosemary was a favourite among topiarists while privet was recommended for shaping by the distinguished sixteenth-century herbalist and author, John Parkinson. In the seventeenth century, the equally renowned Sir Francis Bacon commends the use of juniper and describes '. . . little low hedges round like welts, with some pretty pyramids I like well, and in some places fair columns'.

In the later seventeenth century, French-inspired parterres together with topiary were an important element in garden design.

BELOW: *Topiary was not confined to Europe. This clever topiary elephant, photographed by our son Ian, provides an interesting contrast to the buildings of Bombay.*

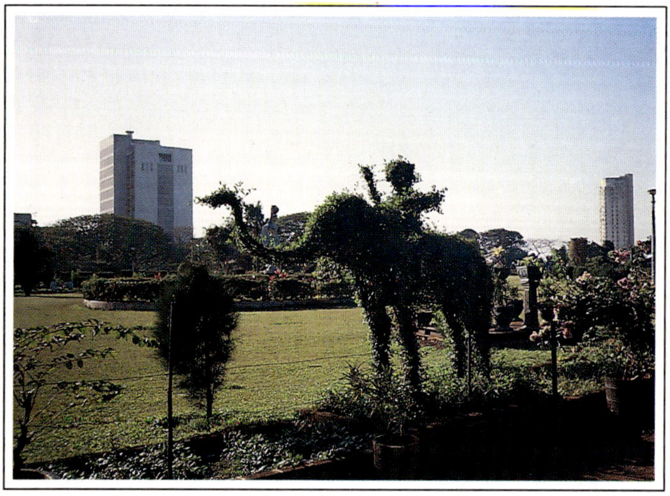

Evergreens such as holly, yew, box and bay lent themselves to shaping. In the eighteenth century, John James noted that '. . . Natural Arbors are formed only by the Branches of Trees artfully interwoven, and sustained by strong lattice-work, Hoops, Poles etc. which make Galleries, Porticoes, . . . naturally cover'd'.

By the second half of the eighteenth century topiary fell into disfavour as it was regarded as being in bad taste, but by the later nineteenth century topiary work, mostly in yew, was greatly admired again, especially by art and craft advocates. Exhibits of shaped trees were presented at London horticultural shows in 1900. *The Oxford Companion to Gardens* regrets that 'topiary specimens are sadly difficult to find in Britain, only standard and pyramid bay and box being easily available'.

Topiary was not confined to Europe. John and Ray Oldham in *Gardens in Time* display colour plates of old Indian gardens. Like the Shalimar Bagh garden in Kashmir, there are successions of water-ladders with gardens on either side of them containing sizeable clipped standard trees all with the Himalayan mountains as a backdrop. Another colour photograph shows part of Nishat Bagh, Kashmir, the Oldham's favourite formal garden in the world. The picture is taken from a pavilion, and through the tall arches you can see water sparkling over ascending stone water-ladders while a straight row of jets sends up small fountains. The eye is taken upwards to green lawns, topiary, and to the awesome beauty of the towering Himalayas beyond. In the seventeenth century, this garden was admired and coveted by Shah Jahan, builder of the Taj Mahal. The owner of the gardens, who was also the Shah's father-in-law, could not bring himself to surrender his cherished pleasure: in his anger Shah Jahan ordered that the water supply to the Nishat Bagh be cut off, destroying the beauty of this splendid garden. Eventually the Shah relented and water was restored to the garden.

Today, enthusiasts the world over create topiary of their own devising. We have seen a topiary bird nestling on the ground in a friend's garden made from a small-leaved creeper growing through and over a wire frame, so that it is completely covered. We feel a little shock of pleasure when we find such a treasure in a secret corner of an interesting garden like this.

When driving through England, we often saw village gardens displaying all kinds of topiary shapes, and we also saw many examples of topiary in the gardens we visited — pyramids, urns, round balls and corkscrews. The most unusual topiary was in the Japanese Garden in San Francisco's Botanical Garden. It was a replica of Mt Fuji in Japan made, we think, of two kinds of box. The clipped sloping green 'mountain', at least 2.4 m/8 ft high, was covered at the peak with white and green variegated box or privet, artfully trimmed into a convincing snow-line.

Herbaceous Borders

Herbaceous borders were a seventeenth-century gardening invention and in the late nineteenth century were thought of as a survival from monastic gardens, forming an essential part of old-fashioned gardens. Gertrude Jekyll, gifted landscaper of the late nineteenth and early twentieth centuries, popularised herbaceous borders in masses of colour arranged in informal drifts, as well as in shades of one colour. These borders are a delightful way of displaying favourite perennial plants that complement one another in colour and height. Borders can be short and narrow or long and wide, depending on garden size; they are usually set against a wall, hedge, or fence. They may be planted in a personal choice of mixed colours, or in brilliant blazes of red, copper and yellow — and white borders or gardens can be most effective with silver foliage and white flowers with varying shades of green leaves.

Herbaceous plants are perennial: the leafy stems die down in autumn each year, the rootstock living on and spreading by sending out underground roots or (sometimes) by self-sowing. Seeds of annuals can be sown among the perennials for added interest. The border, even if narrow, should have two rows of plants, short in front and taller behind. Some suggestions

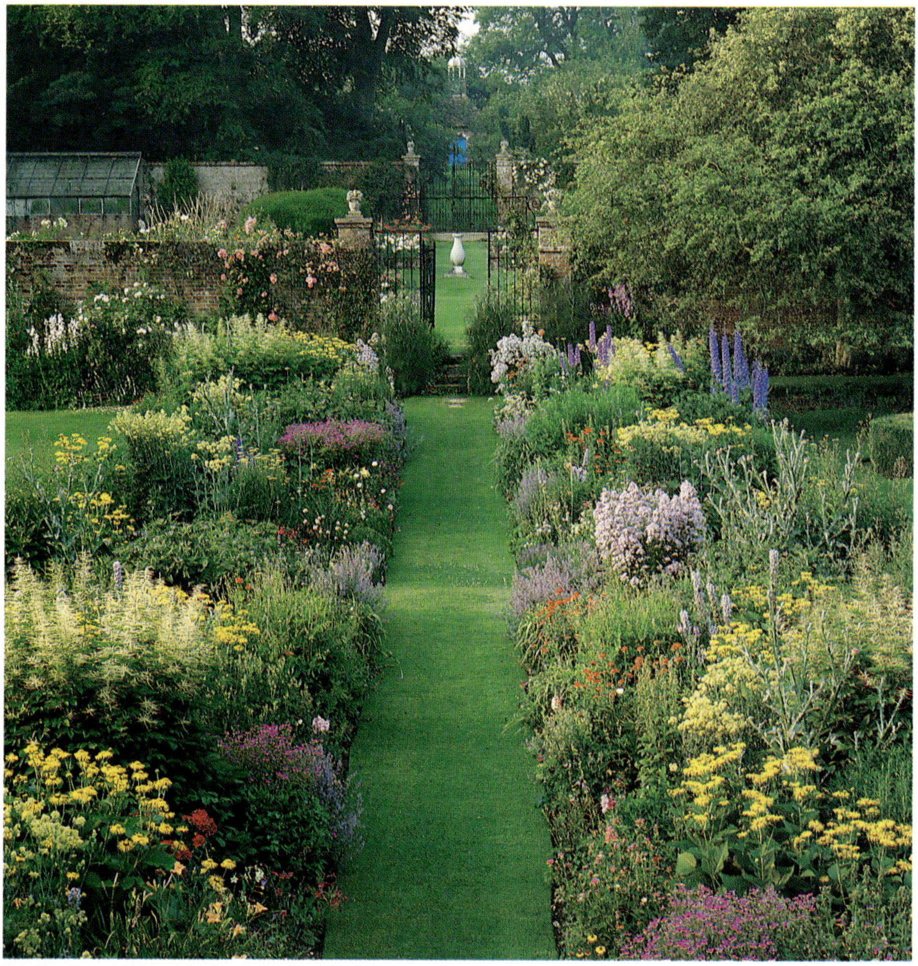

RIGHT: *This herbaceous border at Bramdean House balances perennial plants, allowing them to complement each other in colour and height.*

for low perennials are Ajuga, the 'blue bugle' flower; yellow fumitory, or 'wee folk's stockings' (*Corydalis lutea*), 'ladies' mantle' (*Alchemilla mollis*), Welsh poppy (*Papaver*), chamomiles and pinks (*Dianthus*); 'Bistort' (*Plyganum bistorta*), variegated sages in grey and purple, and grey and gold (*Salvia*) are also useful, as are columbines or 'granny's bonnet' (*Aquilegia*), the 'English' true geranium, or 'cranesbill' grows in compact mounds entirely covered with small, single flowers in pink, mauve, blue, and many more. It is interesting to know that these are all old-fashioned cottage garden flowers, which are also herbs, as are most herbaceous plants (although they are not necessarily herbs for culinary purposes they were used therapeutically in the past).

There are wonderful choices of traditional cottage garden herbs for tall or background plants; we saw a great number of them on our visits to English gardens. They included 'colewort' (*Crambe cordifolia*) which grows to 2.1 m/7 ft, and is a member of the cabbage family: its long branching thin flower stalks interlace loosely, bearing myriads of tiny white blossoms like gypsophila. Other useful plants are foxgloves (*Digitalis*), tobacco plants in different colours (*Nicotiana*), mullein (*Verbascum*), standard honeysuckles (*Lonicera*), and slender-stemmed poppies (*Papaver*). Old roses, grown as standards or climbing up the nearest tree can be used, as can angelica (*Angelica archangelica*), which can grow to over 2.4 m/8 ft tall. An excellent informative plant guide for herbaceous borders is Stirling Macoboy's *Perennials for Bed and Border*.

Mazes and Labyrinths

Mazes and labyrinths are based upon antique designs made up of a complicated, winding route with an entrance and an exit (the exit being very difficult to find, and sometimes the same as the entrance) and a definite centre. The ancient Egyptians constructed labyrinths as early as 2,300 BC and the site of one has been excavated and its foundations exposed. But these styles conjure up Greek mythology and the tale of Theseus, son of King Aegeus of Athens who slew the dreaded Minotaur in its circular, subterranean labyrinth designed by Daedalus, architect for King Minos of Crete. Theseus was saved from certain death by Ariadne, the King's lovely daughter, who gave him a ball of thread to mark his way so that he could escape through the serpentine passages after killing the monstrous half-man half-bull. In Graeco-Roman times labyrinths were generally built underground. The confusing network of paths and passages were purposely designed to make it difficult for anyone who entered to get out again.

The notion of transferring the labyrinth to decorative garden art happened at about the time knot gardens were introduced in the late fifteenth century, and in this setting they became known as a maze or puzzle-garden. The garden writers of the day advised that they be set with similar hedging specimens as a knot garden, although some were planted with hedges which would grow to 3 m/10 ft or more. A seventeenth-century expert advised that a maze should have 'fower sundry fruits to be placed in each of the corners of the maze, and in the middle of it a proper herbe decked wyth Roses, or elles some fayre tree of Rosemarye'.

BELOW: *Mazes exist in as many varieties as there are puzzles and tricks, mythologies and symbols.*

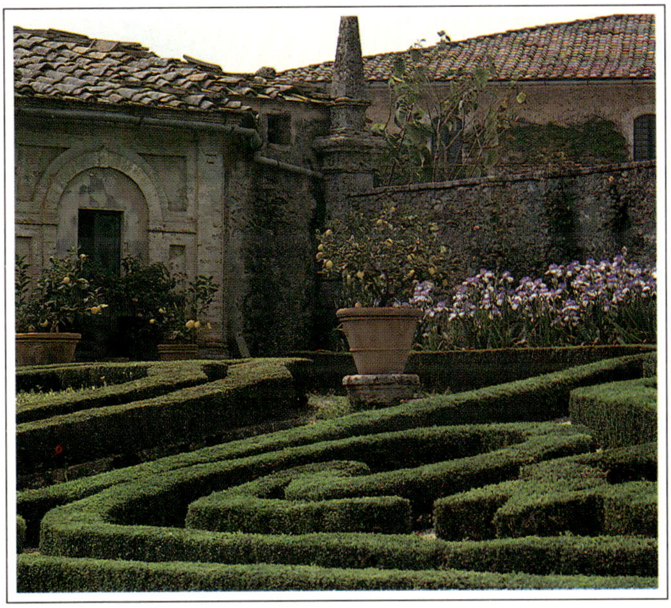

OPPOSITE: *This Elizabethan knot garden at Cranborne Manor can be seen in its entirety, as intended, when viewed from the first floor window.*

BELOW: *The interlacing designs and symbols of infinity present in this knot garden follow its original seventeenth-century design.*

There are countless pathways to follow in a garden maze, and the design is extremely complex. When there are low hedges to step over, it is not impossible to find a way out and there is no need to worry, but some puzzle gardens with high, thick hedges are not appealing. There is a story, true or false, that King Henry VIII of England delighted in a game which involved a pretty maiden being sent into a maze of tall hedges to which only the King knew the way out — so when the lady realised her predicament and called for help, he would come to the rescue!

There is a strange, compelling labyrinth inlaid in the floor of beautiful dynamic Chartres Cathedral in France. To learn of man's destiny, one of us was told, you must step slowly along the appointed way on the mosaic, meditating on this great mystery of life. The answer was not revealed, partly through lack of time, partly because of the depth of this awesome enigma.

Knot Gardens

The number of formes, mazes and knots is so great and men are so diversely delighted, I leave every Housewife to herselfe, especially seeing to set downe many had been but to fill much paper. Yet lest I deprive her of all delight and direction, let her view these few choise new formes, and note this generally, that all plots are square, and all are bordered about with roses, thorne, rosemary, bee-flowers, issop, sage or such-like.

WILLIAM LAWSON, *THE COUNTRY HOUSEWIFE'S GARDEN*, 1618.

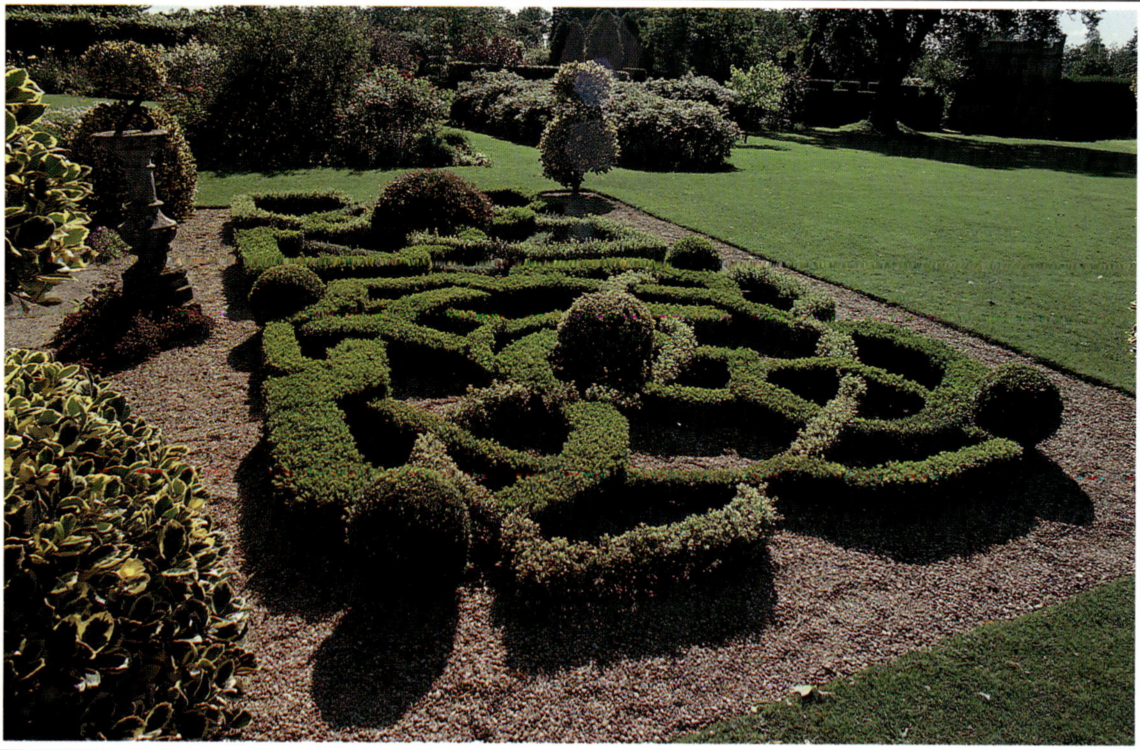

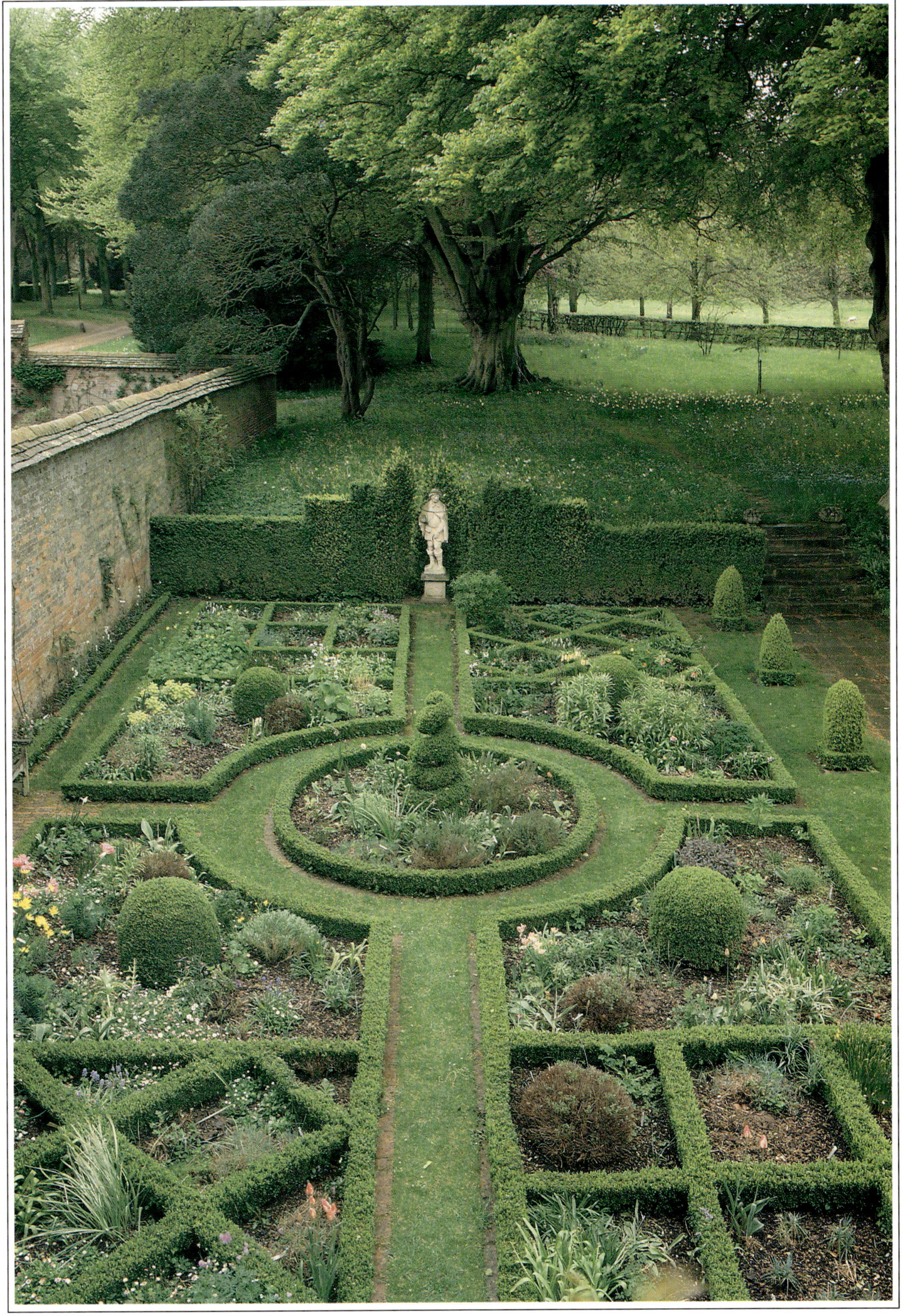

OPPPOSITE:
Parterres, balustrades, statues and formality at Collodi, Italy.

The use of knots as a design — with the knot as a continuous interlacing motif — goes back to the third millenium BC, and featured intertwining snakes. Endless unbroken knots were a symbol of infinity. Knot designs also appeared in Roman, Islamic, Celtic and medieval Christian art. The knot image displaying brilliant flowers on a rug was imported into Europe from the Middle East during the fifteenth century. In 1499 the first known plans and diagrams for using the knot in a garden design were published in Venice. Ideas travelled and knot gardens in diverse patterns became popular in Tudor England; the plant used to delineate the lines of the knot plan was usually dwarf evergreen box (*Buxus sempervirens*), an excellent specimen for clipping into shapes. Other suitable, compact plants were sometimes used instead, or were placed as a variation of foliage colour to accentuate complicated styles: examples are 'golden' box; grey, fragrant-leaved English lavender kept neatly trimmed and not allowed to flower to make a subtle foliage contrast when needed; smoky, pungent santolina (also called cotton lavender); bushy, highly scented thymes; green, peppery winter savory; stimulating hyssop; blue piercing rue leaves; and piney rosemary. These are still followed with great success. Many knot gardens were filled with shells, pebbles, gravel in different colours, or other similar material within the curving, dense hedges, so that their involved form could be seen more clearly. Box pruned into ball shapes and clipped standard bay trees were recommended as appropriate focal points.

In time, knot gardens changed in character, and the interweaving of clipped specimens became more 'open', until in the seventeenth century the term 'knot' and 'infinity' lost their meaning — 'knot garden' came to mean hedged, geometric beds filled with herbs, vegetables, or flowers. Today, a number of knot gardens look like this, although with the nostalgia for old-fashioned manners of planting, together with a fondness for herbs, old roses and cottage flowers, there are now many examples of pre-seventeenth century traditional complex knot gardens to be seen.

Parterre Gardens

Compartiments de broderie or *Parterre de broderie* are French terms for a special garden design. The phrase is made up of *broderie*, meaning embroidered and *parterre*, on the ground. French parterres were laid on level ground in regular, ornamental, swirling patterns, emulating intricate embroidery and glowing, flowery carpets. Sturdy, low box hedges were preferred for defining shapes, and were in-filled with coloured earth or gravel, flowers, herbs, or bands of turf to show clearly the demarcation of undulating patterns. Other bushy, upright plants that could be

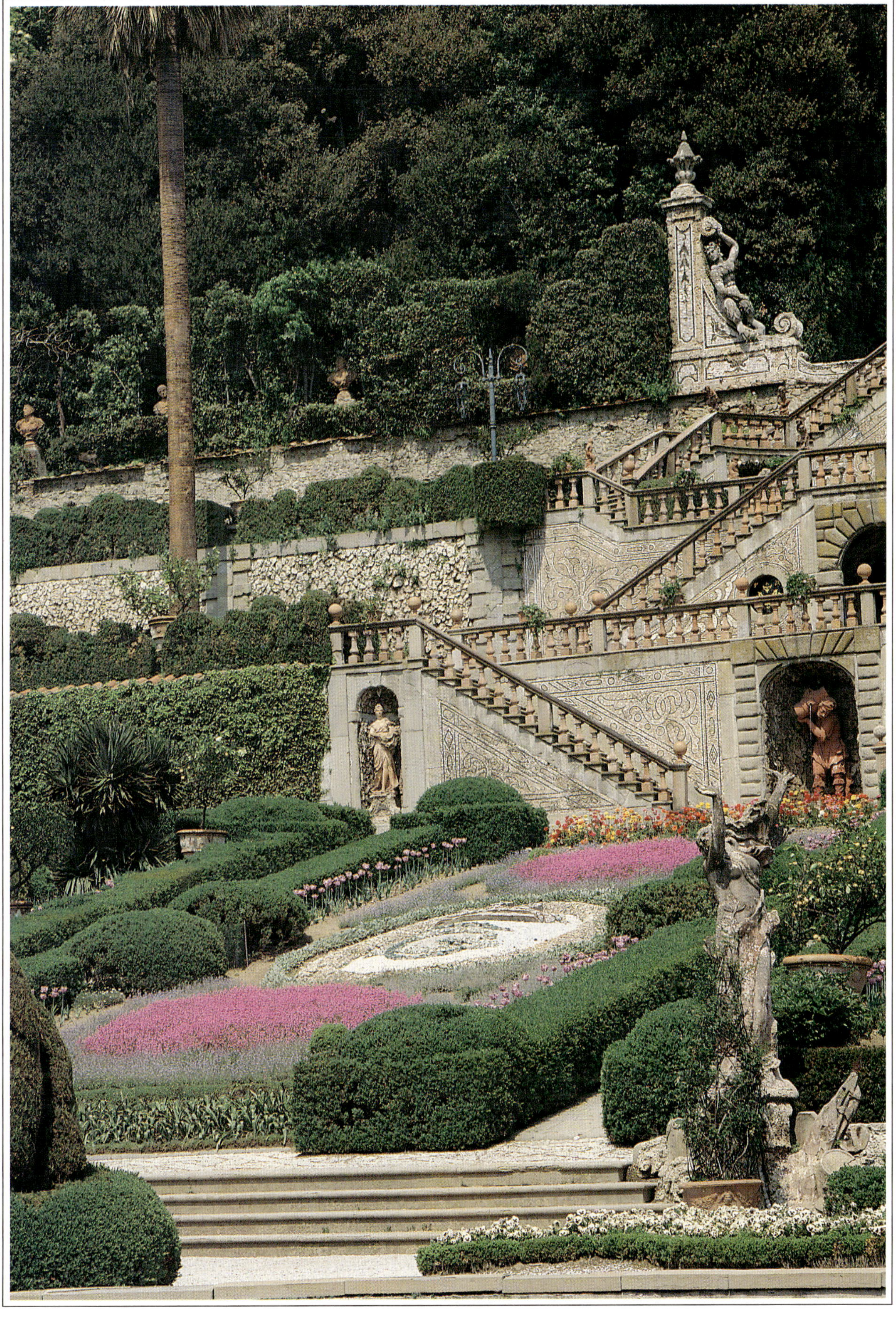

trimmed successfully for outlining and which could occasionally replace box include English lavender, rosemary, santolina, cotton lavender and wall germander. These herbs could also be planted with 'golden' box to emphasise a certain design.

Parterre gardens became popular throughout France during the late sixteenth and seventeenth centuries, although they appeared to have their origins in splendid, older Chinese, Mughal, and Indian gardens, described so well in John and Ray Oldham's classic *Gardens in Time*. Divisions in Indian parterres were defined in various ways: marble, stone, plants, earth or water canals were among the methods for determining shapes. These parterres were decorated with native exotic flowering plants, such as zinnias, marigolds, cannas, balsam, cosmos and amaranth. Indian designs also included water parterres whose solid, carved shapes seem to float on blue pools adrift with carefully placed lotus flowers. Low shrubs and suitable plants were set at intervals in recessed beds of soil, embellishing the substantial carved marble or stone that gave contour to these highly successful and unusual parterres — referred to as parterres, although on

BELOW: *Parterres show a flair for elegance and a sense of symmetry, appearing as embroidery, lace and fine carpets executed in nature.*

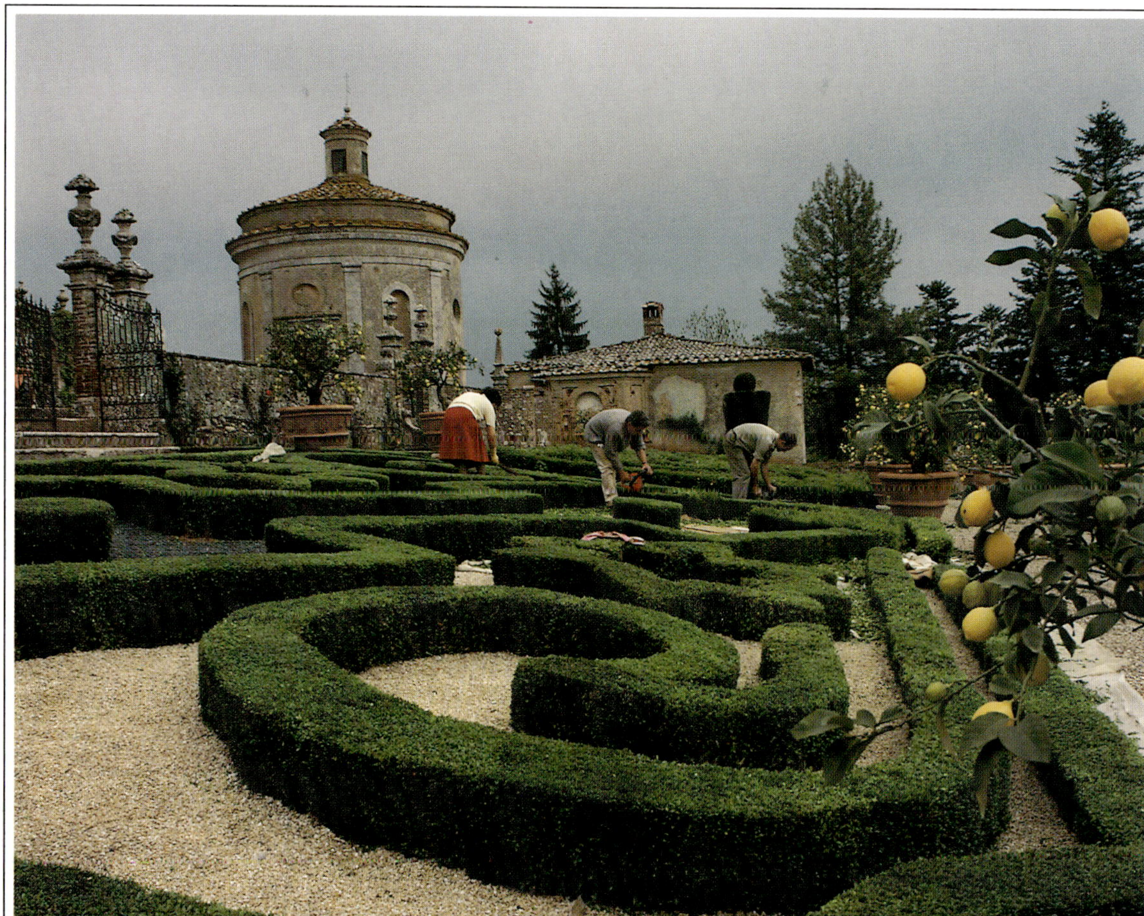

water and not 'on the ground'.

In Europe — particularly in France — in the seventeenth century, parterre gardens became an art form with recognised types and styles. Plans for parterres from the eighteenth century show the French innate flair for elegance and exquisite symmetry in their designs, so like dexterously worked lace or embroidery translated to the larger medium of landscape.

Parterres were placed close to the house so that the whole effect could be admired from terraces and long windows. The French Mollet family, a dynasty of Royal gardeners, and in particular Claude I, is credited with pioneering parterre gardens in France. In the sixteenth century Claude Mollet I served his apprenticeship in the making of parterres at the Chateau d'Anet, once the home of the beautiful Diane de Poitiers, and owned in Mollet's time by her grandson the Duc d'Aumale. Parterres were made at other great Chateaux, including the Royal country mansion at Fontainbleau. It is said that later in the first half of the seventeenth century, Claude II designed the first *parterre de broderie* at Versailles. Later, in the second half of the century, Andre le Notre became the most celebrated French landscape architect, following the Mollets: he designed the world-famous gardens of Versailles and Vaux-le-Vicomte and their enormous parterre gardens. Indeed, this garden style was enthusiastically adopted as a feature of royal and noble residents in the eighteenth century; an army of gardeners was needed to maintain them in perfect condition.

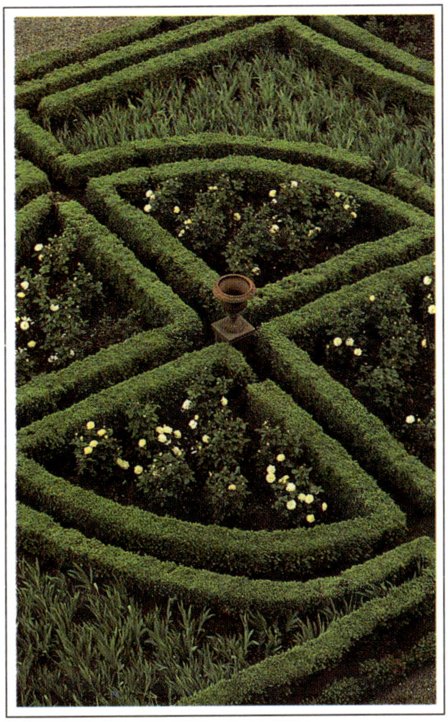

LEFT: *Definitions are hazy in this section of garden and design, and it is often difficult to differentiate parterres and knot gardens — a good way to begin a debate between garden writers would be to ask if this is an open knot garden, or a parterre.*

By the middle of the eighteenth century parterres were out of favour in France, and almost disappeared after the French Revolution in 1789, until their revival in the late nineteenth century. The fascination with parterres spread to England where they also became fashionable, and were known as *Parterres a L'anglaise*, 'in the English manner', and were somewhat simplified. They also suffered a demise in England after some years, and came back into favour in the nineteenth century with the interest of the distinguished garden designer, Humphrey Repton, and they were also boosted with the interest of the equally notable Sir Edwin

Lutyens in the twentieth century. Today, parterres are once more a decorative feature in certain gardens.

Sometimes it is difficult to see the difference between knot and parterre gardens. The former are usually smaller with an accent on the knot design, however simple, whereas parterres may be larger with definite swirls and curves in the traditional complex style. There is a fine line between the two, which depends on the creator of the garden.

Modern Florentine gardens are famed for their charming parterres. We know of one hidden behind

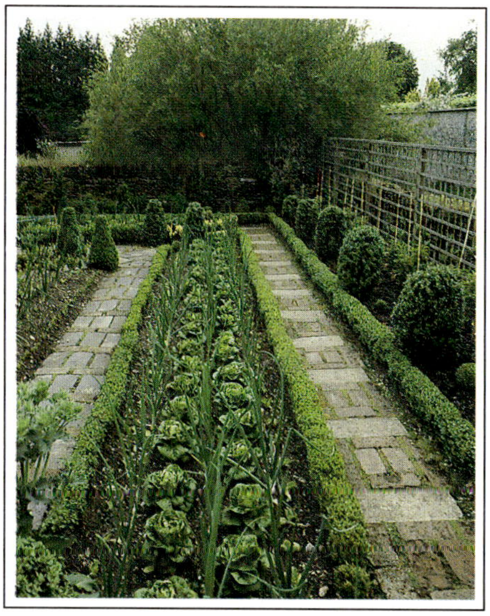

RIGHT: *A vegetable and herb garden at Barnsley House.*

sculpted ancient grey walls hung with espaliered greenery. The parterre was designed in clipped box squares, with curved box ovals within each; on top of every corner of the hedge is box trimmed into balls and there are pathways between the beds; a gentle contrast to the fresh green foliage and old grey walls were cloud-pink forget-me-nots filling the centres of every section. Another Italian parterre covering a large open space in front of the same pale ochre-coloured house was also designed in clipped box squares with balls of shaped box at each corner, looking as if they had been balanced carefully upon the low, pruned hedges. The beds held mists of blue forget-me-nots, while fruiting lemon trees in Tuscan terracotta tubs were in the centre of each compartment, and pathways were laid between the immaculate gardens.

In Australia, we have seen parterre-inspired gardens that are different yet again, made to fulfil the requirements, and space, of the owners. They are plainer than the traditional ebullient curves of ‘embroidered parterres’ without losing the formality and delight of the original concept. Box is generally used in the customary manner, trimmed into low hedges outlining a stone-flagged terrace or a green lawn, with interesting focal points: a fountain, a statue, standard trees in pots, and topiary. One in particular belonging to a friend is overlooked by long, French doors opening on to the paved box-edged parterre.

Formal, traditional parterre gardens have caught the imagination of countless garden lovers in various countries and times, who have interpreted them to suit the surroundings. There are superb coloured photographs of some in the book *English Herb Gardens* by Guy Cooper.

Potager

Herbes ou plantes potagéres, jardin potager or simply *potager* are all French terms meaning a kitchen garden of culinary herbs and vegetables (or pot-herbs). The terms have been Anglicised to 'potager' and is sometimes used when describing knot gardens or separate, low-hedged gardens enclosing cooking or salad herbs and vegetables. Probably the most famous and stunning potagers are those at the Chateau de Villandry, Villandry, France (p. 76).

Another fascinating series of potagers have been planted at Barnsley House, Gloucestershire, England by Mrs Rosemary Verey. Besides her delightful knot garden, herb garden walk, and other lovely areas, Mrs Verey is establishing a formal *potager*. Spreading out from a round central bed, the box and herb hedges are laid out in rectangular geometric patterns, and enclose rows of vegetables. We saw gooseberry bushes growing as standards, and peas climbing up pyramid bamboo poles, as well as other decorative methods of vegetable and fruit planting. It was an example of a wonderfully designed and beautiful kitchen garden.

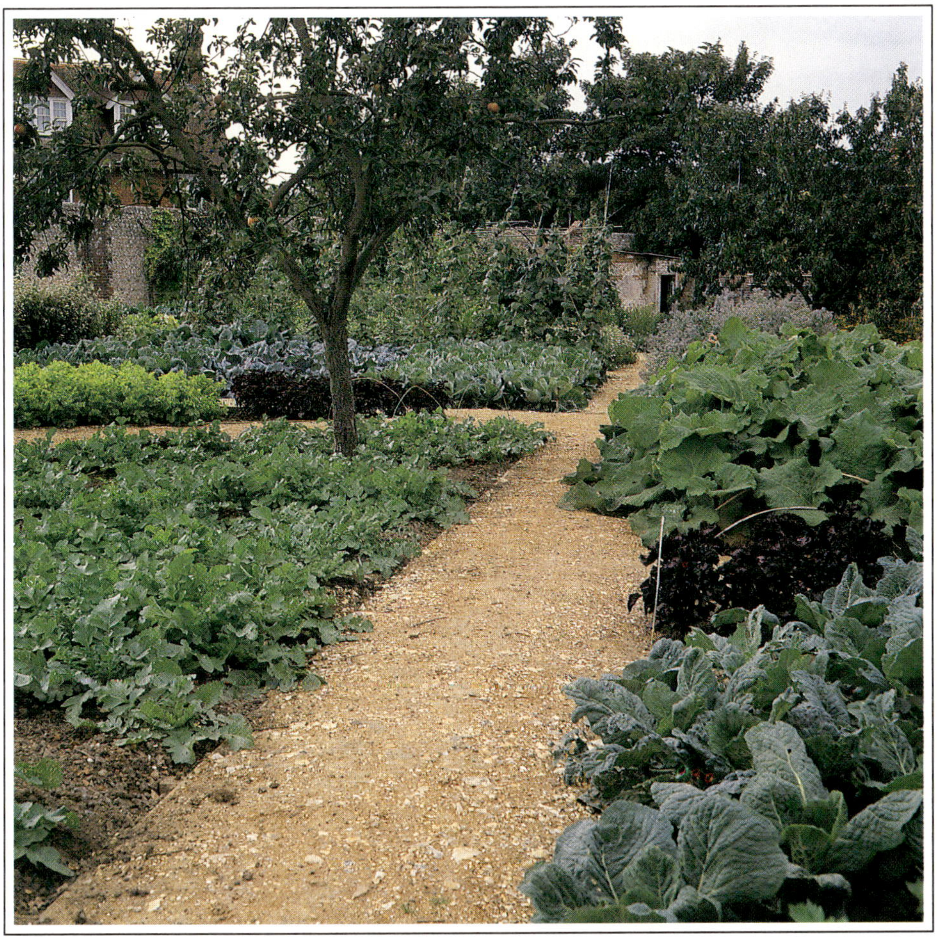

LEFT: *Apple trees, a distant doorway and paths frame this potager, emphasising both its accessability and relation to the house, and its role as a thing of beauty and of domestic significance.*

OVERLEAF: *Herb garden at Kew Palace, London.*

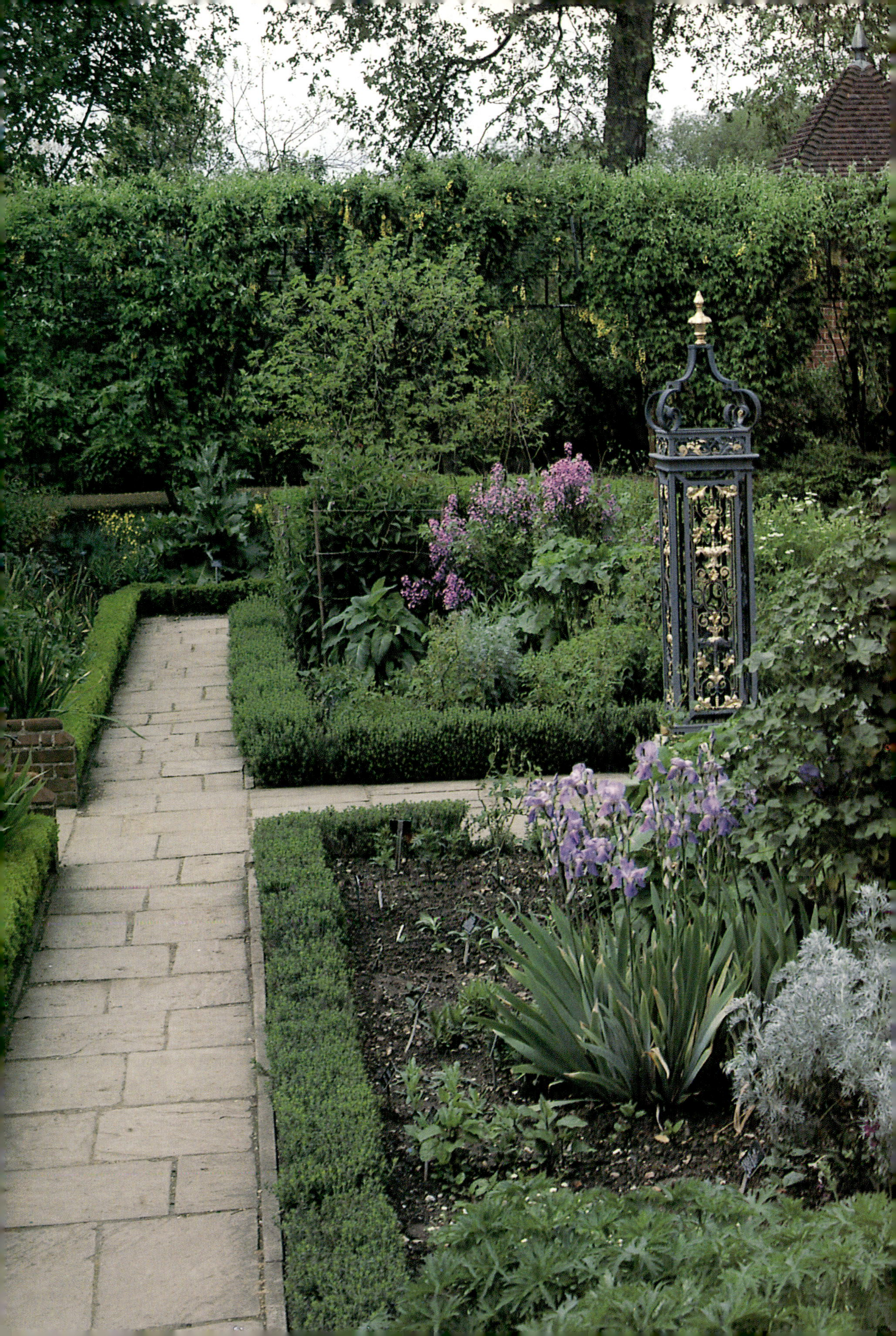

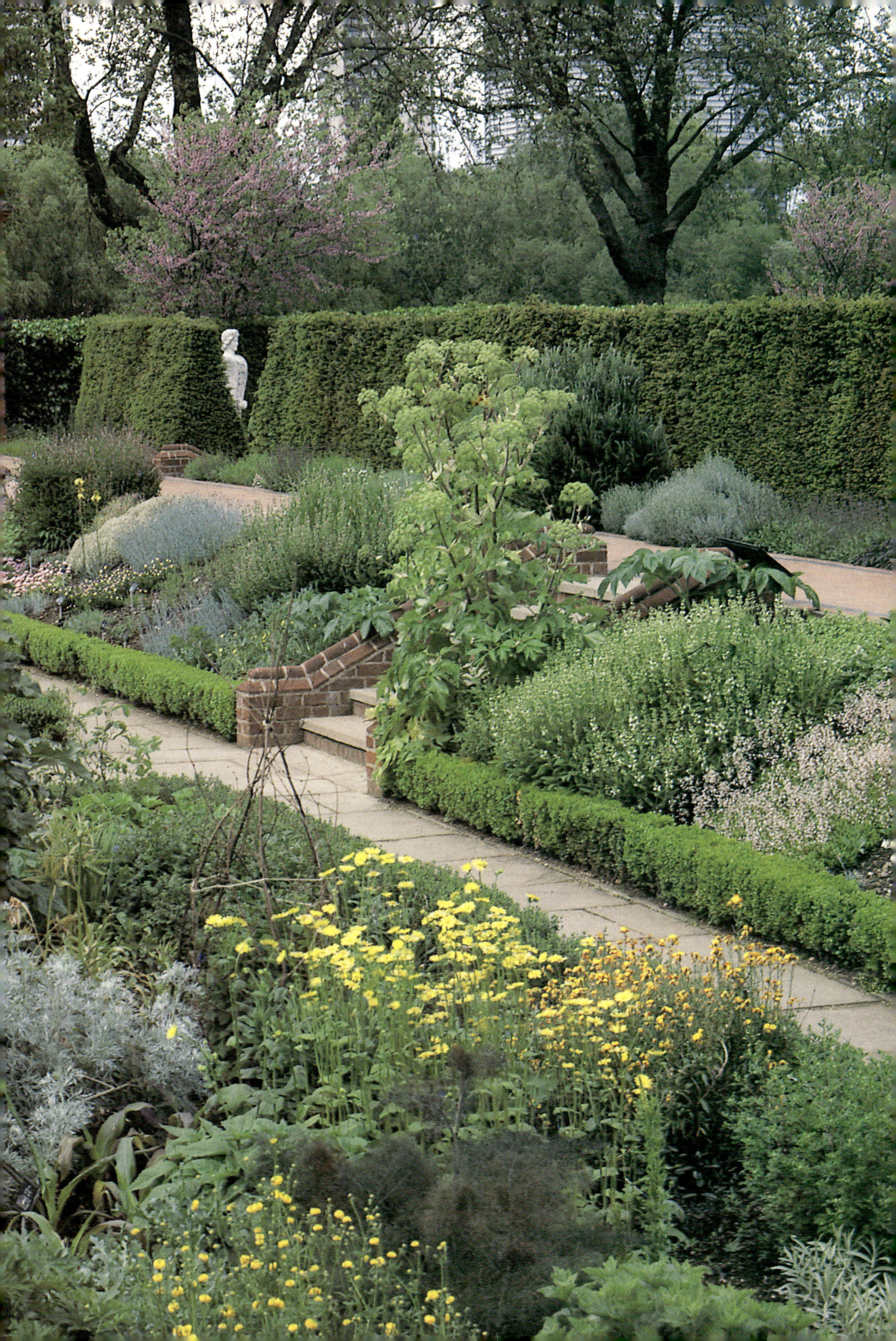

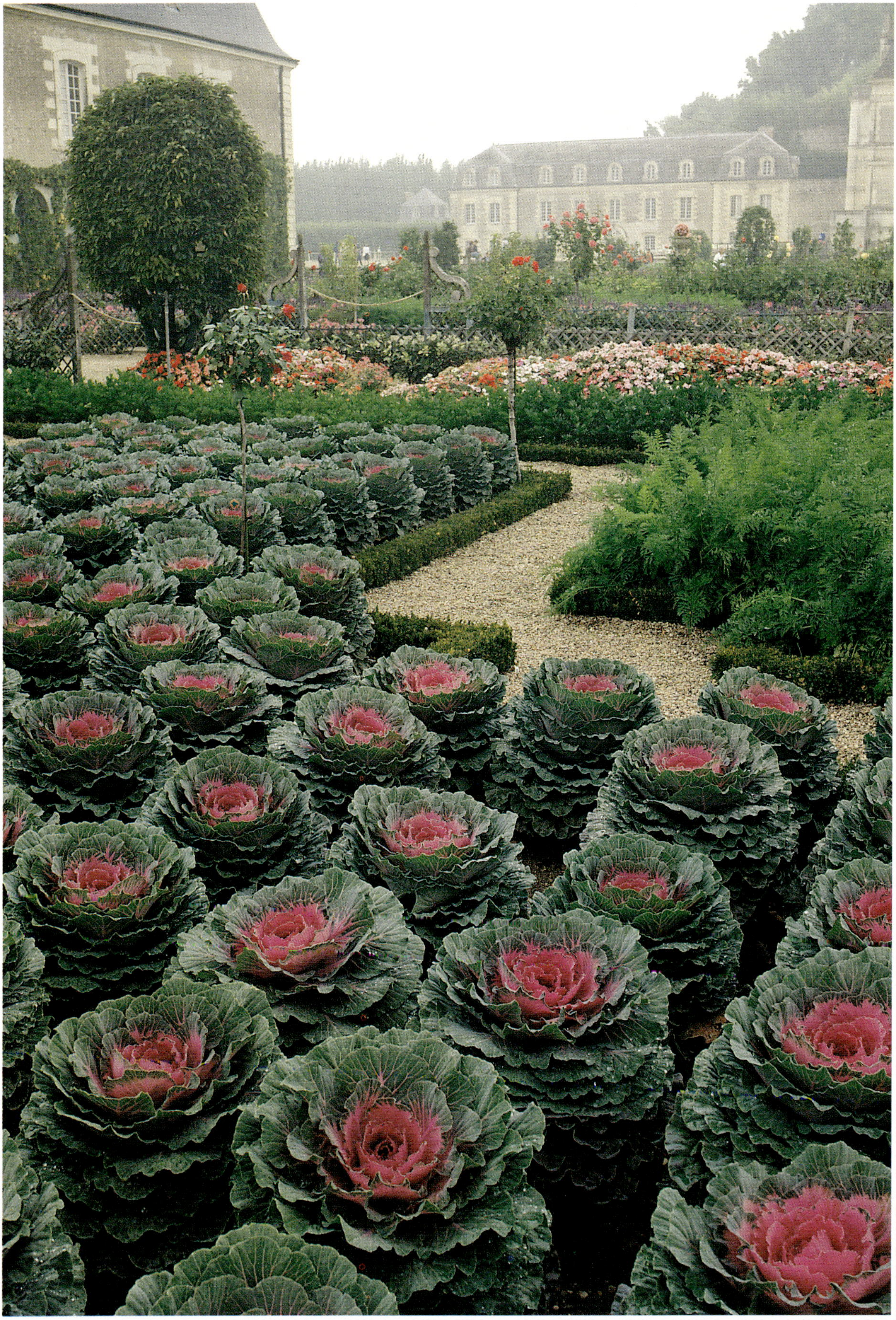

Herb Gardens

There is no question but that very wonderful effects may be wrought by the Vertues which are enveloped within the compasse of the Green Mantles wherewith Many Plants are adorned.

W. COLES, *THE ART OF SIMPLING*, 1656

Herb gardens have been planted since people first grew herbs from necessity, as discussed at the beginning of this book. Then, herb gardens bore no resemblance to the many different forms seen today which are '. . . distinct descendents of the ancient Greek or Roman kitchen gardens, and the medieval monastic collection of plants grown for uses in flavouring food, making medicine or perfume, and decoration'.

Nearly everybody can grow their own herbs, whether in the garden or on a balcony or windowsill. Supposing you decide to grow herbs in the garden, they could be planted in groups beside a path, in a rockery, or in a herbaceous border with cottage flowers, most of which were once used in the household still-room by cottagers, or else they could be grown where one can experiment with companion planting. Herbs can also be grown within box-hedge potagers, knot gardens, or in rectangular beds edged by low-growing herbs or surrounded by suitable hedges. The possibilities for design are endless and there is a wide variety of excellent books to buy full of coloured pictures showing herb gardens in different styles.

OPPOSITE: *The visual definitely dominates practical considerations in this vegetable garden at Sissinghurst: ornamental cabbages, 'Lyssako', create an unusual mosaic.*

BELOW: *Herb garden with standards, Cranborne Manor, Dorset.*

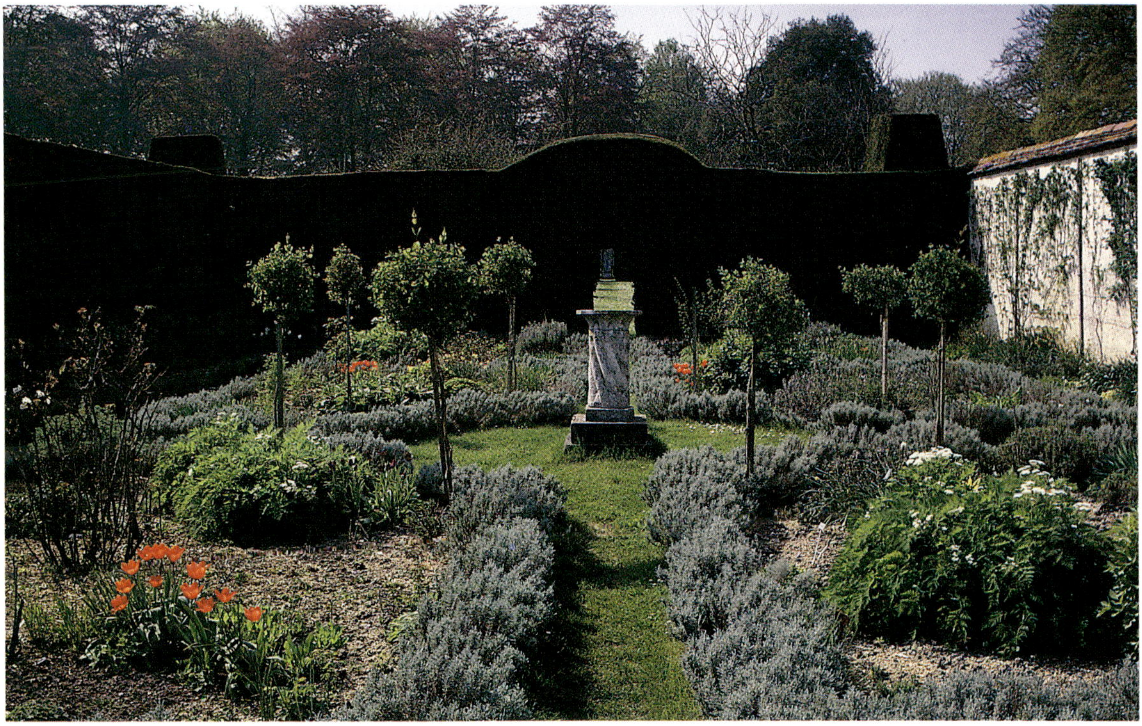

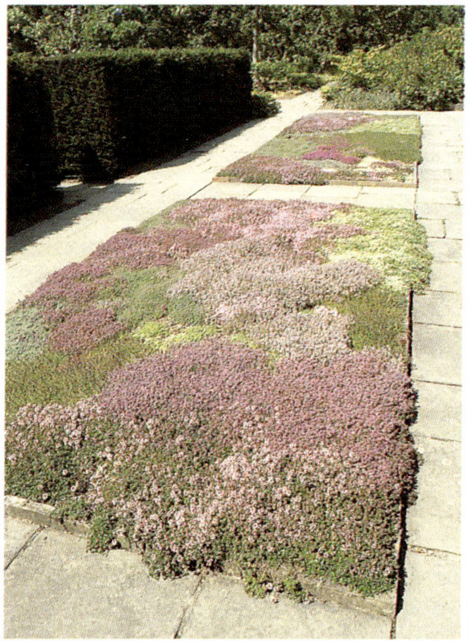

RIGHT: *Carpeting thyme makes this garden more than a herb garden. Its texture can be smelt, seen and touched.*

FAR RIGHT: *Our sundial in the herb garden at Dural, whose golden sandstone and froth of small flowers provide a focus for the whole space.*

Herbs mostly like to grow in well-drained soil in sunny positions. Beds should be prepared by forking in plenty of leaf mould and mushroom or household compost. Add a little river sand if the soil is heavy; river sand contains no harmful salt, and is bought commercially from nurseries. However, if the soil is sandy (and herbs like this type of ground for its level of drainage — watercress is an exception) and needs building up, spread compost for nourishment.

Whatever the size of a herb garden, it needs an interesting focal point — a sundial, suitable statue, a small fountain, bird-bath, or a seat with a herb 'cushion'. The foundation of a herb seat is solid material like brick or stone, with a hollow for the cushion the width of the seat and about 0.3 m/1 ft in depth. The hollow is filled with soil and planted with scented, ground-hugging pennyroyal, or carpeting chamomile.

The herb garden at our Somerset Cottage was a recreation of a monastic cloister garden. We designed and built it with double stone walls 1.2 m/4 ft high. The middle was half filled with rubble, then topped with earth. Lavendar (*Lavendula dentata*) was planted all the way round, which added to the height by 0.9 m/3 ft when in bloom, and gave the impression of an enclosed sunken garden. There were four geometric plots on either side of the central flagged footpath. In the middle a sundial was made from left-over pieces of golden sandstone, giving an interesting symmetry and focus to the garden.

The garden was freshly planted in spring and autumn, except for the hardy perennials rosemary,

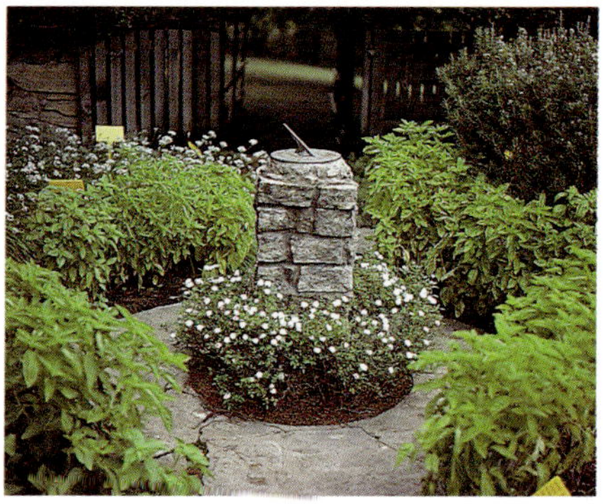

lavender, sage, wormwood, savory, various thymes, and miniature roses around the sundial, which were all pruned at the appropriate times. Oregano, marjoram, catnip, lemongrass, lemon-balm, chicory, salad-burnet, lovage and French sorrel needed trimming back occasionally. Sweet cicely and sweet woodruff did not like our humid summers. In spring we sowed dill,

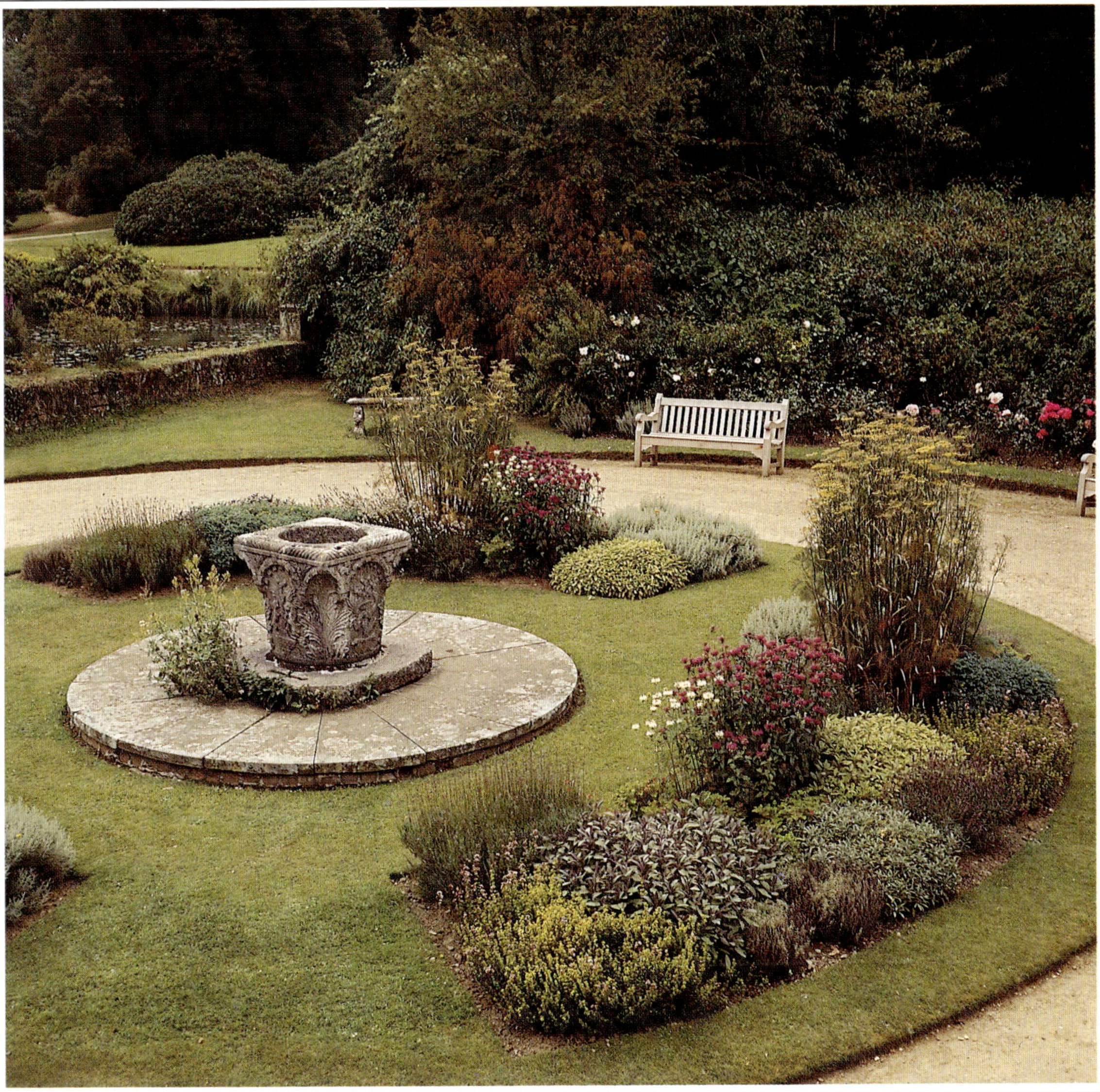

coriander, upland cress, watercress (flourishing in a cool, damp corner), Florence fennel, garlic, Italian parsley, curled parsley, and several kinds of basil. Chervil and borage constantly re-sowed themselves, and angelica seed was carefully collected and sown again within 21 days because of its rapid loss of viability. French tarragon, dormant in winter, sent up new green shoots from its serpentine roots in spring. A repetition of most sowing and planting was programmed for early autumn, except for herbs that do not tolerate a Sydney winter.

Apart from the herb garden, there was 0.4 ha/1 acre around the house planted with many other herbs, old-fashioned roses, and medicinal, fragrant, and culinary cottage flowers. Eight different kinds of mint, as well as pennyroyal, comfrey, yarrow and horseradish all had their own space,

ABOVE: *Herb garden at Scotney Castle.*

OVERLEAF: *A heavy, unrestrained sky provides a dark contrast to the clarity of design that is this herb garden.*

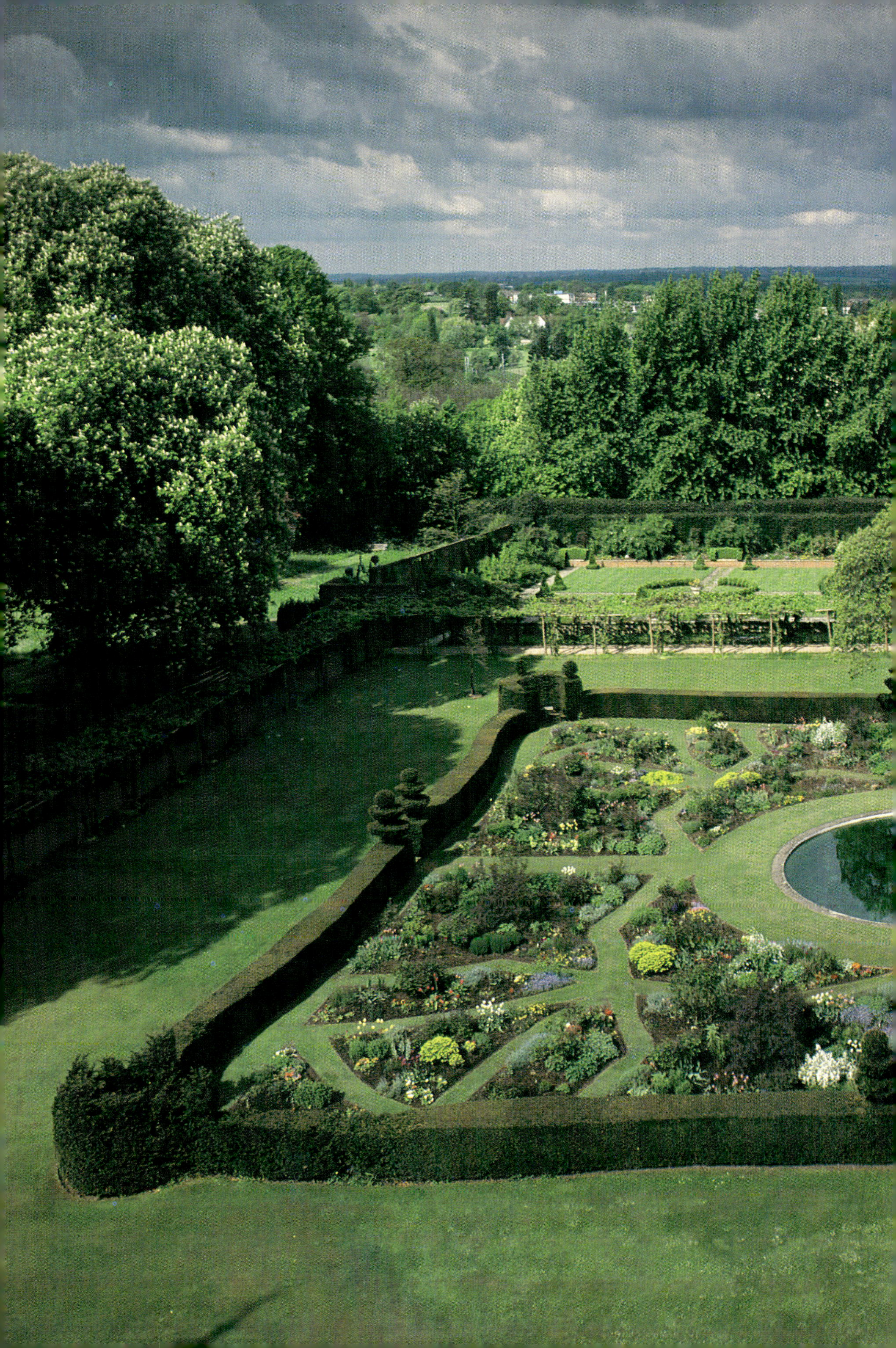

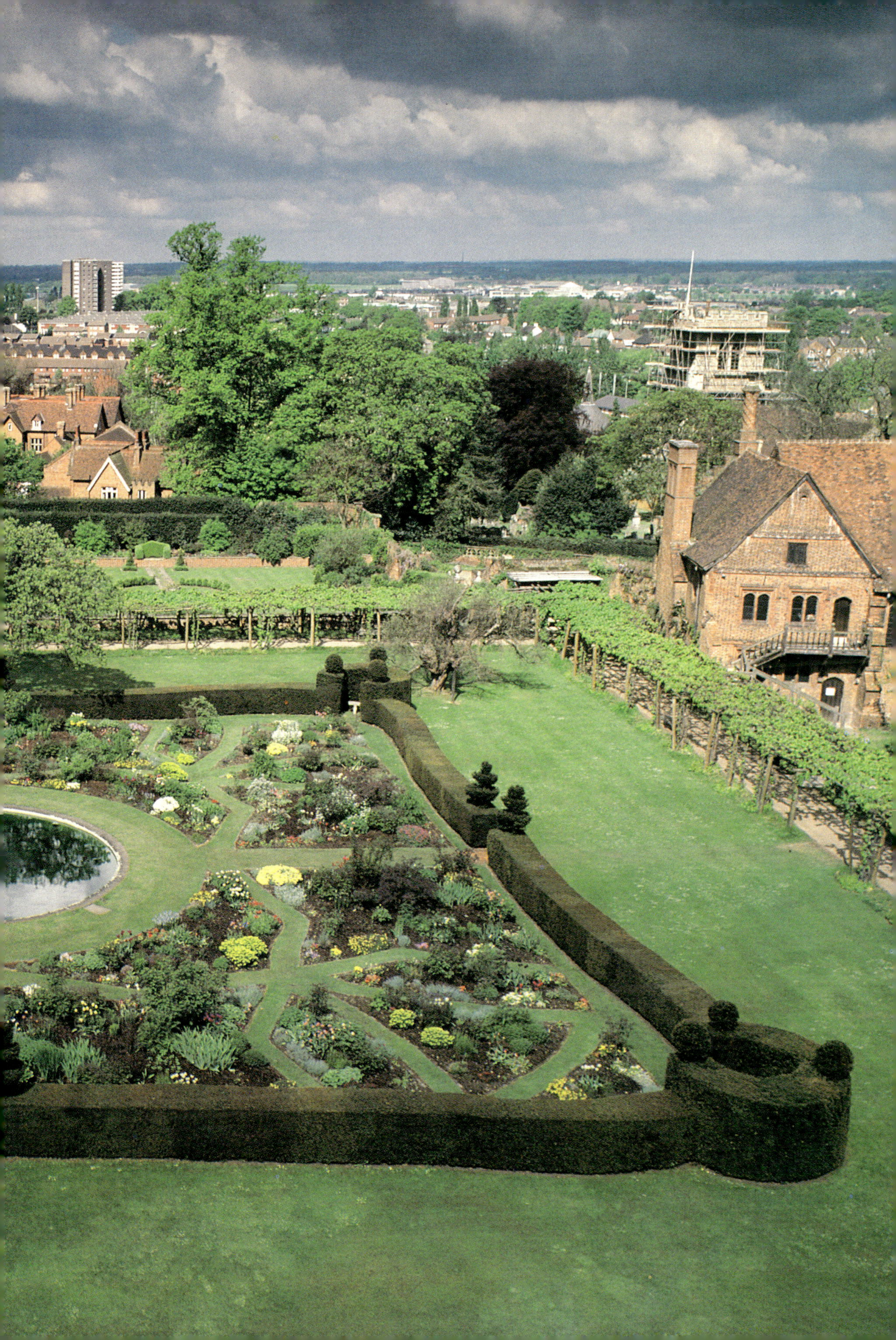

RIGHT: *Curled parsley sits beautifully in our favourite herb pot, with the apostles guarding its every side.*

BELOW RIGHT: *Hypericum in Chelsea Physic Garden.*

allowing for their invasive root systems. Our Shakespeare garden, a tribute to the Bard, was a sheltered plot at the end of an avenue of 6 m/20 ft bay trees, whose branches grew into one another. Next to each group of Shakespeare plants was a sign printed with appropriate lines from a play or sonnet.

In the foothills of Sydney's Blue Mountains where we now live, a potager garden of box is being planted and filled with the herbs we use most frequently.

Suggestions for Planting some Culinary Herbs

Edging: box, curled parsley, garlic chives, onion-chives, miniature basil (in summer only), varieties of chamomile, chervil, upland cress, curled cress, rue, salad burnet, savory, and some of the numerous thymes.

Medium-size for planting behind the edging herbs: anise, lemon-balm, sweet basil, purple basil, bergamot, borage, caraway, coriander, pyrethrums, dill, Florence fennel, Italian parsley, Italian or Spanish lavender (*L. stoechas*), horehound, hyssop, santolina, marjoram, oregano, sage, French sorrel, and French tarragon.

Background: perennial fennel, angelica, lovage, chicory, bay (preferably trained into a standard or pyramid), southernwood, wormwood, tansy, mullein and Great Valerian.

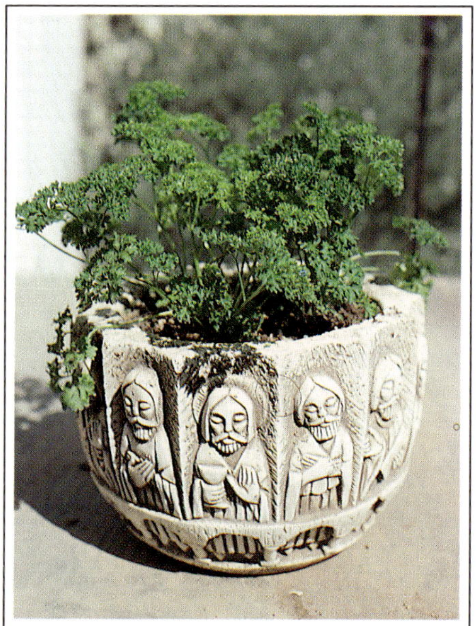

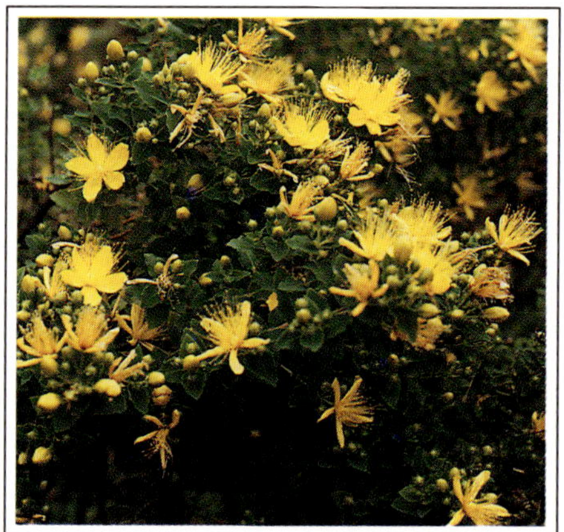

Planting on their own (preferably in submerged containers with both ends removed): mints, pennyroyal (unless developing a small green lawn), comfrey and yarrow. Horseradish should have room for the edible roots to thrive.

Clipping into low hedges: box, santolina, hyssop, rosemary, savory, and English lavender (*L. augustifolia*).

Trees positioned on their own: juniper, elder, and lemon verbena; bay as well if not pruned to a short height.

Pleaching

The word 'pleaching' comes from the French *plessier*, meaning to plait; in Europe, pleaching was a system for making shady avenues to enjoy during hot summers.

Pleached walks and alleys are wide paths made between two rows of trees, whose living branches have been intertwined to make dense hedges up to 3 m/10 ft high. The tree trunks, called stilts, are bare, and remain so by pruning away any side shoots to a height of approximately 0.9 m/3 ft. As the hedge grows and thickens, it is clipped only once a year. This method of making a formal, architectural walk was known in the Middle Ages, and became a favourite device in the sixteenth and seventeenth centuries.

Penelope Hobhouse says in her National Trust publication *A Book of Gardening* that pleaching is first recorded in England in 1324. Some pleaching occurs naturally when trees meet overhead, their leafy branches interlacing and arching high to form secluded green tunnels.

The techniques for pleaching involve first of all the selection of non-suckering lime trees, hornbeams, maples or sycamores. To make a 'walk', the young trees are planted in two lines on either side of a pathway, as long as intended for the walk, and then tied to stakes approximately 3 m/10 ft high. Horizontal wires stretch between the trees, and the side branches are trained along them, and any growth extending in the wrong direction is pruned off.

We noted a small and very elegant street of pleached trees on our way past a French town. In England at Sissinghurst in Kent, we strolled along the famous flagged alley between pleached limes, and at Hidcote Manor in Gloucestershire, another treat was to tread a

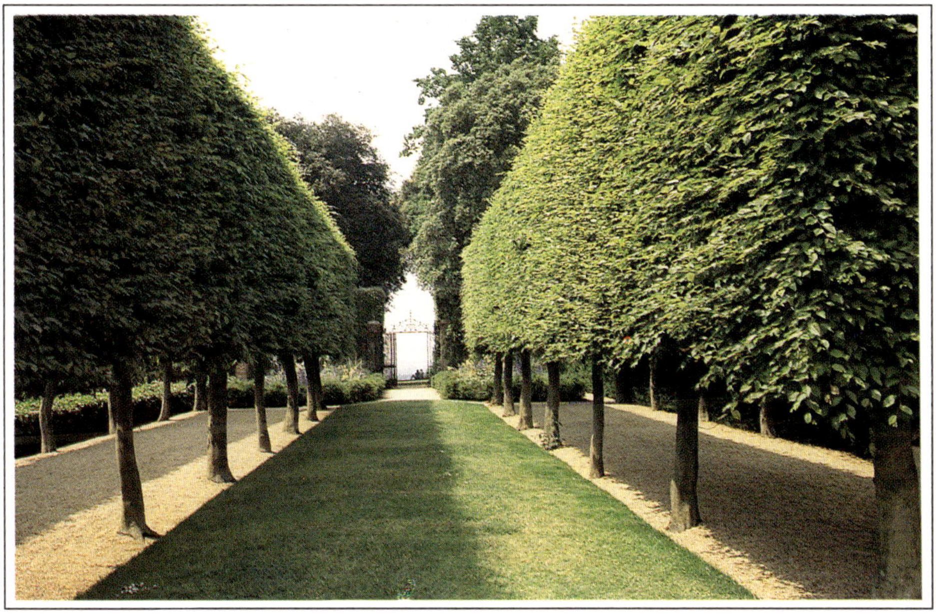

LEFT: *Pleaching is a process that helps to break down barriers between homes and gardens — extra corridors and rooms are formed outside, shade is introduced, and smooth green walls stretch out before you.*

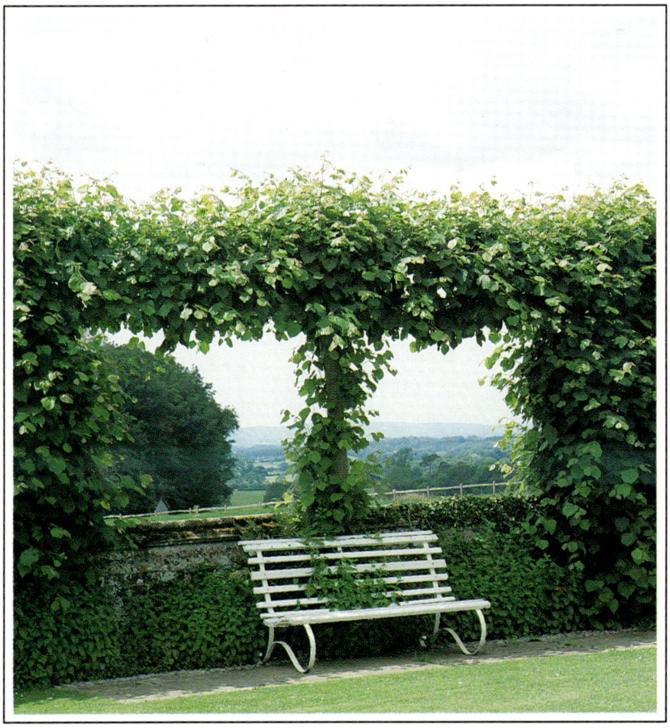

ABOVE: *Not only do they provide walls and divisions, pleached trees provide views and frames for the countryside.*

green lawn between the pleached hornbeams. Here too we saw garden 'rooms', enclosed by some interesting, clipped hedges planted together for their combination of shades of green, and variety of leaf texture. One such room was a green and ruby tapestry of yew, box, holly, beech and hornbeam growing into one another.

Plashing

Having heard of the ancient country art of interweaving twigs and small branches to make hedge thickets, it was fascinating to read Mrs Hobhouse's explanation of the extremely old practice of 'plashing', a term sometimes confused with pleaching. The craft was a necessary way of making impenetrable hedges between fields and roadsides. She quotes a description from 1563 in the *Oxford Dictionary* which spoke of 'cutting young trees half a sunder and bowying down theyr toppes to the grounde, and *plassying* the boughs that growe thicke oute of the sydes wyth bushes and thornes betwene them, they brought to passe that their hedges were as good as defence to them as wal'. They also make a sanctuary for small birds and their nests.

Espalier

Espalier comes from the Italian word *spalle* (shoulder, to lean on) and refers to trees or bushes whose branches are pruned and trained horizontally against a wall or fence, so as to make the most of space, sunshine and warmth.

Fruit trees and climbing or 'piller' roses make excellent subjects for espalier-work. The central trunk is left intact and the side branches are stretched along tight wires against walls or fences or, as often happened in the past, espalier-trained fruit trees are planted in rows to mark out free-standing divisions in walled 'kitchen' gardens. We saw long rows of espaliered apple and pear trees trained along low wooden trellises in this manner, forming divisions between gardens, at the Chateau of Villandrey in France; on closer inspection we found that the interwoven branches were carrying an abundance of maturing fruit.

For wall espaliers, plants are placed no more than 4 m/13 ft apart, then methodical pruning and tying of branches takes place as they grow — these tasks are necessary for maintaining the shape, and to encourage flowering and fruiting. Plants for espalier work are usually first trained by a professional, who knows how to select and tie the most suitable shoots as a basis for the best structure. Once the espalier plants are firmed into the ground, and wires are in place for the branches to be trained along, pruning for the production of fruit and flowers starts in winter. Pruning in summer is important to remove any unwanted foliage, and to maintain the architectural shape.

Espalier work is a technique which some people know instinctively how to carry out, however, exact directions should be followed for guaranteed success. *A Book of Gardening* by Penelope Hobhouse is a highly recommended guide and she has precise information on various other gardening skills.

There is an unusual orchard of fully grown peach trees where we live, and which we pass nearly every day. When the trees were bare in mid-winter, one could see by their skeletal forms that they had been pruned into free-standing espalier trees. Now, the pink blossoms crowd the long, horizontal branches which touch one another. They are not trained on supports, and although the procedure was carried out for easier picking of the fruit, the two-dimensional picture of graceful outlines with delicate blooms sparkling in the sunlight is breathtaking.

Grandfather S's espaliered peaches were a childhood treat. They covered a long section of rosy brick wall protecting the old kitchen garden. Returning home from the city he and Grandmother would walk arm in arm through the long-loved garden, weather permitting. In summer, the espaliered peaches were inspected every day, and if one was declared ripe it was carefully picked and handed to the lucky hoverer to be eaten at once, fragrant and warm from sun and wall.

Ha-Ha

Ha-ha: what a wonderful word to describe an ingenious garden design, invisible to the eye over a distance, resulting in an open vista of parkland or of rustic peace.

'Ha-ha' as a garden term means 'a dry ditch with a raised retaining wall, used to conceal the boundaries of an estate or a landscape'. The idea was originally a French one, an '*ah-ah*' which appeared at Versailles and other estates in France in the seventeenth century. A French gardener introduced the ha-ha to England in 1695 and the device, where suitable, has been widely used ever since to give the illusion of a garden's uninterrupted panorama.

We saw this clever, subtle deception when spending a weekend at a friend's country house in the quiet of a half-forgotten

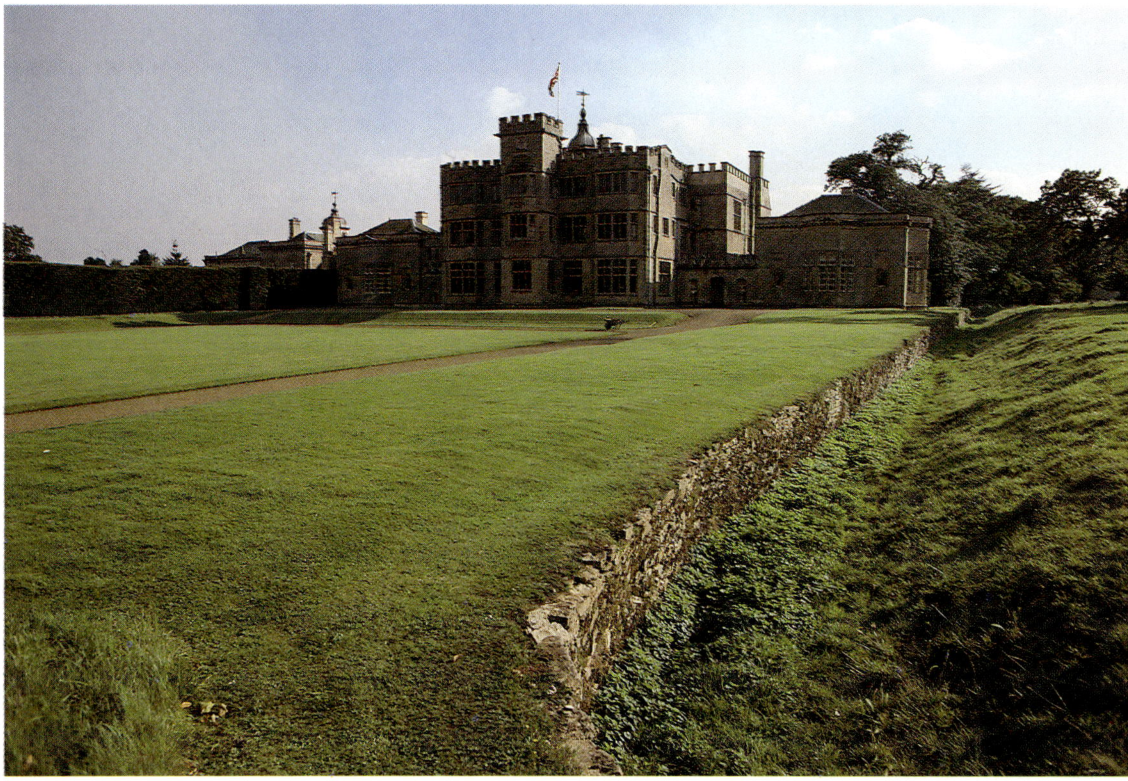

ABOVE: *'How do you keep the cows from coming into the garden?' we asked, and to our delight we were answered, 'Because of the ha-ha!'*

OPPOSITE: *Formal garden meets formal architecture.*

English village. On walking outside onto the flower-bordered lawns, the garden seemed limitless, an endless continuation of green sward under the summer sky and, in the distance, cows grazing near a 'folly' — this one an artfully constructed 'ruin' of a Roman temple. 'How do you manage to keep the cows from coming into the garden?' we asked, and to our delight we were answered 'because of the ha-ha!' Having heard the term, and knowing a little about it, it was very interesting to find exactly how this one was constructed. We walked some way to the garden's boundary, and there saw a steep grass-covered fold of earth going down to an almost-buried wire fence; another fold rose just as steeply on the far side. This was the effective deterrent to straying livestock. Some ha-has, additionally, retain stone facings which are very strong.

Formal Gardens

When describing a garden as 'formal', the term indicates a structural, regular style such as a parade of clipped hedges, neat trees and shrubs — some pruned into topiary and others grown as standards, or dwarf specimens — low stone walls with tidy ranks of plants and geometric flower beds. It could also indicate mown strips of lawn, paths that are well delineated, statues and ornaments in proportion to the garden, and pots filled with greenery whose shape, texture and shade contrast with one

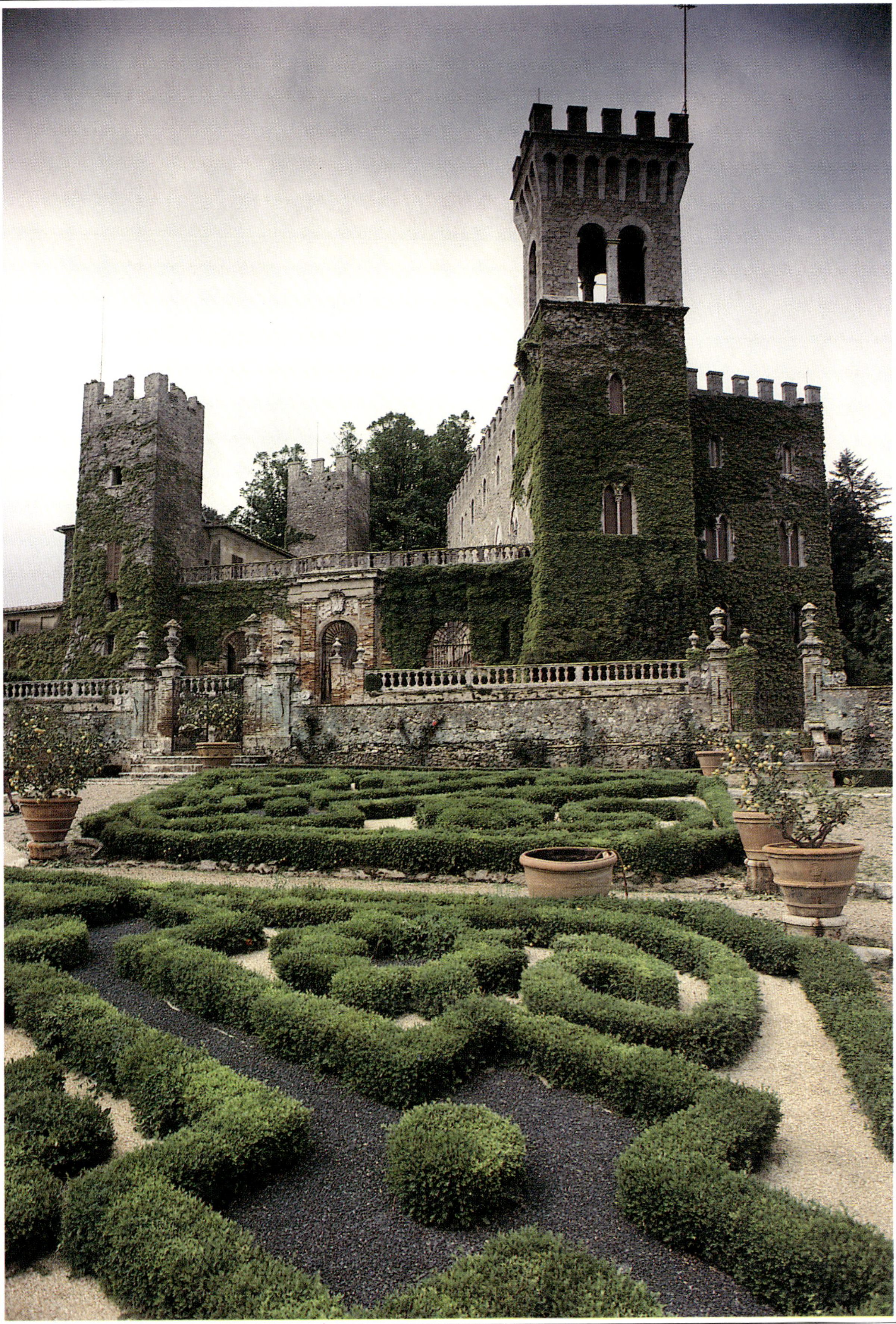

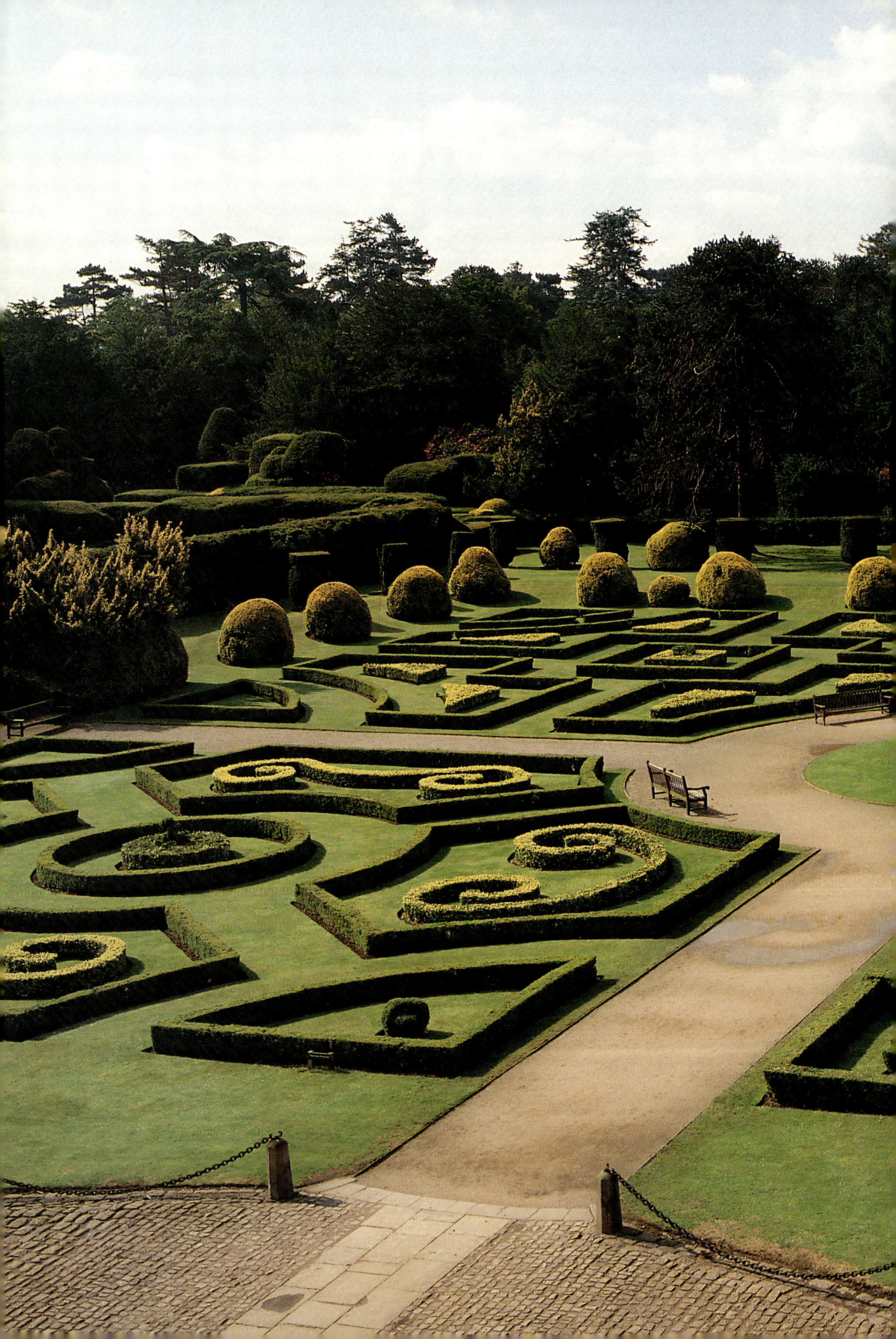

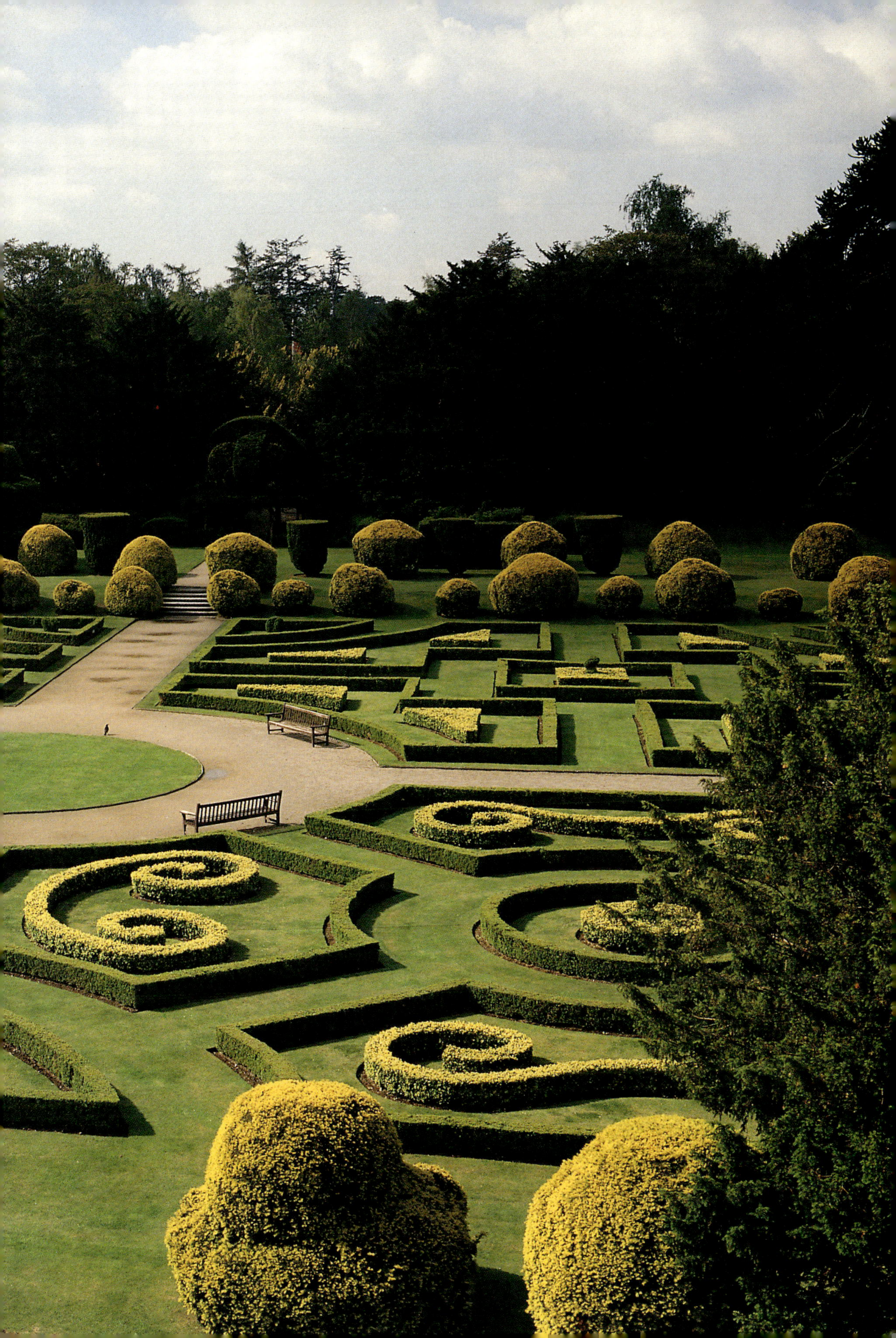

another. The eye is always led onwards when different areas of the garden are thoughtfully placed.

'Formal' does not mean 'big', although there are many large formal gardens. Small gardens can look much larger when the space is treated with formality. We visited a perfect example of formality in a medium-sized garden; notes written at the time remind us of all the requisites for formality given above. Well remembered are two rosemary bushes on either side of stone steps, leading to a straight flagged pathway hedged with a row of deep-pink, single old-fashioned 'Rescht' roses from Persia.

We also saw large formal gardens in England and France. Most of them were divided into 'rooms', separated by brick walls or hedges. Formal gardens like these require intensive care to maintain the neatness of topiary and standards, to mow vast stretches of lawn, and to keep low, clipped hedges of knot gardens and parterres immaculate. Formality requires shearing high hedges smoothly and continually pulling out stray weeds whose presence immediately ruins the effect. It requires constant watering of ornamental pots, whether full of plants or holding a single standard, ensuring that fountains continue to work, and watching over pleached trees and espaliered plants, pruning away rebellious sproutings.

The tiny frontages of inner city terrace houses with a little more space at the back lend themselves superbly to manageable small formal gardens. The making of parterres and knot gardens is ideal for a site like this, just as they are for limited space in any location.

PREVIOUS PAGES: *The centrality of box in the formation of structured gardens is clear in the Parterre Garden at Elvaston Castle Country Park, where green and yellow box work together to form stylised curves and frame sweeps of symmetrical lawn.*

BELOW: *Packam Park herb garden.*

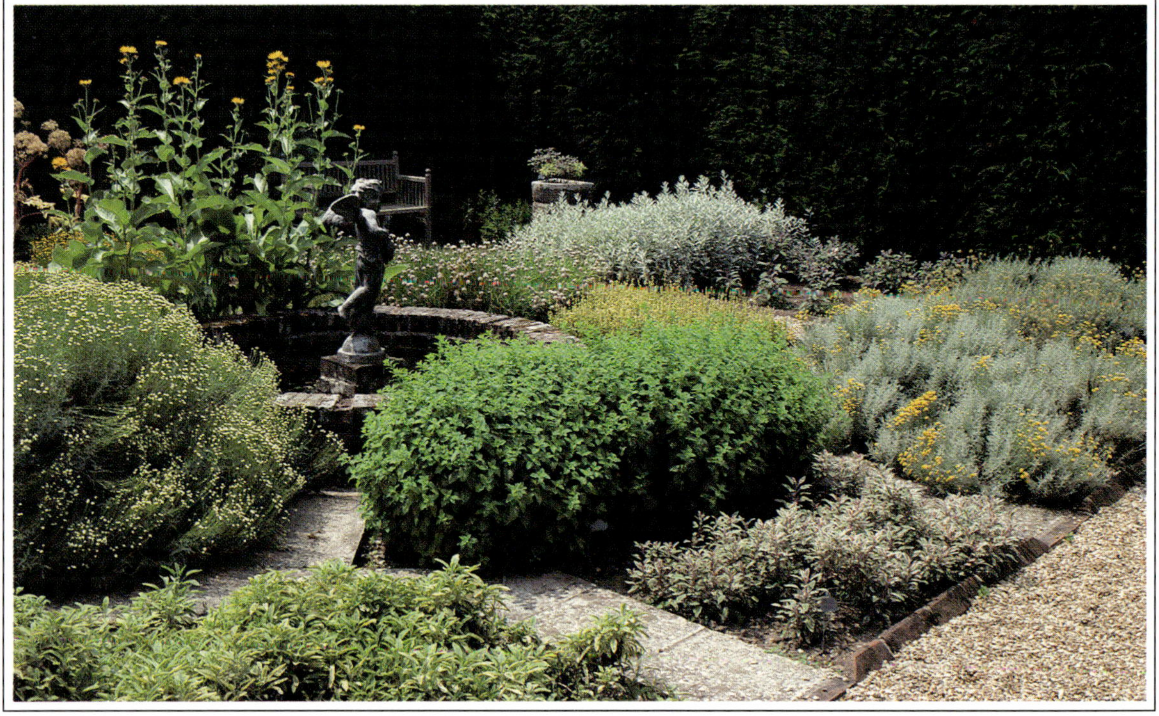

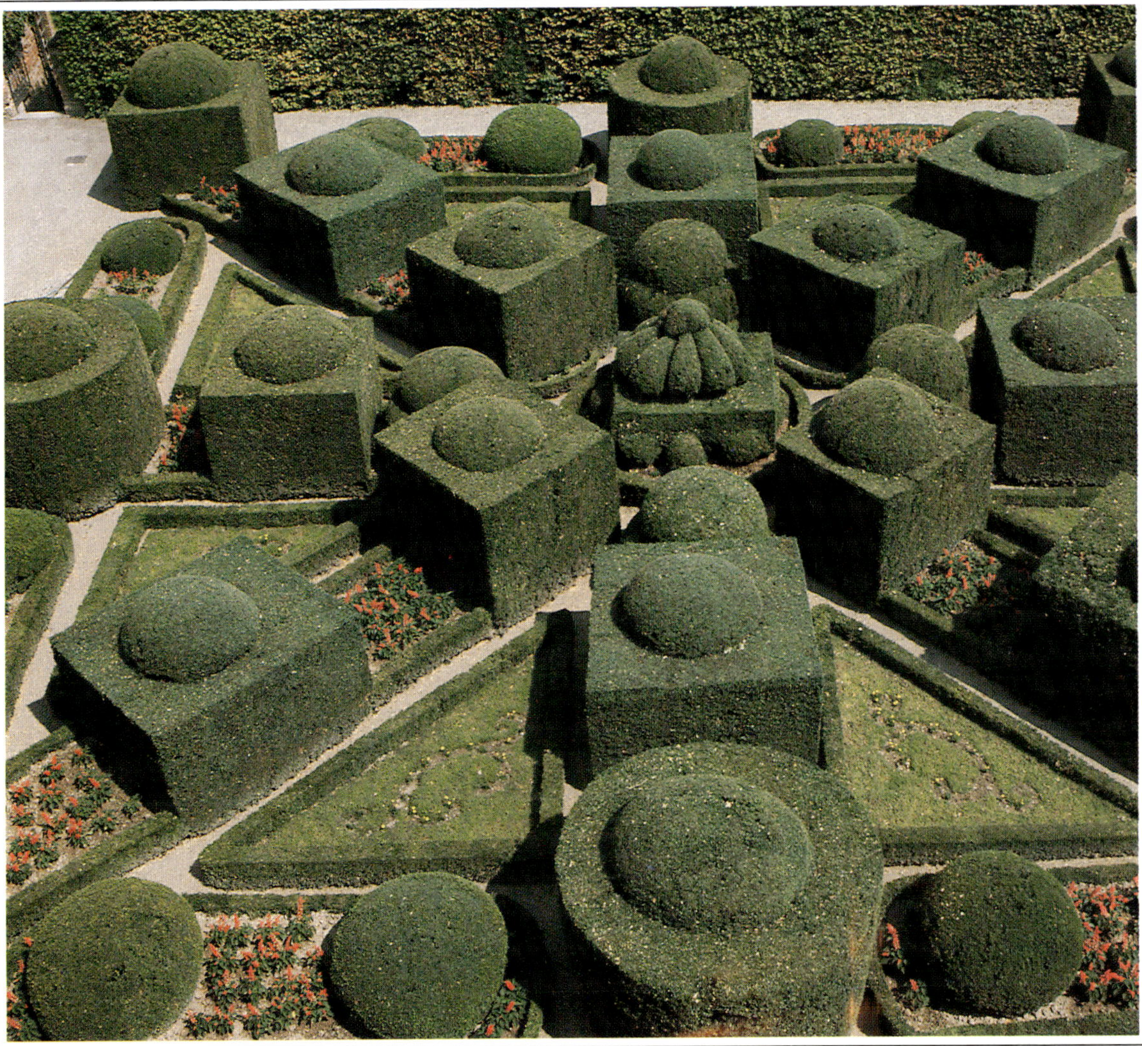

ABOVE: This elaborate garden, with its stylish squares and very geometric form is not quite a knot garden, and neither is it a parterre. It is, however, undoubtedly a formal garden.

The planning of and caring for knots and parterres are a source of creative pleasure for frustrated gardeners unable to spread themselves in larger surroundings.

A simplified fantasy reminiscent of a parterre can be achieved by edging an entrance path to a front door with neat box, and putting a well-placed standard tree or two near the porch. A pocket-handkerchief sized lawn, or stone flagging, edged with box and a green hedge or a straight bed of old-fashioned roses along the front fence, completes the picture, and is an appropriate way of complementing the charm of a period house like this. Modern townhouses are suitable for the same kind of gardens.

The formal garden first described is by Mrs Avilde Lees-Milne of Essex House, Badminton, England.

Anne Scott-James says in her book *Sissinghurst*, that Vita Sackville-West loved *looking into* plants, observing with rare sensitivity the form, colour, and texture of a flower, and she planted

OPPOSITE: *While hardly as informal as some gardens might be, this collection of colourful plants provides a more casual contrast to the inscrutability of the stone architecture.*

BELOW: *For all its apparent informality, a lot of thought and planning has gone into this garden.*

those of particular delicacy where they could best be seen. She writes 'her friend, Mrs Avilde Lees-Milne (herself a superb gardener), first drew attention to this quality of Vita's planting . . . few people, unless they are painting a flower in detail, or are botanists dissecting it, know plants in this way'.

The back of a house is a perfect place for an 'open-plan' knot garden: vegetables, herbs, and flowers for the house are grown within box hedges, or 'potagers' intersected by pathways (see knot gardens, p. 66 and potagers, p. 73). For a purely ornamental look, the type of knot garden at Moseley Old Hall, Wolverhampton (England) is ideal. It is a repetition of geometric patterns in box, in-filled with different coloured gravels, and with judiciously placed standard bay trees at intervals. If there are walls separating each house in city townhouses or terraces espalier-work trained along and up them is an excellent idea (see espalier section, p. 84).

Informal Gardens

It may not seem so, but planning an informal garden takes as much thought and designing as a formal one. Instead of straight lines and architectural garden features, there are gentle curves for beds and lawns, winding pathways, stepping stones, or grass paths to walk on, flowers that are bright and splashy

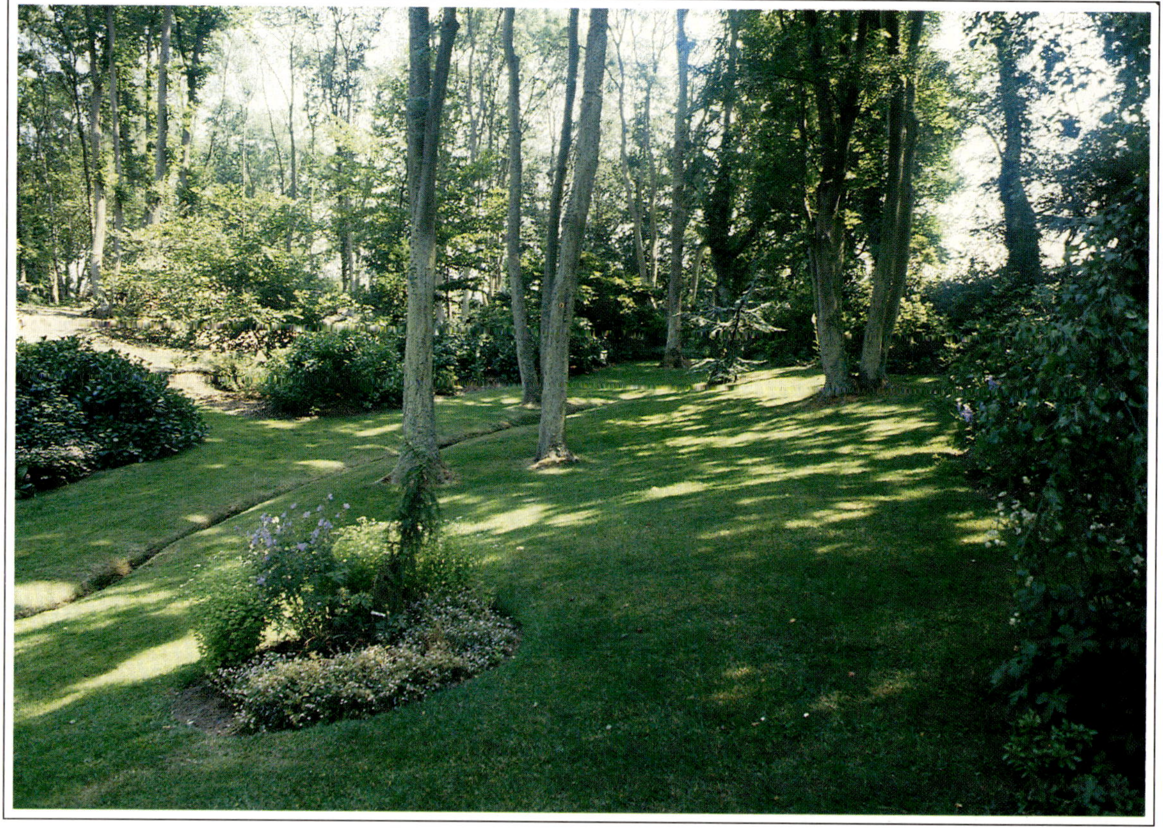

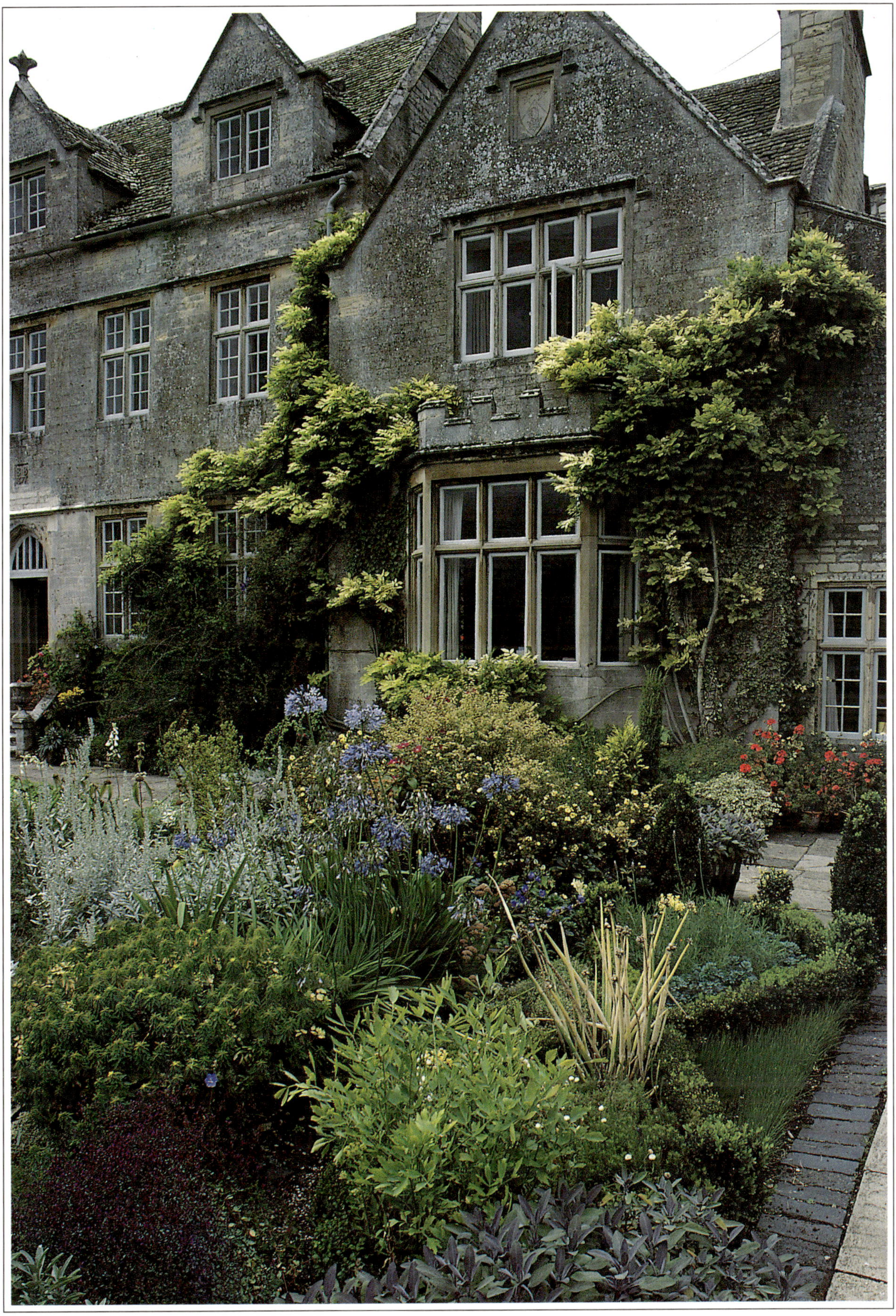

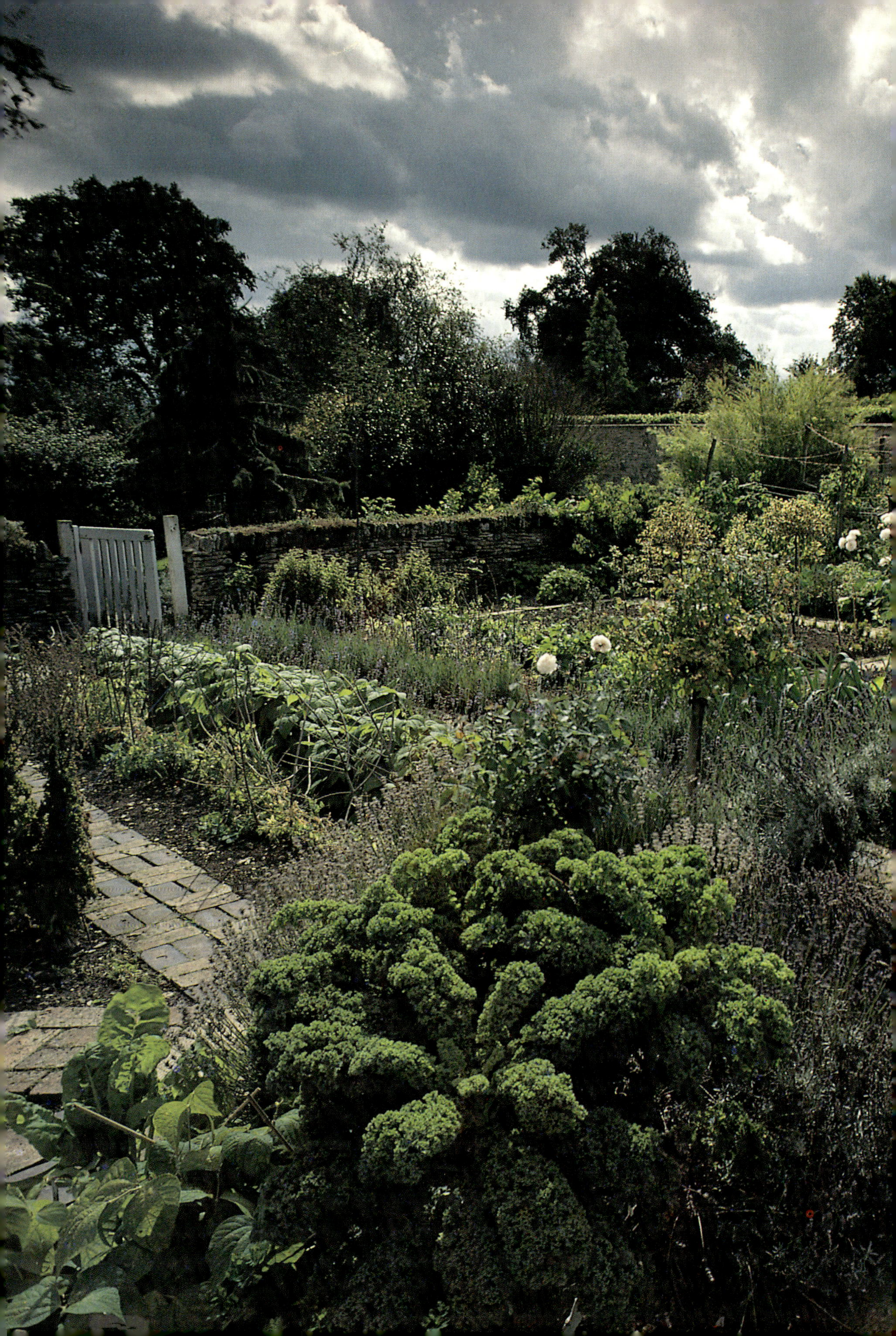

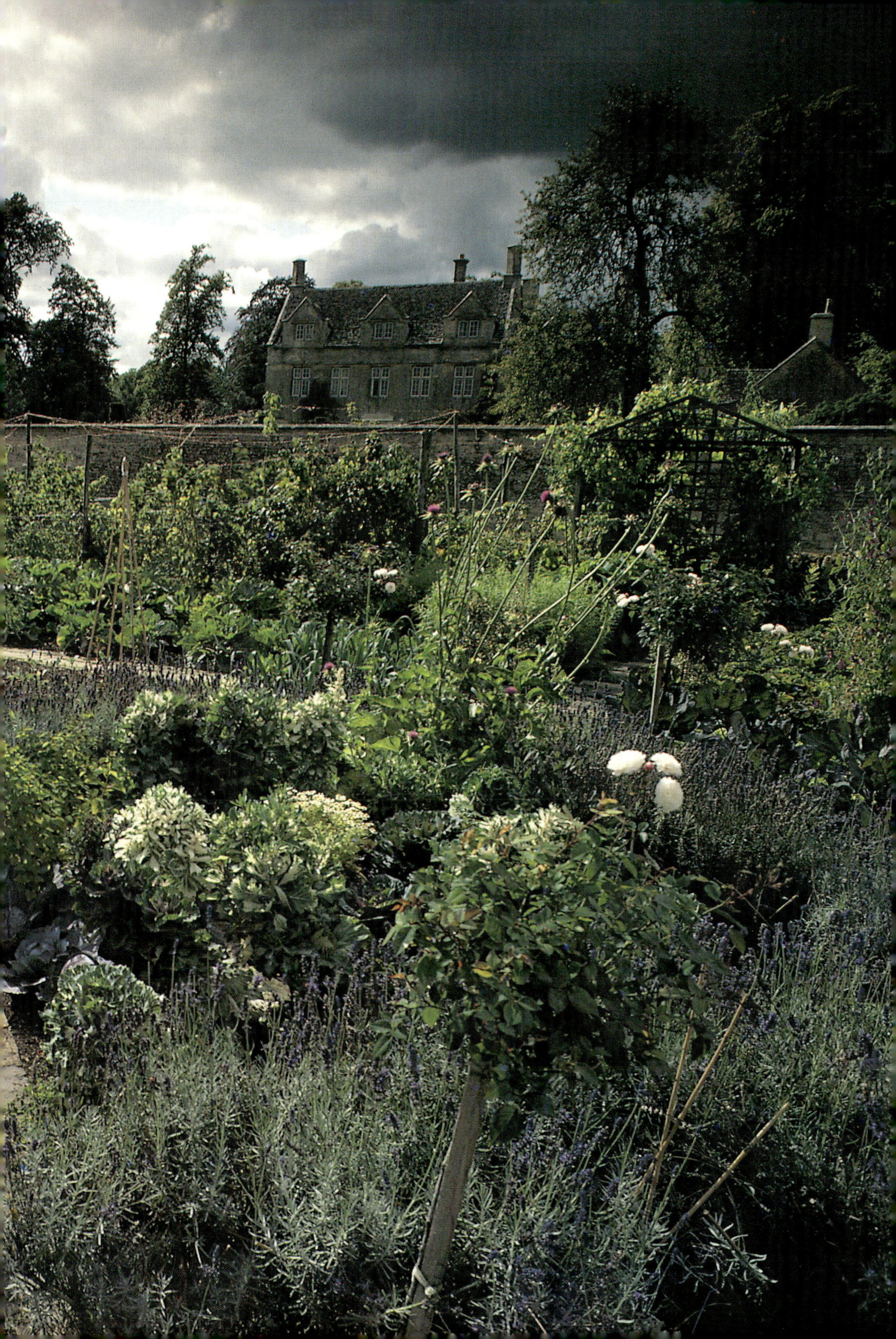

PREVIOUS PAGES: *Barnsley house garden, with its shades of green, seems to converge into the grey sky and the horizon.*

BELOW: *This relatively small garden has been made interesting by the clever placement of a seat, a pond, and framing shrubs.*

BOTTOM: Corydalis lutea, *or 'Wee Folk's Stockings'.*

(consider Monet's garden in summer, p. 136), or flowers in various complementary shades to tone and blend with one another, as at Sissinghurst (p. 109). Or else you may find a rose-canopied arbour, arch or pergola, a rustic summer-house or a plain wooden bridge crossing — those and other features are characteristics of an informal garden. A cottage garden is the epitome of informality, reminding us of the cottage-shaped tea cosies our grandmothers embroidered . . . roses climb up to the thatched roof; honeysuckle and clematis frame the front door; delphiniums, hollyhocks, and foxgloves nod at the windows, and a patchwork of old-fashioned flowers fill the tiny garden.

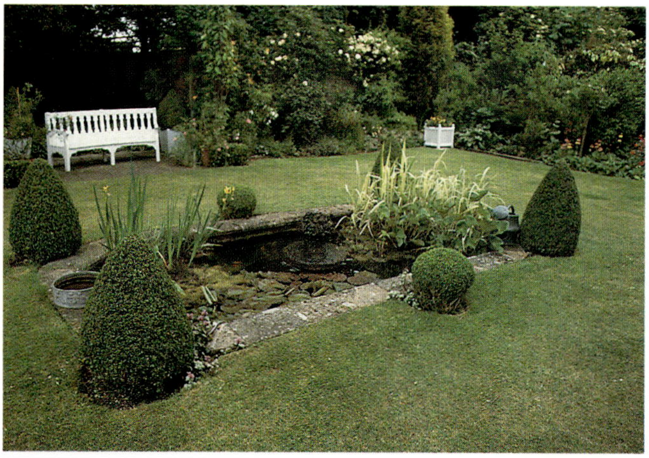

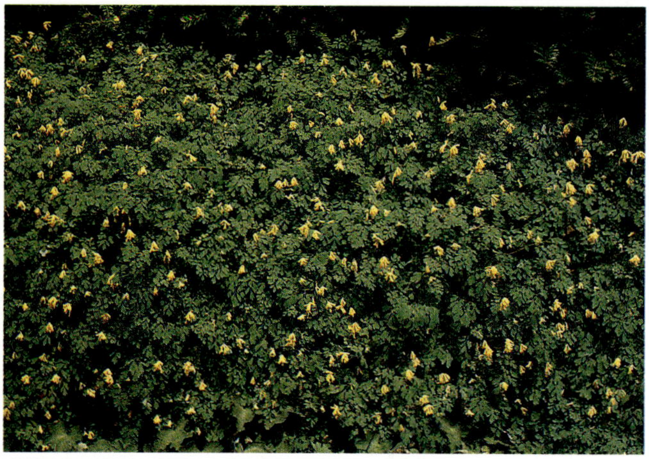

Follies are not usually seen in informal gardens; they were the whim of the rich, much favoured in the sixteenth century when sham 'ruins' of towers, temples, castles, and even churches ornamented the acres of formal gardens. However, authorities have said that a true folly is an accompaniment to the landscape rather than the formal garden. An informal garden may simply appear to be part of the surroundings, although a great deal of work has been done to achieve the result.

Informality for old times' sake often includes a herb garden, a small knot garden, and potagers within a walled kitchen garden. Informal and formal gardens can be cleverly combined, as at Sissinghurst.

An historic and beautiful house and garden that we saw in Normandy, France was designed in a formal manner: there was a roomy courtyard tiled in a two-colour symmetrical pattern, and an arch in a high wall led to a stately semi-circle of shallow steps taking one down to a spacious, enclosed garden with lawns and flowers, and a long bed full of summer-blooming plants complementing espaliered roses behind. Unexpectedly, there was then a whimsical touch of French elegance and a rejection of too much perfection: on top of a cream stone wall was a self-sown 'herbaceous border' bright with flowers — allowed to flourish, it gave an unforgettable air of informal exuberance to the vast expanse of this memorable garden.

In contrast we saw another extensive garden in Normandy planned with informality. Windbreaks of sheltering trees in various greens with different leaf textures and height protected softly rounded beds full of flowering perennials, shrubs and accent trees. Immaculate stretches of undulating lawn took us past headlands of glowing flowers to others just as lovely, but different: there were gatherings of yellow foxgloves, long and slender, snowfalls of giant gypsophila, spires of airy Japanese anemone, flotillas of shining arum lilies and, everywhere, scented clouds of roses clambering up tree trunks and looping themselves over leafy boughs in joyful celebration of summer.

This most delightfully informal garden is a tribute to the owner's hard work, understanding and care for each plant. They were pruned to help the garden's condition, natural growth habit for every specimen was allowed and composting and no digging was also part of its care. The landscape flows naturally, beckoning you on over simple plank bridges, crossing brooks and taking you around bends to yet more scenes, each as superb as the last. It is said that the plants here grow more luxuriantly and that their blooming season is longer than elsewhere.

The sun shone gently over the garden on that still day. It seemed as if the lambent light caressed each flower. There was an atmosphere of harmony, and of nature spirits weaving their magic spells around us; suddenly we were aware that there was no time as we know it, instead a calm span of being with no beginning and no end.

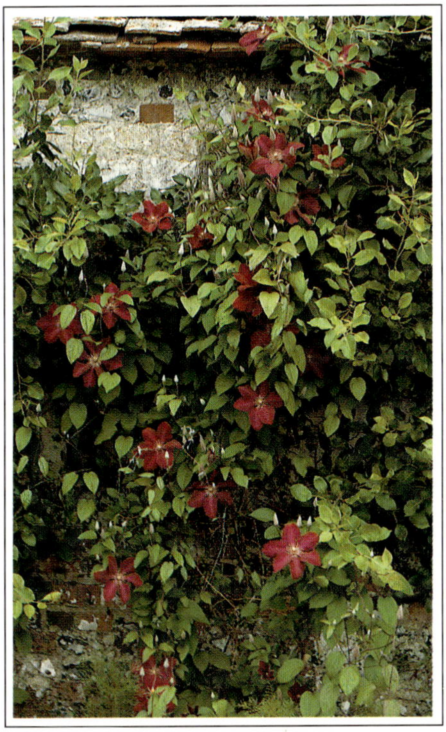

LEFT: *Red Clematis.*

OVERLEAF: *A meadow scattered with flowers is another interesting way of presenting colour and exploring landscape.*

This kind of garden can be used for large or small areas; the lesson we learned by example was that for success a deep involvement with everything that grows and nourishes plant-life is necessary, as well as a knowledge of the soil's particular composition and the aspect of the garden.

In complete contrast to large informal gardens is a miniature one for even small blocks like city terraces or townhouses. This is described by Vita Sackville-West in

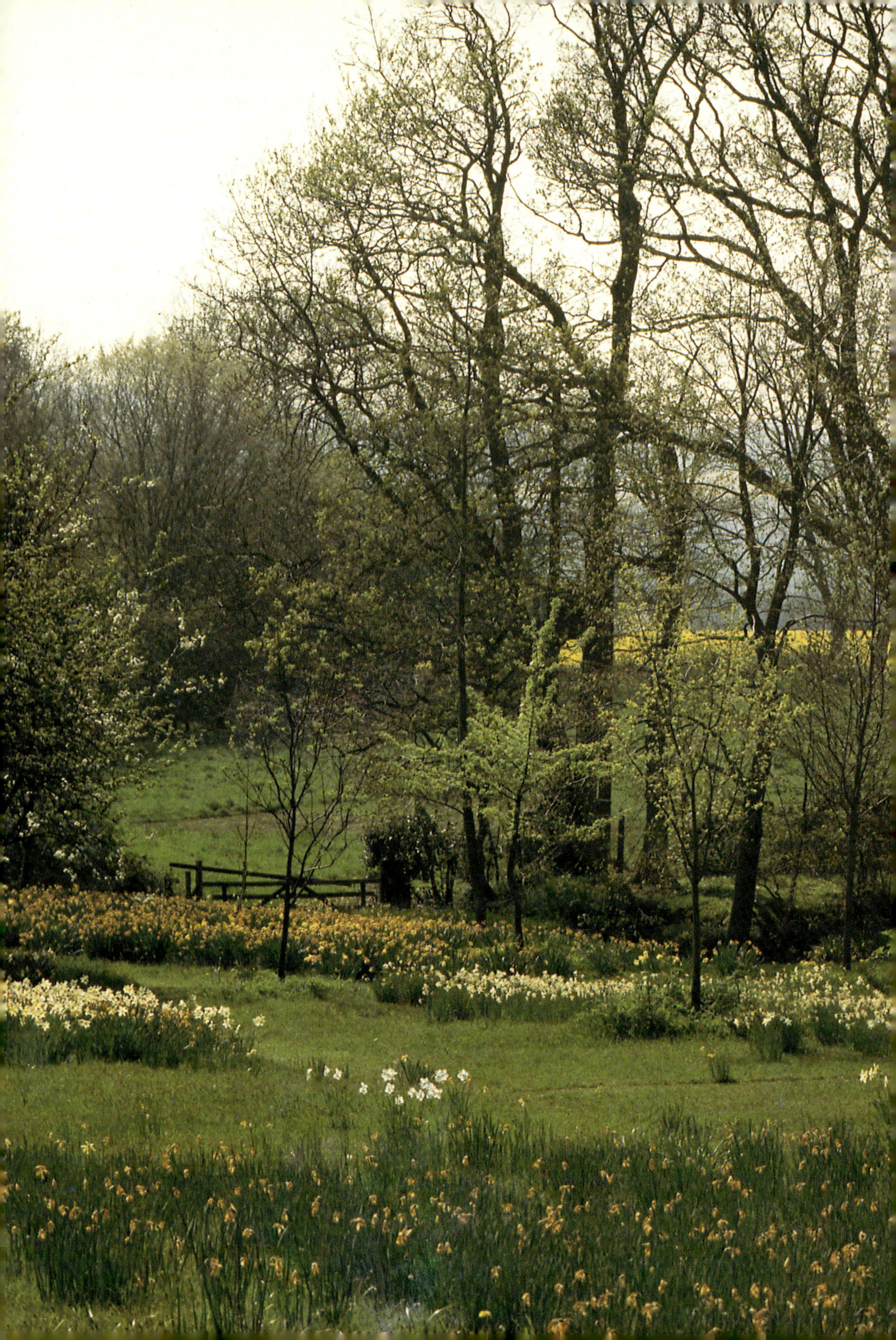

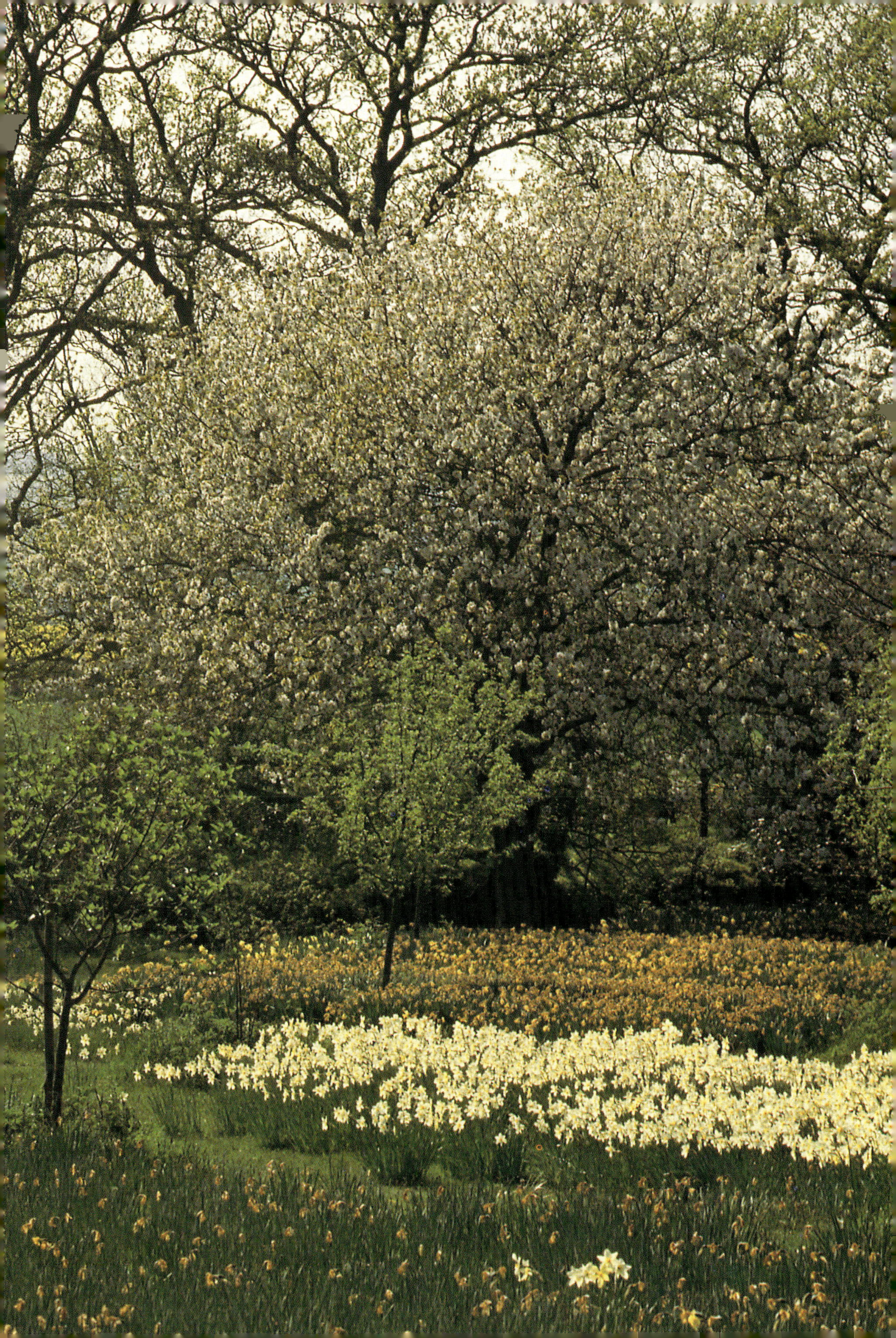

her own special way, where a paved area is allowed to become a rug of flowers and '. . . it seemed a solution to the recurrent problem of the pocket-handkerchief garden, which is all that many people are now able to enjoy. It would be extremely labour-saving: no mowing, no weeds. And very pretty and original . . . Lakes of aubretia, bumps or thrift, mattresses of yellow stone-crop, hassocks of pinks, rivulets of violets: you see the idea'.

Small blocks, too, lend themselves to becoming bright little cottage gardens, completely informal and full of loved old favourites, providing flowers for picking.

OPPOSITE: *The standards, parterre lawns and statuary lead us onwards and into views of distance.*

BELOW: *Red lavender is another plant that would go well in a bright little cottage garden.*

BOTTOM: Achillea, *Coronation Gold.*

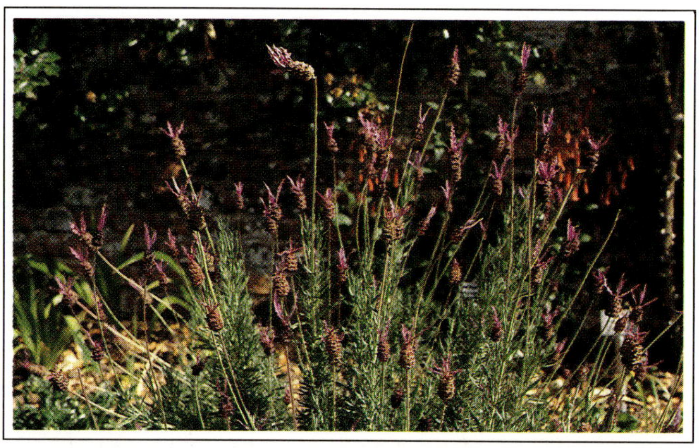

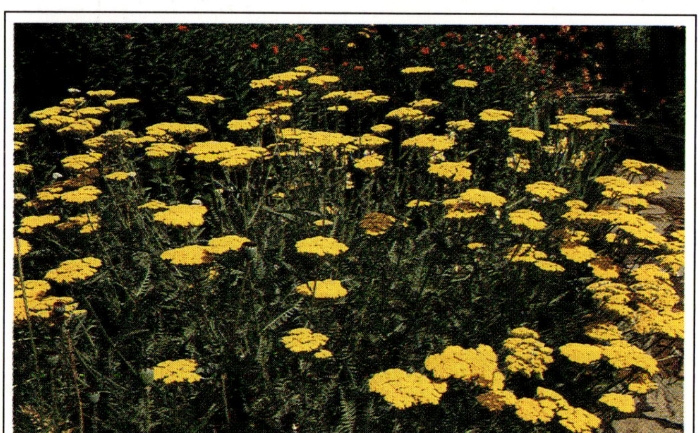

Meadows

Another way of enjoying wildflowers and rescuing them from near oblivion is to grow a wildflower meadow. The idea has gained so much favour that seed merchants in many countries are packaging mixtures of native wildflowers and appropriate grasses to sow in a particular area of garden — perhaps instead of a lawn. Wildflower meadows attract wildlife too — birds, bees and butterflies. Advocates of native wildflower meadows do not defend growing seeds like vigorous thistles and invasive tough grasses which would strangle the flowers, but the more subtle grasses have been selected for the special mixtures.

Nostalgia for herbs and old world wildflowers have made designs on William Morris (1834–1896) wallpaper, chintz, tapestry, tiles and stained glass lasting favourites. Some of the appealing old flowers depicted in his work are marigolds, honeysuckle, corncockle, chrysanthemums, sweet peas and many others. He once said 'Have nothing in your houses that you do not know to be useful, or believe to be beautiful'. We bought a charming notebook decorated with William Morris's long-loved flowers, with information that many of his firm's designs are now part of the design archive of wallpaper and fabric manufacturers Arthur Sanderson & Sons Ltd (Morris & Co was established in 1875).

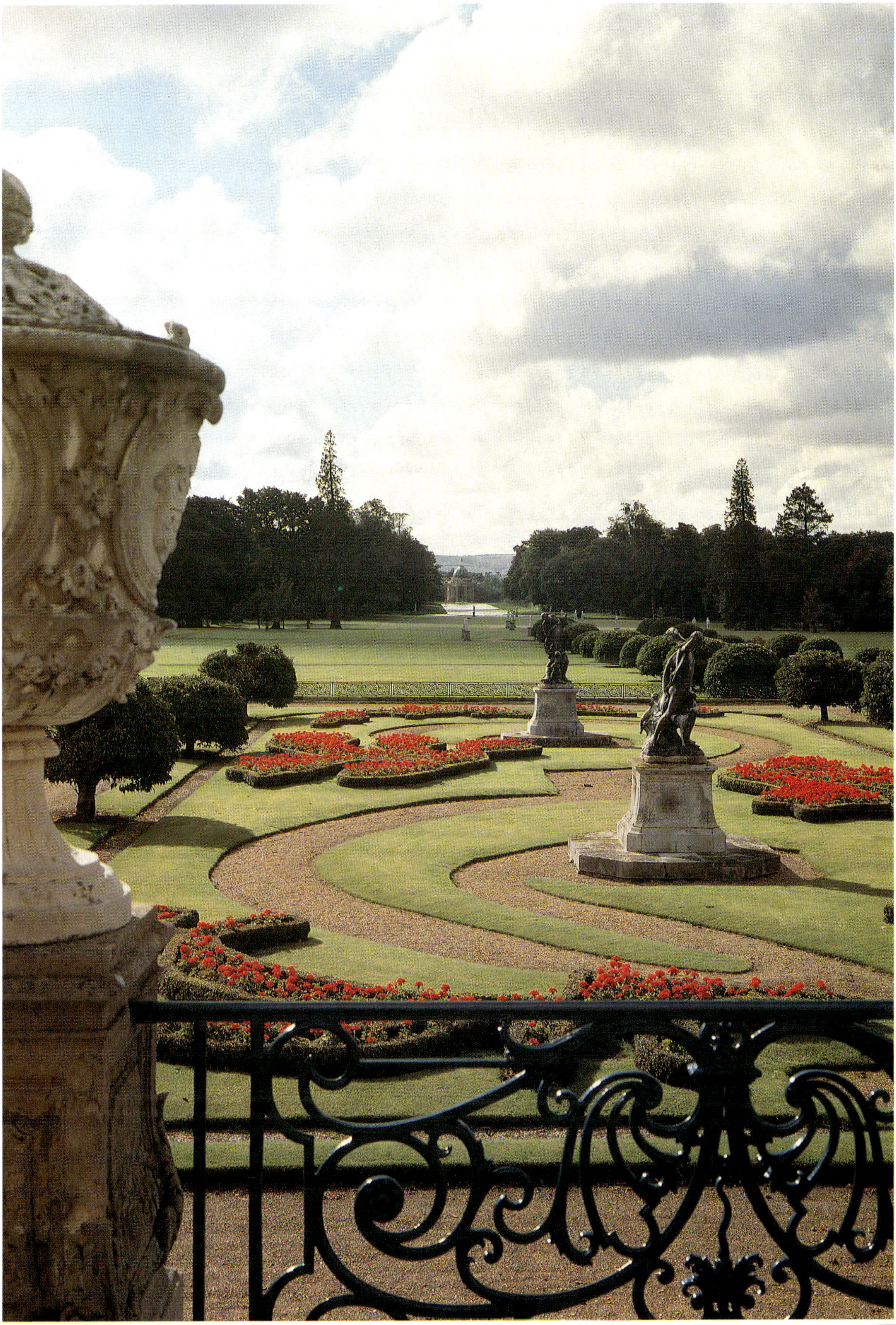

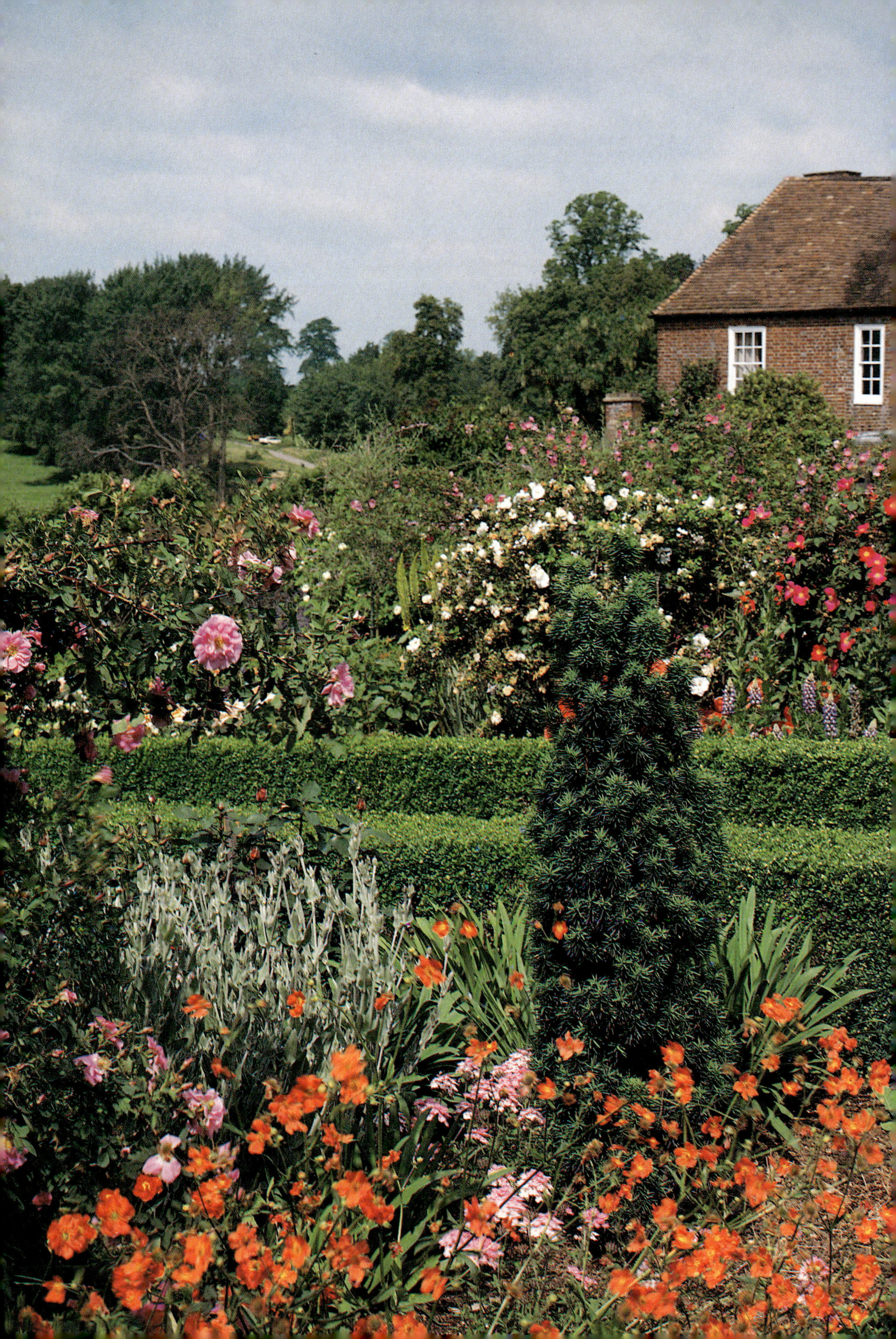

PART THREE

Our Favourite Gardens

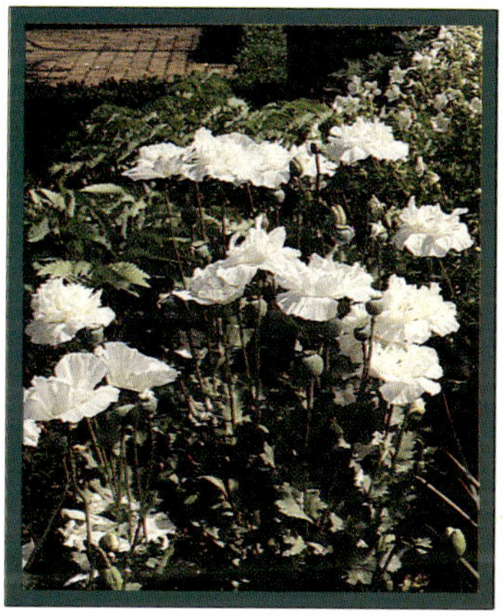

The Journey

We set out from Australia with the express purpose of visiting some especially lovely and historic gardens in England and France. Our main objective was to note and photograph gardens that had set aside a particular area for herbs, and which were now established as a delightful and useful legacy. We looked at the diverse manner of planting herbs, sometimes within elaborate knot gardens, sometimes confined in

PREVIOUS PAGES: *One of our favourite gardens in England, the Culpeper Garden of Leeds Castle, Kent.* INSET: *White Poppy.*

formal separate beds and wholly enclosed by high hedges, or just meandering in scented clumps beside pathways. Fragrant 'cottage' flowers also captured our interest, some nearly lost to intense use of herbicides and cultivation, leaving no space for them to grow. Some have been rescued from oblivion, such as 'corncockle', which is included in the English Heritage group of packaged seeds. We brought a packet home, and sowed the seeds immediately in spring, whereupon they came up and flowered all summer, quickly self-sowing again in clumps.

Our stay was limited so we were unable to see every garden of interest in either country, although wherever we went remains in our memories as a glimpse of heaven. It was summer — still and warm — the sun shone each day, and the herbs and flowers seemed to be caught in a time-warp . . . as if they had always been in abundance, their full perfect blooms and colour being like this forever.

ENGLAND

Travelling through England meant driving within an endless garden full of marvels: wild rose hedgerows starred with miniature five-petalled blooms of pink or white bordered lanes and highways. Bright wildflowers splashed ribbons of colour in unexpected places, while filmy, white Queen Anne's lace frothed lavishly wherever it could. Sloping fields blanketed hillsides, or came to the road's edge, dazzling in their different greens and contrasting with other fields of vivid yellow-flowering rape.

We passed fairy-land groves of silver birches, their slender trunks clad in gleaming bark. Sometimes the leafy branches of stout oaks, elms and beeches met overhead, forming arched sun-speckled tunnels.

As we absorbed this lovely landscape we saw villages and remote farmhouses built long ago of local stone or brick, and half-timbered houses with black beams placed over white, ochre, or 'ox-blood' washes. Picturesque thatched cottages with honeysuckle and roses framing their windows and doors were another treat for the eyes.

The experience of seeing all this, as well as the gardens, revealed the continuity of a loved inheritance, providing us with a new awareness of how much is based on the past and how history in these countries is revered.

Coming so swiftly from our own dry continent of Australia, we were sensitive to the dewy softness of the English air, which seemed to caress us with a balmy breath faintly redolent of old roses, wildflowers, green grass and rich brown earth. Added to this was the music of countless tiny birds chirruping in protecting thickets.

Never had we seen England looking so beautiful, and we recollected William Shakespeare's inimitable description:

This royal throne of kings, this scepter'd isle,
This earth of majesty, this seat of Mars,
This other Eden, demi-paradise . . .
This precious stone set in the silver sea . . .
This blessed plot, this earth, this realm, this England.
(*Richard II*, Act II, Scene 1.)

Leeds Castle

Leeds Castle, built in the thirteenth century, is the most romantic of castles. Its setting is equally picturesque: approximately 200 lovely hectares/500 acres of rolling lush parkland with stands of old trees in the distance.

We visited historic Leeds Castle in the Weald of Kent on a memorable, calm and sunny day in summer. Before we left Australia an English friend had told us that this was the castle Henry VIII liked to take his favourite of the moment to dally awhile, and so it became known as 'Lady's Castle' — shortened to 'Leeds' over the passage of time.

There are two ways of approaching the castle: you can walk the private straight drive, or go via the duck pond. We chose the winding path by the duck pond, past banks of wildflowers in bloom and a wide stream, tall trees making a sun-dappled canopy above. We came upon brilliant sapphire and emerald peacocks, and among them an all-white fellow spread his tail feathers for us, quivering them and turning slowly so that we could enjoy the full breathtaking effect, reminding us of intricately designed lace sewn on to fans, or perhaps those made of ivory filigree.

The pond widened as we walked up towards the castle. Rounding a corner there was the blue moat surrounding the ancient grey stone fort, looking as impressive as it

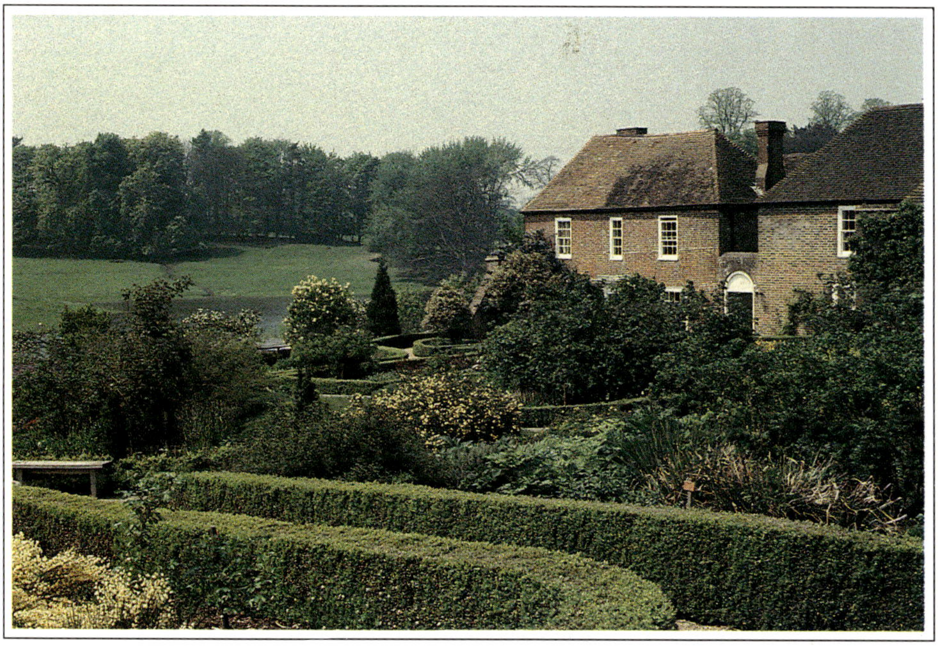

LEFT: *We visited historic Leeds Castle in the Weald of Kent on a memorable calm and sunny day in summer.*

OVERLEAF: *The sun shone each day, and the herbs and flowers seemed caught in a time-warp, as if their full perfect blooms had been like this forever.*

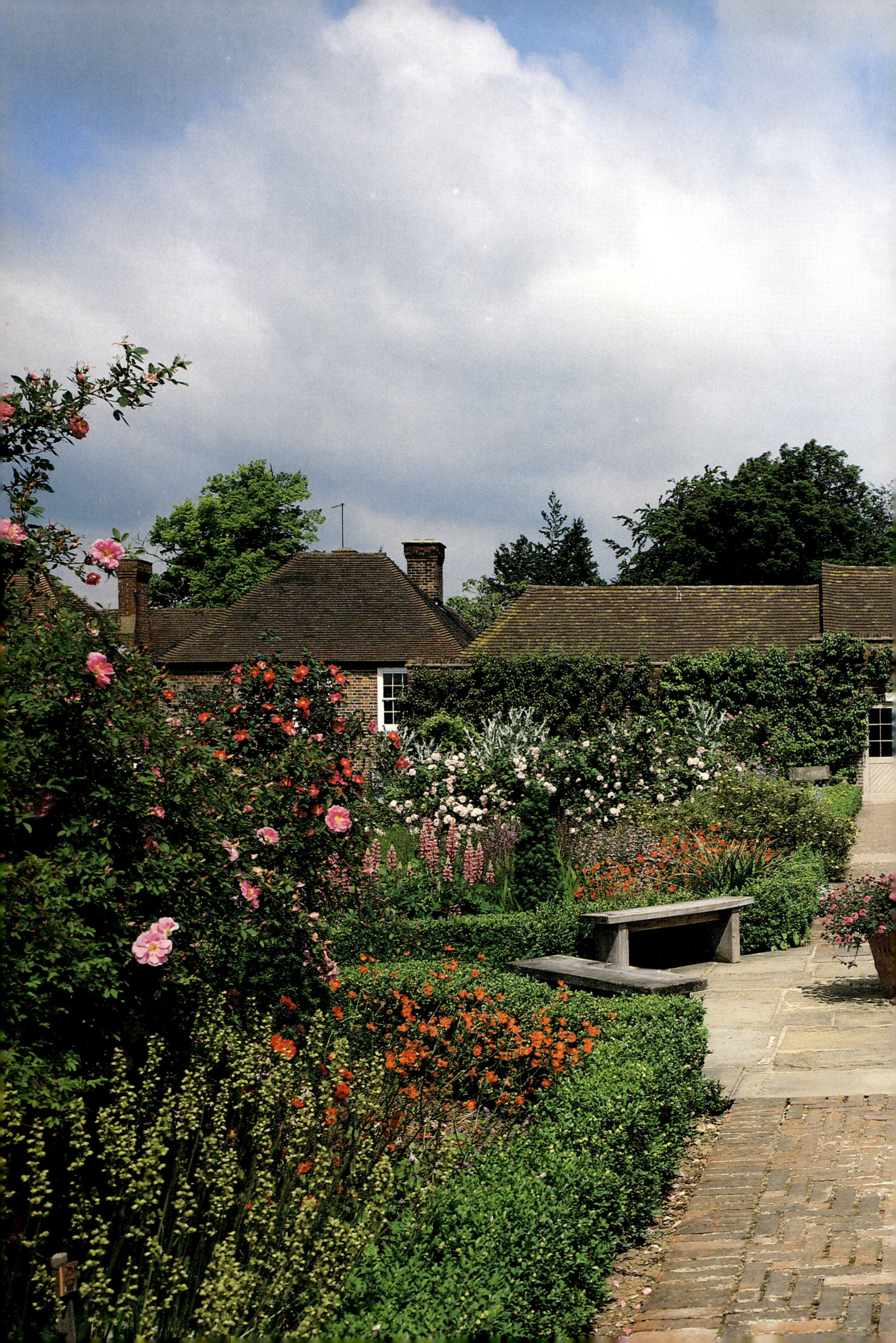

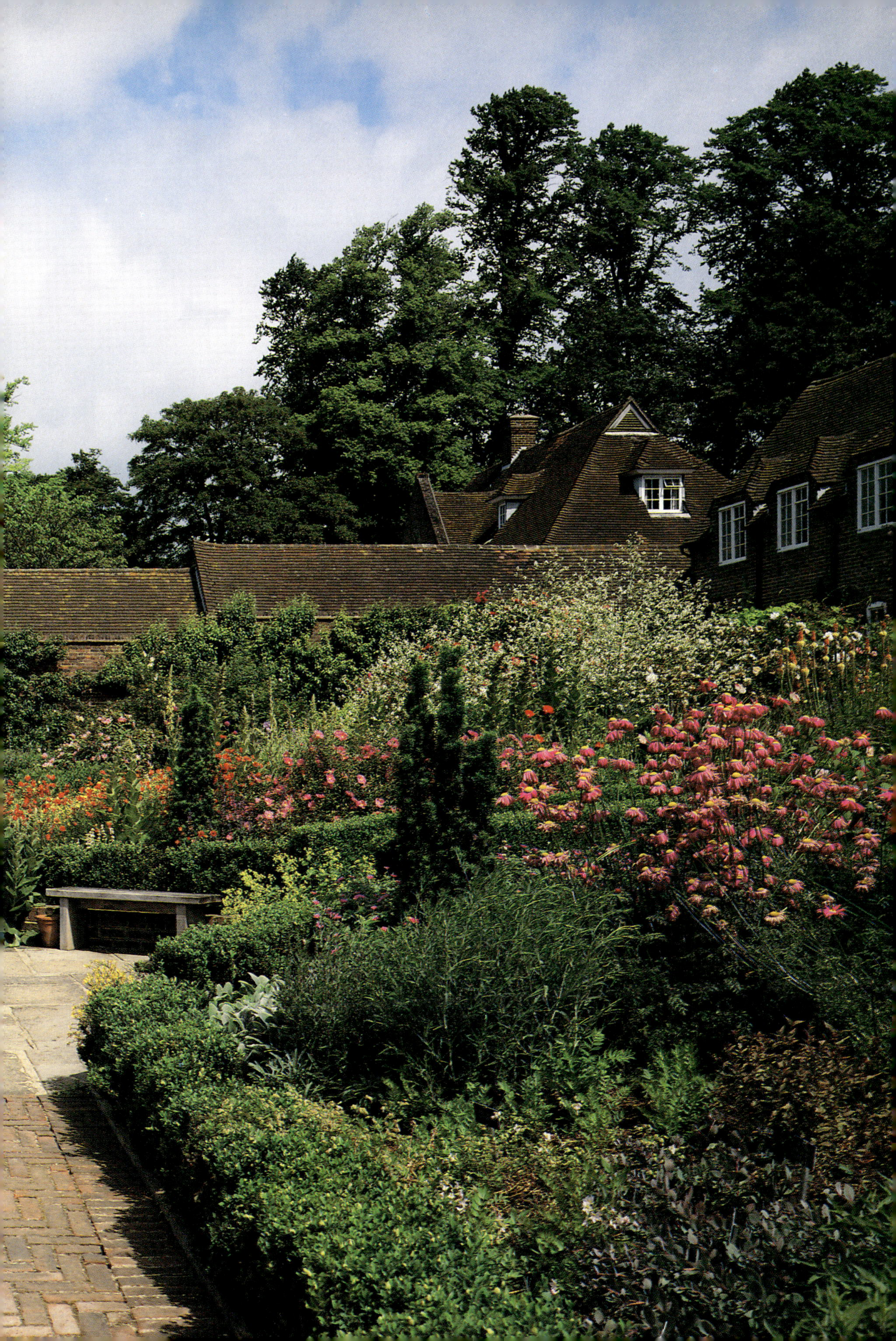

must have when built in the thirteenth century. The castle is sheltered on three sides by out-buildings and a rosy brick wall. The fourth side, left open, allows full view of the 'Great Water', a lake covering 2.5 hectares/6 acres, once a mediaeval water defence.

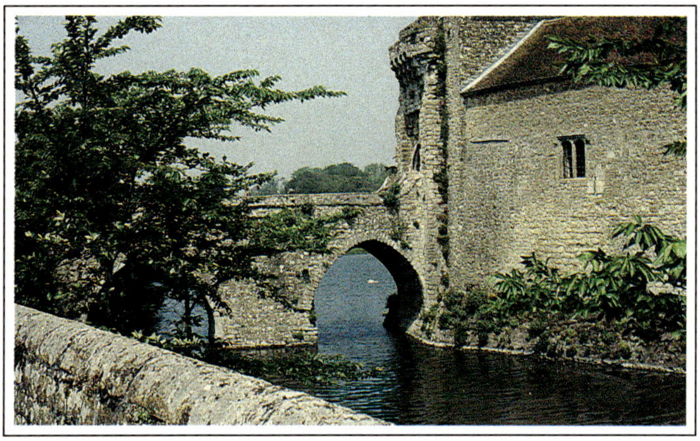

ABOVE: *Thirteenth century Leeds Castle is the most romantic of castles.*

Beyond is the valley, and serene vistas of green undulating land.

Relatives of Nicholas Culpeper, the famous herbalist, owned the castle in the seventeenth century. In the twentieth century the castle came into the hands of the Hon. Lady Baillie, a member of the Whitney family of America. She restored it and, on her death, left a bequest to the Leeds Castle Foundation for medical research and conferences to be held at the castle.

In 1980 Russel Page was asked to suggest appropriate planning to replace the old cutting garden behind the estate cottages and stables. Stephen Crisp created the planting scheme, and the result is now known as 'The Culpeper Garden'. Low, clipped box hedges provide four formal enclosed areas for beds of herbs, old-fashioned roses, bulbs and colourful cottage garden flowers with pathways between the hedges.

Nostalgic plantings within the box hedge compartments give variety from late spring to early autumn. There are many kinds of lovely, low-growing geraniums covered with small single flowers in different pastel shades. There is also Lady's mantle (*Alchemilla mollis*), five varieties of sage, numerous thymes, lavender, rue, ten kinds of mint, and a long border of thirty different herbs.

Old scented roses abound with silver-leaved plants providing foliage contrast. Russel lupins, delphiniums and forget-me-nots are delightful additions. Clambering up walls are clematis, climbing roses, ivy and, from another era, espaliered pear trees. A feature of the garden is the marvellous range of bergamots (*Monarda*), originally from the American continent.

There are, of course, many more interesting and beautiful plants at Leeds Castle — the atmosphere is gently suffused with their combined fragrances, seducing you to stay and never leave.

About 400 000 people visit Leeds Castle and Culpeper Garden each year. As there was no conference in the castle when we were there it was open, and we enjoyed the truly wonderful experience of walking through it. Friends spent half a day at the castle one early autumn; it was exquisite then too, the whole scene capturing, they said, 'the subtle mistiness of a Constable painting'.

Sissinghurst Castle

Sissinghurst Castle in the Weald of Kent has been a mecca for garden lovers for many years. Victoria (Vita) Sackville-West and her husband Sir Harold Nicolson, both unique and gifted people, started the garden when they rescued the derelict buildings of Sissinghurst in 1930. Many books have been written about them and their inspired achievements at Sissinghurst.

Vita Sackville-West's background was privileged British aristocracy. She was born in 1902 at historic Knole, a huge Tudor Palace in Kent which had belonged to her family for hundreds of years. She knew every corner of the 365 room mansion and the 404 hectare/1000 acre estate on which it stood. However, because she was not a male (her father Lionel became the third Lord Sackville in 1908), she could not inherit her beloved home. However, in time the Nicolsons created a magnificent substitute for Knole at Sissinghurst.

An Illustrated Guide to Sissinghurst Castle by N.N. tells us that the site was occupied as early as the twelfth century, and called Saxingherste; the first owners took as their name 'de Saxingherste'. Over the next three hundred years the property was owned by several different people, until the Baker family bought it in 1490. A son of the Baker family built an impressive house of rosy-pink brick, where Queen Elizabeth I stayed during her progress through Kent in 1573.

It is fascinating to learn that an ancestor of Vita Sackville-West lived at Sissinghurst. She was Cecily Baker, who married Thomas Sackville-West, first Earl of Dorset, in the sixteenth century.

By the time the Nicolsons

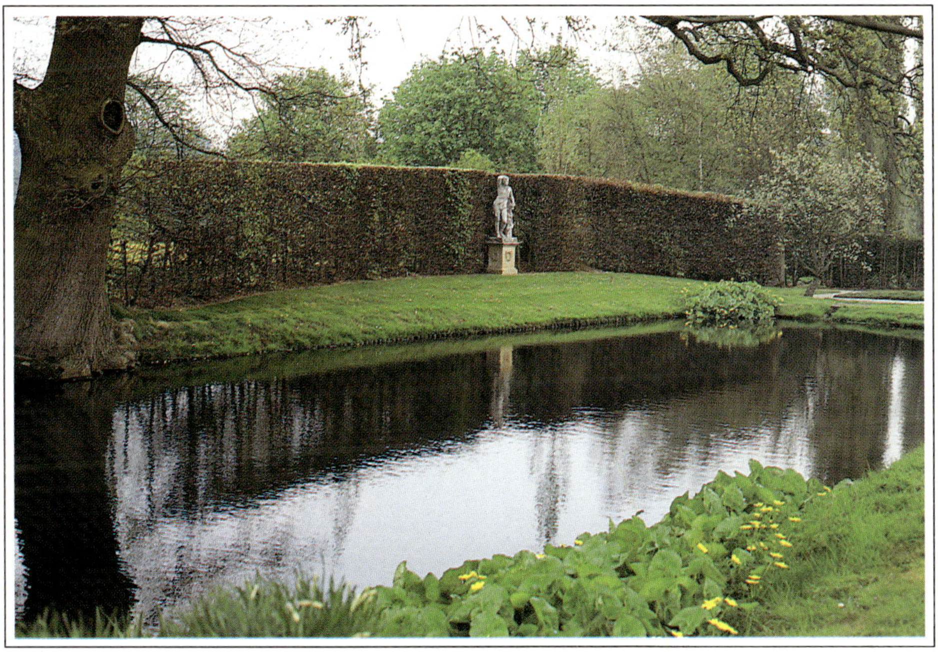

LEFT: *Moat at Sissinghurst Castle.*

bought the property it had been passed on to various owners until eventually it fell into decay. When Vita saw it in the spring of 1930, she 'fell in love' and knew she could make something of it, but not without much planning and hard work. Harold Nicolson designed the garden, and divided it into many 'rooms'; Vita Sackville-West planted it. They decided on strict formality of design and informality of planting. On their travels, the couple collected various treasures including wonderful antique ornaments to enhance the garden. These can be seen today, each one augmenting its setting.

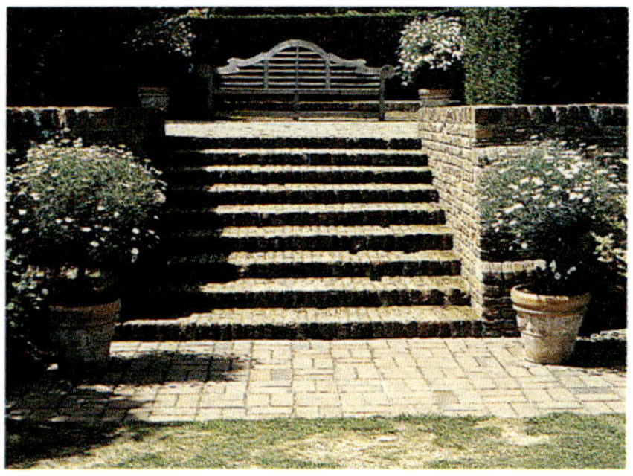

RIGHT: *Even the symmetry of these stairs is agreeable.*

OPPOSITE: *Occupied as early as the twelfth century, Sissinghurst was originally called Saxingherste.*

Once more we drove to Sissinghurst on a perfect summer's day in June, and our diary entry says 'Sissinghurst even more beautiful than last time . . . roses perfection, White Garden design and choice of greens and white, heavenly'.

As you walk from the car park you come to the imposing entrance and courtyard, and then to the long, rose-brick buildings. Rising from them is the commanding tower with its two octagonal turrets. It was in one of these turrets that Vita Sackville-West wrote much of her work. We climbed the spiral stairway to her sanctum and felt grateful for the experience of seeing this very personal room.

We moved on to the grounds where the garden rooms are divided by either high brick walls or neat yew hedges. Honeysuckles adorned the walls, their fragrance pervasive. These gardens are completely different from one another, and are called the Rose Garden, Cottage Garden, Moat Walk and Nuttery, the Herb Garden, Moat and Orchard, the Tower Lawn, the White Garden, and the Lime Walk. All are superb and a tribute to beauty in the realm of garden design and planting.

In June, the Rose Garden was in full flower, most of the roses being the old-fashioned kind, supplemented by other flowering shrubs in the long border along the wall. The robust rose bushes were cloaked in a gloriously scented profusion of blooms. Old roses were a favourite of the Nicolsons and, beside the collection in this garden, they are to be found everywhere at Sissinghurst. The rondel (round) lawn in the centre of the garden is outlined by a closely clipped yew hedge, and there are four pathways leading to it from the outer garden.

Harold Nicolson's study overlooks the Cottage Garden, full of warmly coloured old cottage flowers — a joyous glow of yellow, orange and red in summer. 'Planned with a controlled untidiness' as the guide book puts

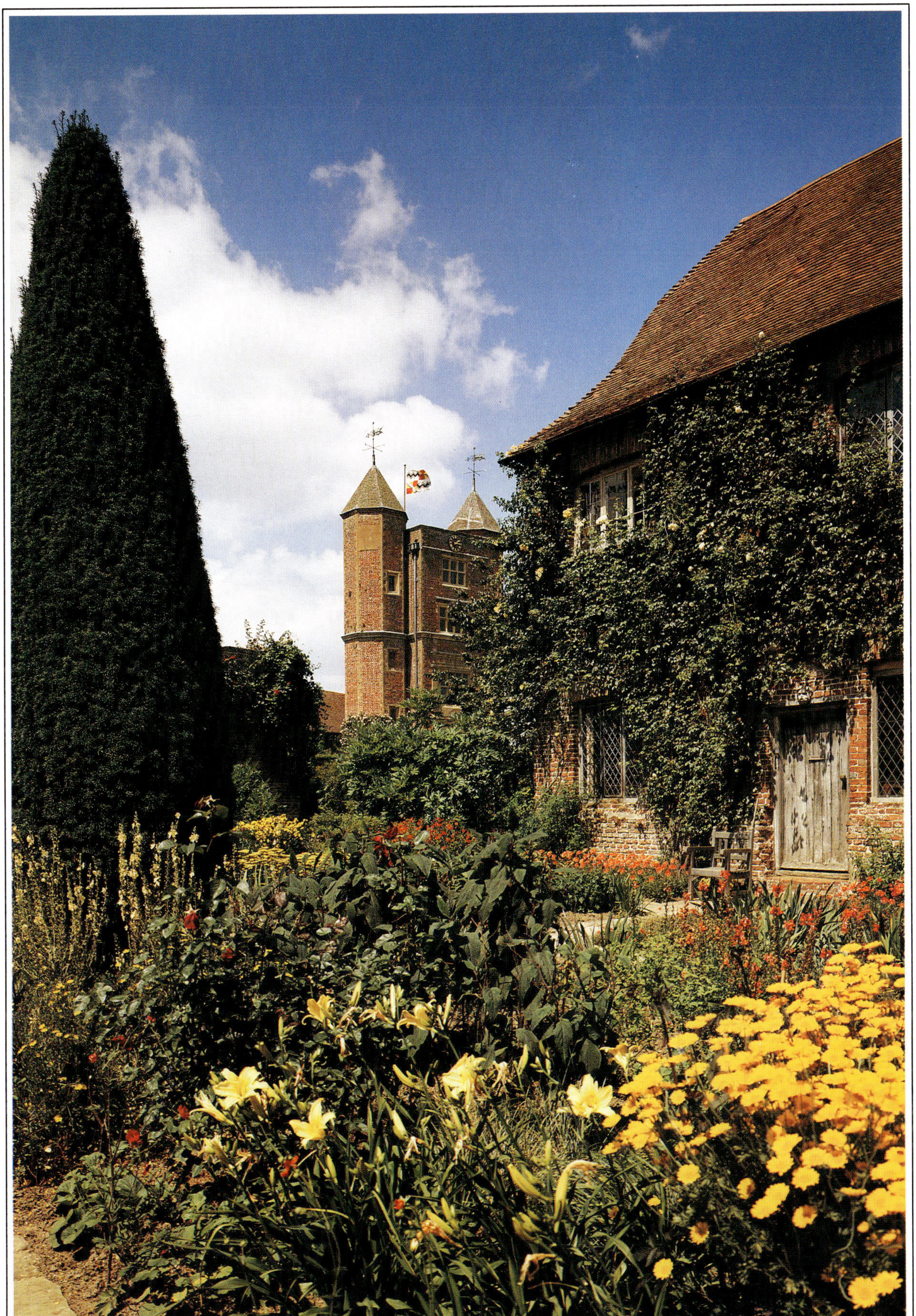

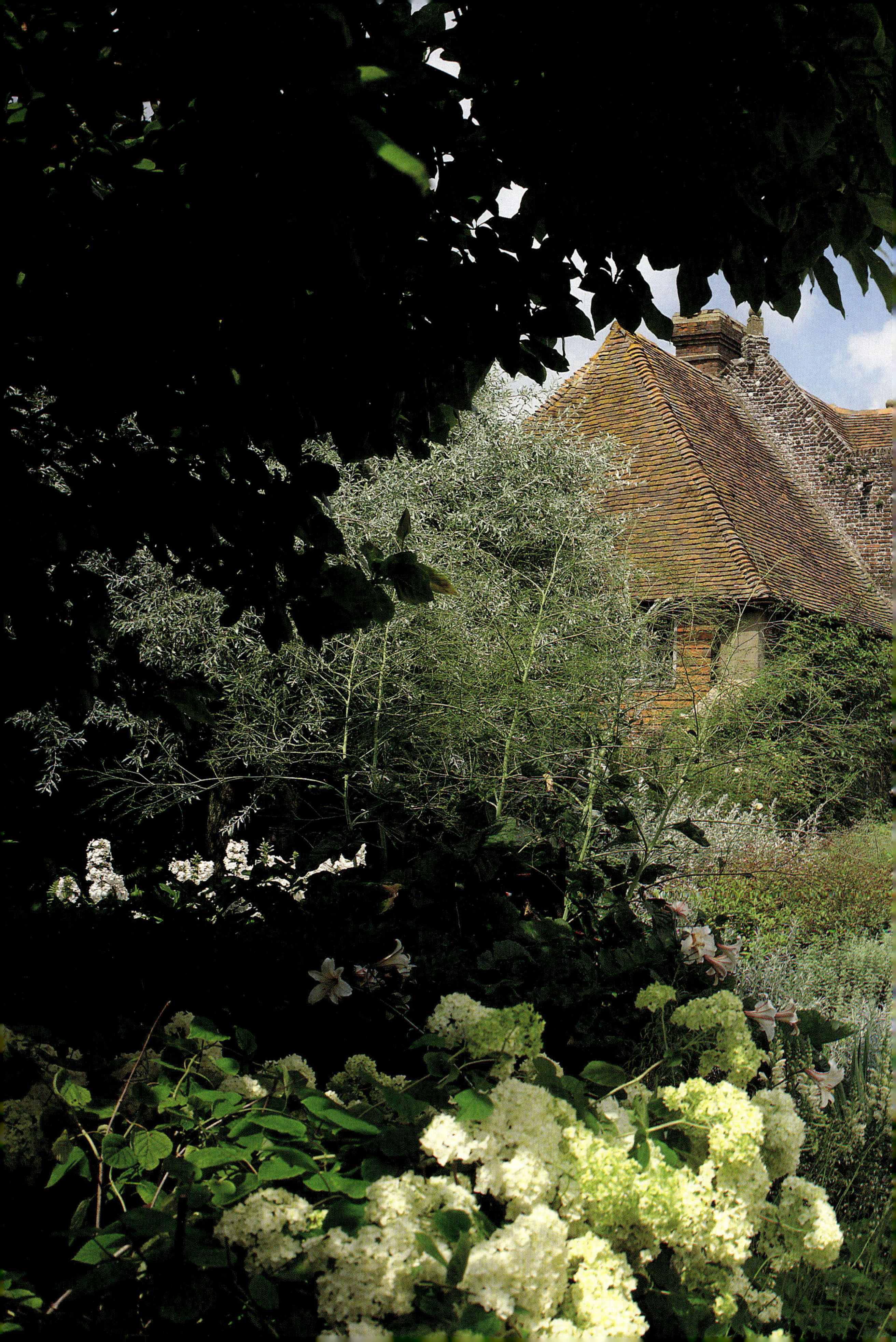

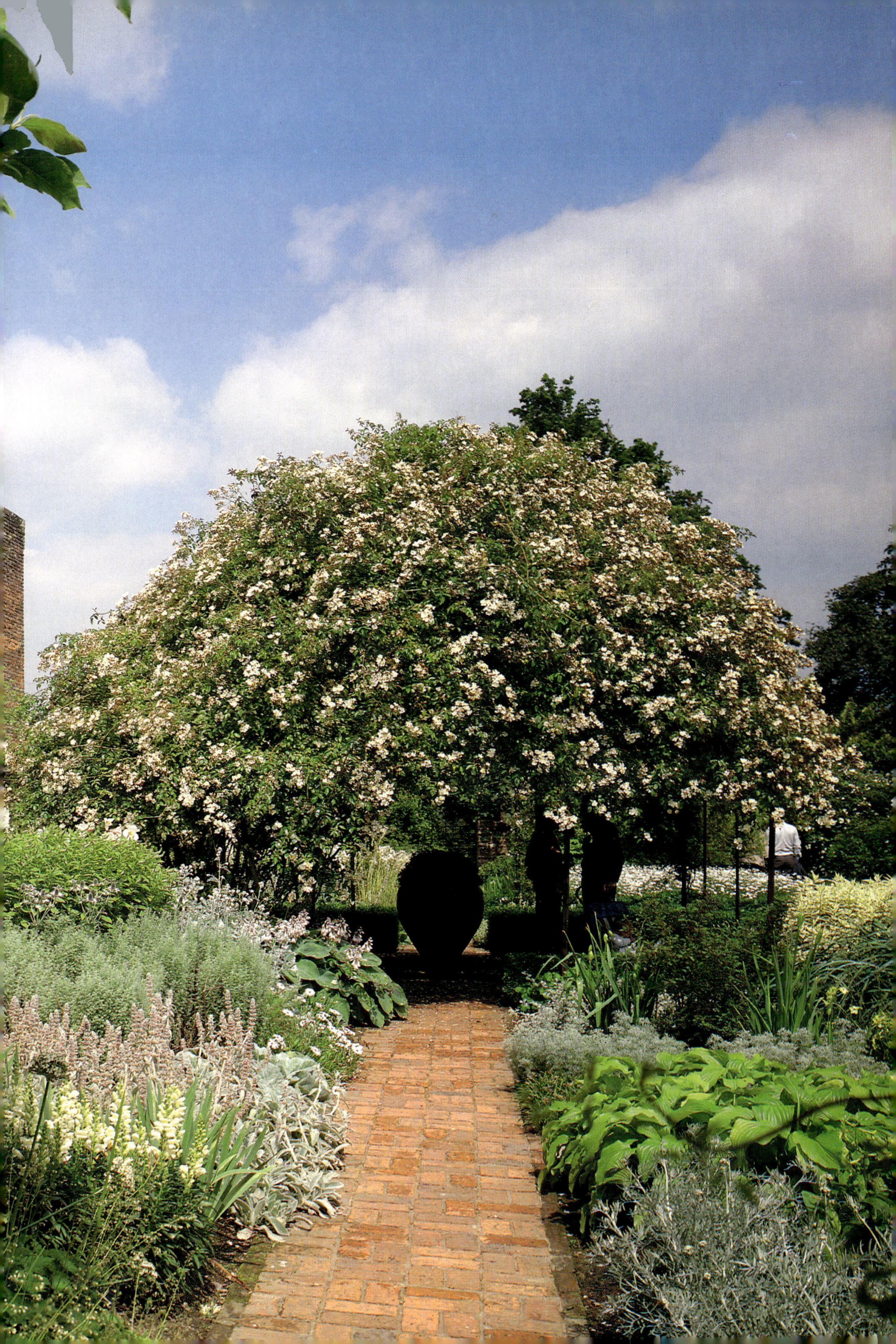

PREVIOUS PAGES: *When you enter the White Garden you enter a completely different world of light.*

RIGHT: *The Rose Garden and Rondel at Sissinghurst.*

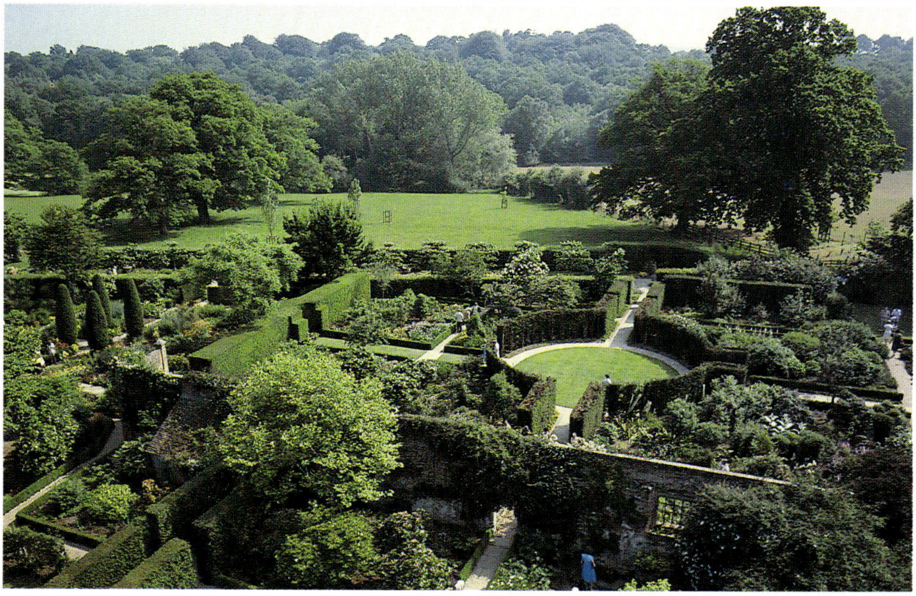

it, the Cottage Garden also boasts dahlias, iris, tulips and columbines. The paths here are a mixture of paving stones and old bricks. Above, and covering the front walls of the South Cottage, is a majestic white climbing rose, 'Mme Alfred Carrière'. A big old copper is the centrepiece, filled with flowers in season.

The Moat Walk and Nuttery lead from the Cottage Garden down some steps and along the moat wall, or through the Nuttery. The very old nut trees are underplanted with a blaze of polyanthus.

In front of the Herb Garden, there is a small lawn of thyme (*Thymus serpyllum*), a dense mat of pink and crimson flowers. Then you once again pass into a room with walls of yew and formal beds within which are a prodigality of useful herbs: some for the kitchen, others for medicine, for dying cloth, or for making scented articles. There is also orris root, iris, and woad, thymes, sages, rosemary, mints, caraway, garlic and fennel among others. From the fragrant leaves and flowers a pot-pourri was made at Sissinghurst to an old Knole recipe, said to have originated in the time of King George I. The blend contained dried lavender, verbena, geranium, double violets, rose petals, balm, rosemary, musk, bay, salt and spices. There is a seat of aromatic plants at one end of the garden, and the centrepiece is a bowl of fine marble.

The moat and the orchard beckon. There is a grassy walk beside the dark waters of the moat and roses climb through the old apple trees growing in the middle of the orchard. In spring daffodils and narcissi light up the grass under the trees. On coming to the Tower Lawn, a mass of roses cling to the walls on either side of the Tower, along with trees, shrubs and flowers, and a charming, small sunken garden greets you.

When you walk into the White Garden you enter a completely different world of light within its own sphere of flower-hung walls and lofty hedges — a picture held in the memory to dream about. It has been described as 'the most beautiful garden at Sissinghurst and indeed of all England'. As expected, it is composed entirely of white flowers, silver leaves, and green hedges. There is a canopy of rose garlands (*Rosa longicuspis*) deeply thatching an arched iron frame in the centre of the garden, and a Ming pot. Clouds of gypsophila, spears of gladioli, rare white heartsease, stately lilies, translucent iris with grey leaves and huge frilled poppies delight the senses. A silver willow-leaved pear protects a lead statue of the virgin; lavenders, artemisis, santolina and dianthus are among other plants with grey foliage. On a clear day there are contrasts of bright light and dark shadow — sunlight shining on a low box hedge, white flowers and silver leaves with the luminous quality of moonlight, and for perfect harmony shades of green from lime to nearly black . . . the most romantic garden.

We waited until last to stroll along the flagged path sheltered on each side by pleached limes. The Lime Walk was Harold Nicolson's inspiration. The elegant trees are underplanted with flowers that open in the garden's yearly wealth of blooms, a sumptuous Persian carpet of eastern hues; pots from Tuscany overflow with even more flowers.

Sissinghurst is the result of a collaboration between husband and wife, a blending of their great artistic talents.

There is now a restaurant in one of the outbuildings run by the National Trust, and a delightful shop. One may spend a whole blissful day there in comfort.

Chelsea Physic Garden, London

In our nostalgic pursuit of garden styles and plants from former times, we were eager to see the Chelsea Physic Garden for ourselves, an old and highly esteemed educational garden founded by the Society of Apothecaries more than 300 years ago in 1673.

The first such garden had been opened in Europe at Pisa University in 1543. Plants at that time were still the major source of medicines, and physicians and apothecaries were taught how to recognise and use them in physic gardens.

Carried on from antiquity was the prevailing belief that all plants had been put on Earth by God for people's use, and that what was not already known about them could be studied further, and improved upon. The examination of a plant's therapeutic properties lay behind the establishment of these gardens, although not all were grown for such study.

When the Society of Apothecaries chose the site for their physic garden, the grounds were part of a riverside village which already boasted large gardens and orchards surrounding magnificent houses, where once Henry VIII and Sir Thomas More had owned mansions. In the seventeenth century when the Apothecaries began to establish their garden, there were no convenient roadways on which to travel to Chelsea, the only safe and convenient access being by water. In those days the estate went down to the river where there were steps, which were approached by boat. Today, there is a wall-tablet commemorating the boathouse which once housed the Apothecaries' barge.

The garden started well, and then went into decline, until Sir Hans Sloane (1660–1753), a leading physician and former student at the garden, resurrected it. He had bought the Manor of Chelsea in 1712 and in 1722 he granted the Apothecaries a conditional lease in virtual perpetuity and at a nominal rent.

Sir Hans Sloane was an extraordinary man of many talents, and one of the great individuals of his time. His intellectual

BELOW: *Chelsea Physic Garden was founded by the Society of Apothecaries in 1673.*

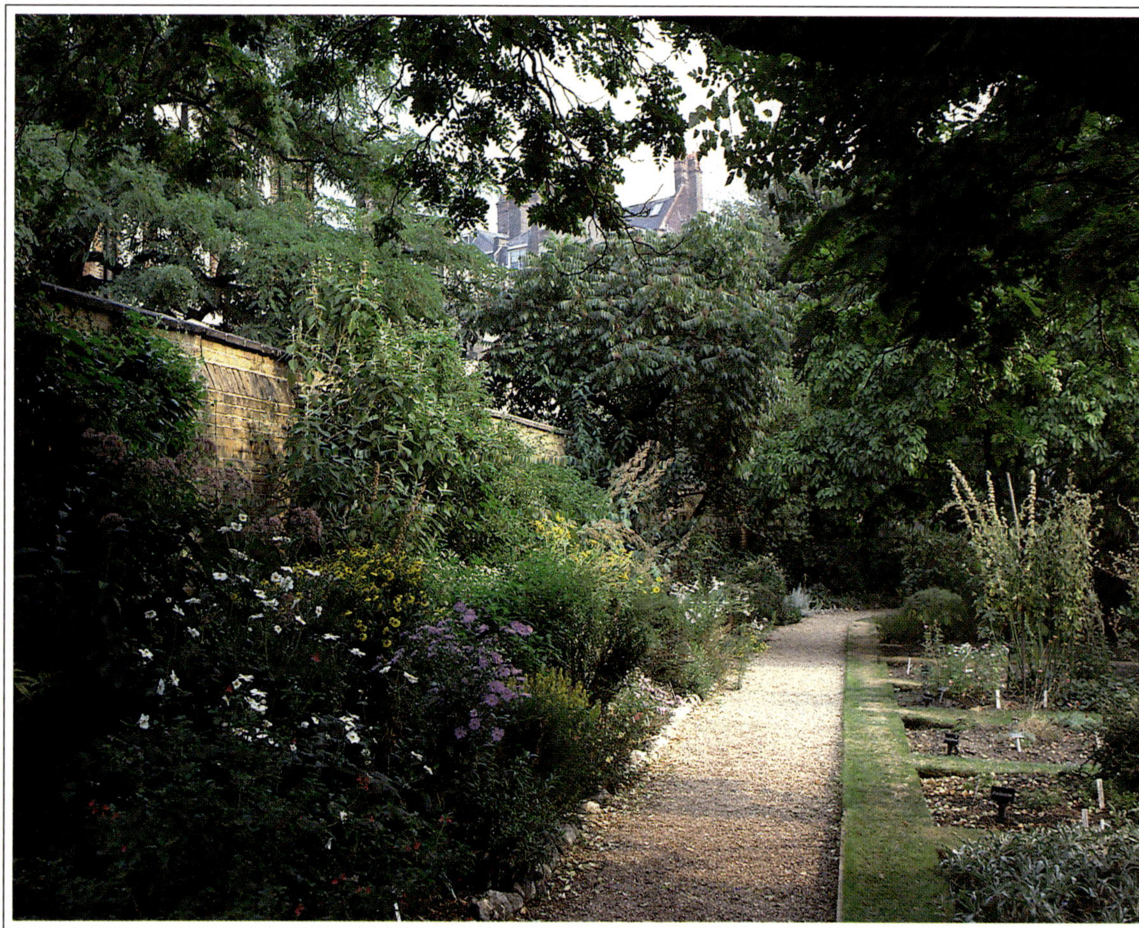

contributions were outstanding on several fronts. It is fitting that he is not only remembered in the Physic Garden, but also commemorated by Sloane Street and Sloane Square. Moreover, the Cadogan family, his heirs, are still the owners and benefactors of the large Chelsea estate.

The Physic Garden remains a source of analysis and study — various plants are grown there for investigation and evaluation and the gardens are used by medical and botany students, schools and visitors. All of these people continue to use the garden, and are made welcome.

Sitting on a comfortable seat in a roomy London taxi with big windows for a perfect view of the passing scene, we arrived at Chelsea Garden; the thoughtful driver stopped his black cab at an anonymous-looking entrance while explaining that from here we could walk through the grounds, making our way to the other end and another gate from which to leave.

On the summer Sunday of our visit many fragrances mingled on the still air. Golden sunlight splashed on to leaves, enhancing their shades of green and grey. Bird song uplifted the heart, seats were everywhere for resting, and so we assimilated the prodigious diversity of herb plants and the manner of their arrangement. The atmosphere was that of an old country garden, a wonderful achievement in the heart of a busy city.

The Garden covers 2 hectares/ 5 acres and includes office, lecture rooms, the curator's house and greenhouses. One area contains a vast herb garden of about 300 different species. All are named and are classified into their various uses: culinary, medicinal, fragrant and dyeing. Brick and grass pathways intersect the neat square and rectangular beds.

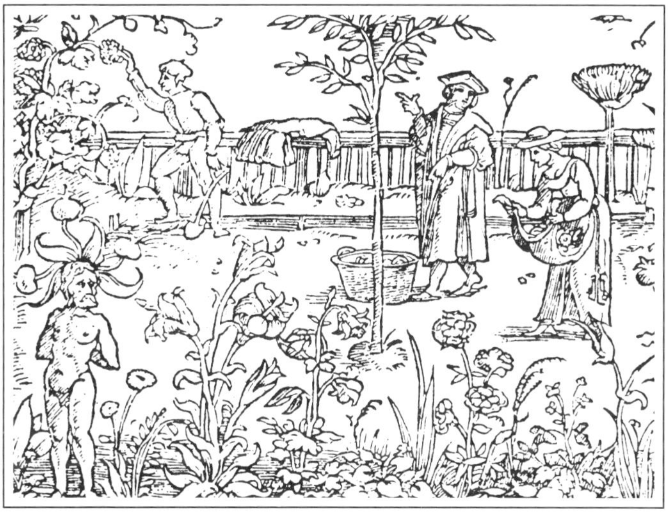

ABOVE: *Physic Gardens such as this were established principally in order to examine the therapeutic properties of plants.*

The camera was adjusted and a jotter pad made ready. Printed on a notice for all to read are the wise words of Sir (Dr) Hans Sloane, one of the most significant forces in the history of Chelsea Garden:

What is a Herb Garden? A place in which you can learn better to distinguish good and useful plants from those that bear resemblance to them and yet are hurtful.

Continuing on our way, a long border of flourishing, fragrant mints drew our delighted attention. There was a spectacular variety, including an upright pennyroyal, Bowls mint, white peppermint, fine spearmint, variegated ginger mint with golden streaks, eau-de-cologne mint, spearmint, variegated applemint, grey-leaved woolly mint and horsemint. Another few steps and more herbs subtly invited us on with their perfume and attractive shapes. There was a compact type of pungent winter oregano and garden purslane with its lemon-tasting succulent leaves (so refreshingly delicious in salads and in thinly cut brown bread sandwiches). Here also was hypericum, its clear yellow flowers radiating light. This herb is also known as St John's wort, being in full flower in the northern summer on St John's Day 24 June. It has been revered since the earliest times for its magical and medicinal properties, and is still used today in natural ointments for healing wounds and burns.

In another bed were the green and the silver santolinas (cotton lavender), both with the fine aromatic foliage detested by moths and silverfish. Silver santolina is very pleasing when used for foliage contrast in low hedge-work or in green-box knot gardens, and is equally striking on its own. Clumps of tansy or 'buttons' were there, the fern-like leaves long a prized insect-repellent. Next to the tansy were spires of pretty fairy-like white yarrow. This herb was also called achillea, woundwort, milfoil and carpenter's weed for its ancient use was healing open wounds and stemming the flow of blood; the classical Greek hero Achilles is said to have cured his warriors with it.

There are many beautiful and rare trees growing in the garden, besides numerous botanical specimens of importance. The earliest rock garden in Europe is here, and water plants grow in a pond nearby. The embankment is an enchanting wild area of flowering shrubs and uncommon peonies. These unusual varieties, along with the rest of the garden, make a great attraction to wildlife — amazing in the middle of London.

The afternoon had passed quickly and, reluctantly, we knew it was time to leave. As we walked towards the exit gate we discovered an interesting little shop to browse in. English friends and relations have bought herb plants at this shop, but as we were travellers this was not possible.

Chelsea Physic Garden is open to the public on Sunday and Wednesday afternoons from mid-April to mid-October, and during Chelsea Flower Show week, also at other times to groups by appointment.

Garden Cottage, Surrey, Mr and Mrs Carl Upton

An especially fulfilling experience for us when in England is to call on Mr and Mrs Carl Upton at Garden Cottage in Surrey. As we drew near our destination there is a happy expectancy; the roadside becomes leafier and the trees more enveloping, until it is like driving through a secluded forest. A tree-topped hill encloses grassy slopes, and nestled there is Carl's office and Garden Cottage, reposing among the herbs and flowers of Myfanwy's physic garden.

On arrival this time we stopped, opened the gate, and immediately walked into another world; into a secret garden with a feeling of pervading peace. It is difficult to describe the sense of having passed through an invisible veil into another level of existence different from everyday life. Quiet feelings of tranquillity that come when one lives in harmony with nature were very real that day; looking back, they still are.

Carl Upton practises a branch of medicine not widely known, called Psionic medicine, which may be partly defined as a singular method of skilled, sensitive diagnosis, analysis and treatment of a patient. The whole procedure is carried out on a subtle or unseen level, revealing the onset of an illness sometimes before it has manifested itself physically. This process has had outstanding success with patients, including ourselves. If during analysis specialist orthodox medicine is indicated to be necessary, Carl Upton recommends it before healing with his correctives can be complete. This mingling of orthodox and traditional (or alternative) medicines is an ideal combination

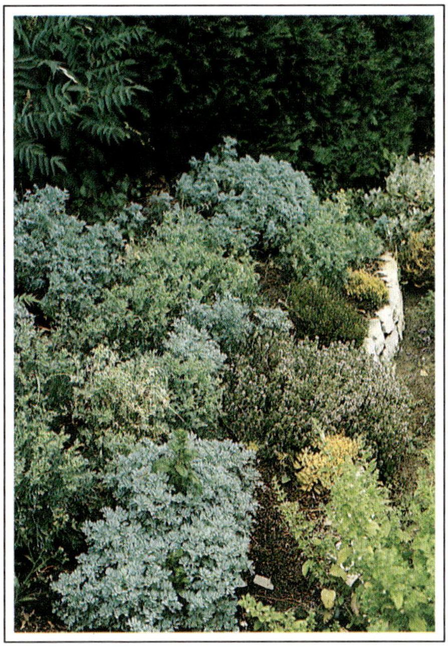

LEFT: *Various medicinal herbs in the Upton's garden.*

when expertly handled by both practitioners and is gaining ground today.

Carl is not alone. Today, there are other highly qualified practitioners, as well as books and papers on the subject. In England this branch of medicine has a considerable following. As laypersons we will not attempt to explain further such a complex medical procedure, as we may unintentionally give a misleading impression. Suffice to say, if the concept appeals to you, and a full elucidation is wanted, we recommend a book called *Psionic Medicine: the study and treatment of the causative factors in illness* by J. H. Reyner BSC, DIC, FIEE in collaboration with George Laurence MRCS, LRCP, FRCS (Edinburgh) and Carl Upton LDS (Birmingham) published by Routledge and Kegan Paul, London, 1982.

When Carl Upton has analysed

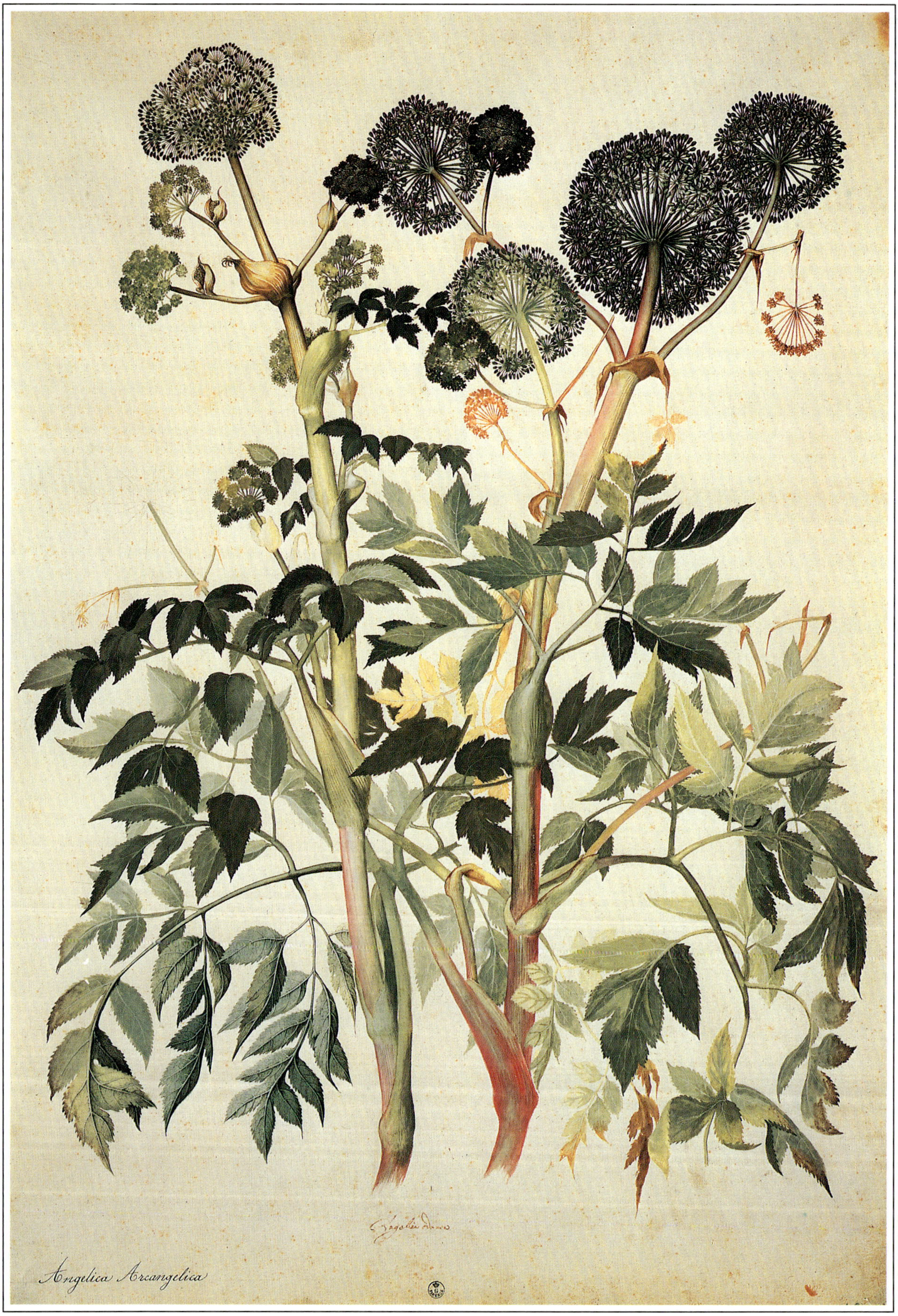
Angelica Arcangelica

a patient, the prescription is sent to Ainsworth's Homeopathic Pharmacy, New Cavendish Street, London which displays at least two Royal Crowns signifying the 'By Appointment' patronage. When the prescription is received by the pharmacy, the remedy is prepared in a special way to suit the particular requirement of the patient.

Myfanwy Upton grows some of the herbs needed by Ainsworth's pharmacy in her garden. When we were there, herbs were flourishing in their special plots (hypericum, rue and mullein). A large bed of marigolds (*Calendula officinalis*) were flowering, their yellow and orange blooms in abundance. These are not the huge 'improved' marigolds, the flowers of which burst with tightly packed petals, but the old-fashioned calendula, the layered blooms of which carry a deep-gold button in their centre. This marigold was a valued medicinal, culinary and cosmetic herb in ancient Greek, Indian and Arabic cultures, and has endured throughout the centuries as a highly useful plant. A fourteenth-century poet wrote, 'Only to look on the flowers will draw eveil humours out of the head and strengthen the eyesight'. 'Ye golde flour' he aptly describes as 'good to see' and its odour 'good to smelle'.

The yellow-flowering mulleins (*Verbascum*) in Myfanwy's garden grew tall and straight, rising high above the rest of the herbs, illuminating the air like candles. This is a common sight, growing wild not only in Europe but in Australia and other continents, having been introduced by settlers coming to unknown lands. Mullein is a true cottage garden plant, having old associations and scented nectar-laden blooms clustered tightly together along their stalks. Gertrude Jekyll, well-known for her garden, grew several types of mullein and esteemed it for its height, colour and ability to grow in shady places. She describes the branching variety as 'A towering candelabrum of pale yellow . . . [which] is only seen at its best in shade, for except at dusk or in cloudy weather the flowers are never properly expanded in open situations.' Mullein was also known as Aaron's rod, donkey's ears and bunny's ears, the last two names referring to the size and shape of its felt-like foliage. Our ancestors made use of the plants around them for countless reasons: mullein is not only a medicinal herb, it was once cut and dried and the long stalks were dipped in tallow, lit and used as tapers. Some of the plant's medicinal properties are employed in sedative mixtures, cough mixtures, herbal smoking blends and some cosmetic preparations. It is also used as a natural dye for cloth, the flowers yielding a light yellow tint.

During that memorable day in Surrey, Carl and Myfanwy drove us through sylvan glens and pastoral countryside to a quaint old inn at Chiddingfold, much of the building dating back to 1285. We lunched there before returning to

OPPOSITE: Angelica arcangelica *by Ligozzi Jacopo (c. 1547–1632)*

Garden Cottage, where we continued our discussions and gained further insight into human relationships with the plant world. Carl's comprehension of Nature, and our part in it, is absorbing and informative. A revealing image of our close connection with the plant realm comes with the understanding that we carry the vegetable kingdom within our makeup. We begin to understand why, in one way or another, our instinct draws us to Nature's many facets and commands our respect. When we look at plants and flowers, it is appropriate to think about their unseen vital energy and the individual plants, which are in themselves distinct entities.

The gentle wisdom and beautiful philosophy of Carl and Myfanwy Upton is reflected in their work and surroundings, giving their small corner of Earth a mysterious loveliness and a rare sanctity.

OPPOSITE: *It was exciting to arrive at the Château de Villandry, renowned for its unique gardens.*

BELOW: *Calendula at Garden Cottage.*

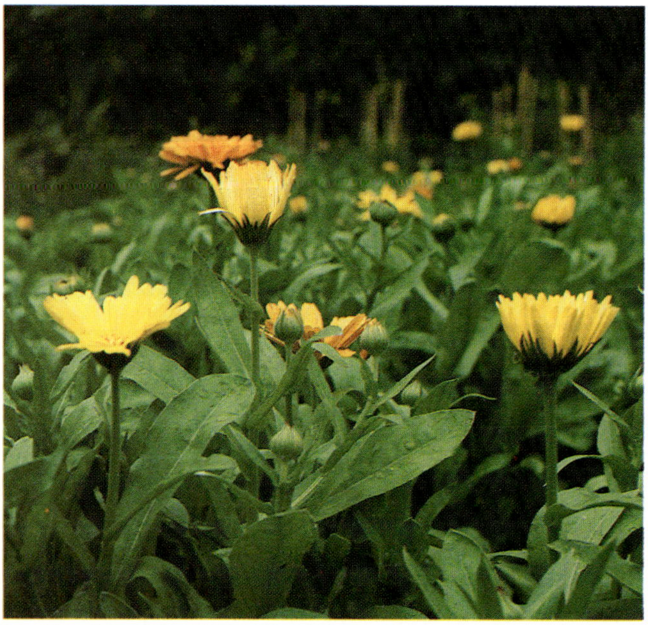

FRANCE

The ferry was full, loaded to capacity with cars and buses, excited schoolchildren and tourists. Leaving the long, white coast of England behind the boat cast off, taking us to France further on our garden quest.

We appreciate our burnt ochre coloured homeland, yet 'down-under' is a long way from most Australians' roots. Europeans leaving home for another destination in Europe take at most a few hours to travel across a border into another country. The language changes, not to mention the currency; the community is different and the landscape is foreign.

There were nostalgic sights to recall in Paris and new ones waiting to be enjoyed; the harmony of roof-lines, wide boulevards, tree-lined avenues, meandering streets full of surprises, and stately broad '*places*' all with magical names. History and art are absorbed in museums and galleries. The bridges of Paris beckon. The River Seine flows on. Cars hurtle along roads patterned with ancient bricks. The musical language enchants the ear, just as delicious food delights the palate.

In search of gardens, we set off for the countryside. The speeding train raced past fields of red poppies, acres of purple lavender, and tilled earth nourishing rows of leafy grapevines. We caught a swift glimpse of an old stone farmhouse among green meadows and fruit

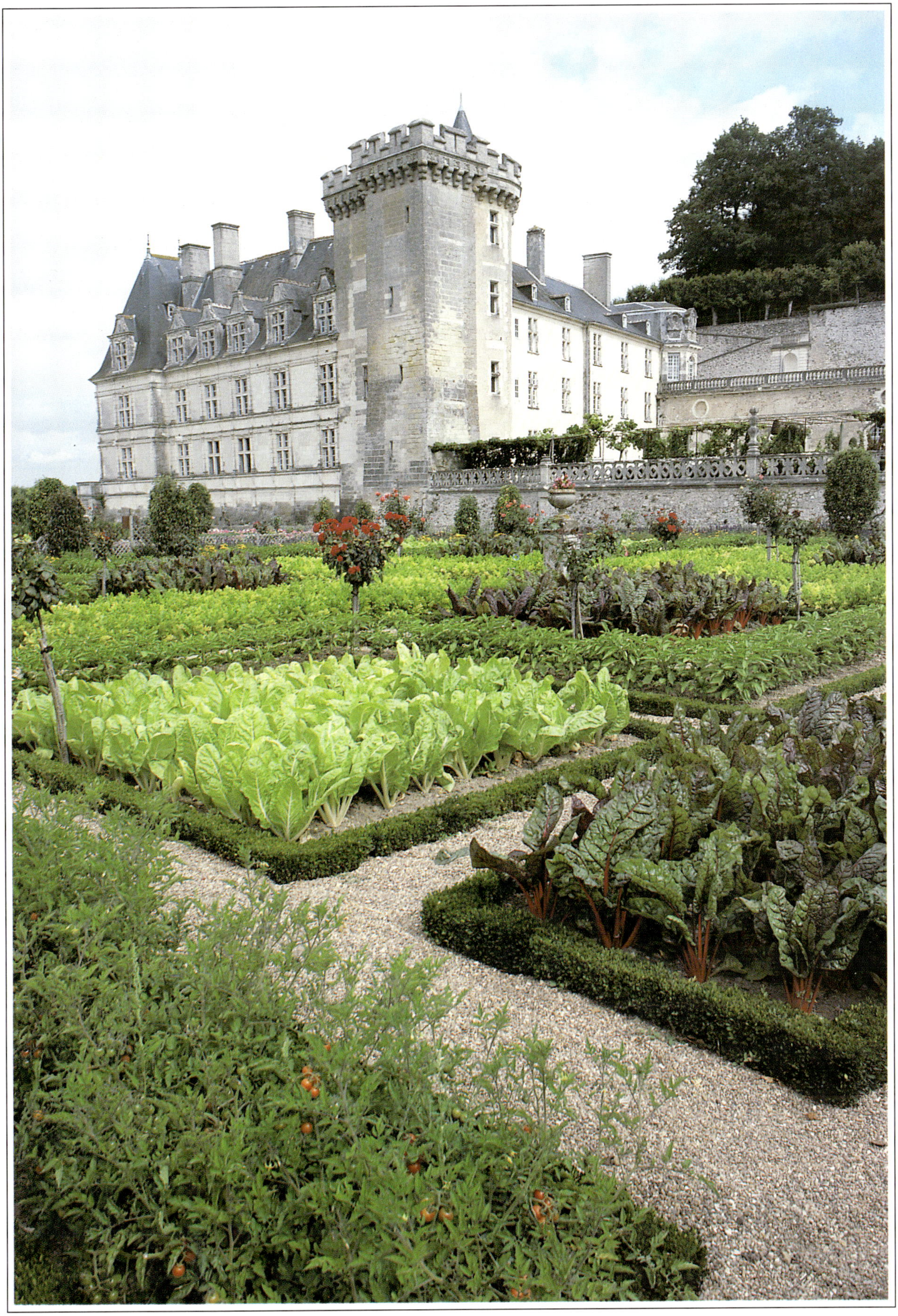

trees. Secret dark forests loomed and were gone. The train stops at a town only briefly before rushing on its way. Villages flashed by, their houses individual and narrow, almost austere, yet quaint and appealing.

We arrived at Barbizon (near Fontainbleau) and began to explore its cobbled streets. Monet once lived here in his struggling days with his artist friends because it was cheaper than living in Paris. The village houses were two or three storeys high, some with balconies holding pots of hanging ivy, and roses in brilliant shades. Bright gardens overflowed with flowers and we were able to stroll through a large kitchen garden full of fragrant herbs and tall-stemmed flowers hedged by clipped silver santolina. Tile-topped walls separated the verdant village gardens evoking French writer Colette's stories of her childhood in rural Burgundy. 'I could gain my liberty at any moment by means of any easy climb over a gate, a wall, or a little sloping roof, but as soon as I landed back on the gravel of our own garden, illusion and faith returned to me.'

Some villages cling like limpets to hillsides, climbing one upon another to the top. Weathered grey and golden stone houses blend into their surroundings, seeming to be part of the rugged earth itself.

Other villages on the Mediterranean coast looked as if they were part of the oyster-white limestone cliffs . . . stark — bleached by the sun. Curtains of bright geraniums in every shade from pink to mauve, scarlet and red: their soft flowers hugging the unyielding stone walls were an unforgettable sight of texture and colour. Bougainvillea and roses bloomed in profusion. The scenery blazed vividly from twisting hairpin bends on the Grande Corniche; impressions that linger are of an azure sky and sheer white cliffs dropping down to the sea. Long twilights of shifting colour slowly turned the sea and sky from aquamarine to pale opal, from translucent moonstone to sapphire velvet and finally to eternal violet.

The many unique villages and their balcony gardens or small flowering patches are a charming contrast to equally beautiful, but infinitely more grand, Palaces and Chateaux standing in spacious, ornate grounds.

Gardens in France have much the same background as English gardens. In bygone days, plants — mainly herbs — were grown from necessity. Scented flowers also had their use, as did fruit trees and vegetables. Mediaeval monastery gardens grew all types of plants, for medicine, for flavouring food, as insect repellent and for perfume to cover unwanted odours. The noble ninth-century French Emperor Charlemange ordered that herbs be grown for the welfare of his people in all his large dominions. Throughout the ages and from every country in the world ideas have been borrowed from one another and the past.

Renaissance Italian gardens were

influenced by Rome and the French, in turn, were effected by the resurgence of great style. It is said that the first illustrious French Renaissance garden to be planned was at the Château d'Anet, designed by Philibert de l'Orme at the request of Diane de Poitiers in the sixteenth century. This was the beginning of developments in this type of large French estate, with open vistas, decorative fountains, elaborate parterres, long avenues bordered by trees, fanciful shapes made with box hedging, and rugs of colourful flowers. These features were made to be admired from above, from the salons or from a carriage. In time French gardens began to emulate the English, just as English gardens were influenced by the evolution of new ideas from France.

In the seventeenth century, André Le Nôtre (considered to be the greatest landscape gardener who ever lived) designed a number of magnificent gardens. Le Notre came from a gardening family. His father was in charge of the Tuileries and his godmother was the wife of Claude Mollet, another great horticulturist and landscape gardener. In 1637 he succeeded his father as head gardener of the Tuileries. Le Notre designed one of the greatest gardens at that time — the garden at Vaux-le-Vicomte for the luckless Nicolas Fouquet *Surintendant des Finances de France*, who had commissioned the garden. When King Louis XIV saw the final result at Fouquet's invitation to attend a grand entertainment there, he was both impressed and infuriated — it was obvious that an enormous amount of money had been spent, and that the imposing grounds were far superior in design and embellishment to any owned by the crown. The King commanded Fouquet to prison where he died 19 years later, and Le Notre was required to design Louis' huge estate at Versailles. The outcome was spectacular and majestic.

French gardens differ from one another in their appeal and manner of planting, because of the variations in climate between the north and south of the country.

Château d'Anet and Diane de Poitiers

FLOWER-de-LUCE
Born in the purple, born to joy and
pleasance,
Thou dost not toil nor spin,
But makest gald and radiant with
thy presence
The meadow and the lin . . .
O Flower-de-luce, bloom on, and let
the river
Linger to kiss they feet!
O flower of song, bloom on, and
make for ever
The world more fair and sweet

LONGFELLOW

Having been enraptured by the real-life story of the romance, four hundred years ago, between King

OPPOSITE: *Diane de Poitiers was said to be highly intelligent, witty, and generous of nature.*

BELOW: *Hibiscus and petunias abound in Diane de Poitiers' garden at the Château de Chenonceaux.*

Henri II of France and the beautiful Diane de Poitiers, it was a wish-come-true to visit two of her Châteaux, Anet and Chenonceaux. Both Châteaux are exquisite reminders of this unique woman of the sixteenth century.

Château d'Anet passed to Diane on the death of her first husband Louis de Brézé, who was 40 years her senior. It was an arranged marriage. Diane, a teenage girl, became the wife of Louis de Brézé, a dignitary of the French Kingdom with the titles Comte de Maulievrier, Seigneur d'Anet, Grand Sénéchal of Normandy and 'Grand Huntsman' of France. Diane herself was descended from an ancient aristocratic family, entering this world on a still and frosty night silvered by a full moon, on the eve of the year 1500. The baby girl was destined to become one of history's most intriguing women. It is said that there was a mysterious allure about her which enslaved Henri all his life. Indeed, it was believed that she was gifted with magical powers, which enabled her to remain agelessly beautiful, white-skinned, shapely and forever enchanting.

As a result of her marriage to de Brézé, Diane was called to the French Court, where her bright intellect and good looks made such an impression that she became Lady of Honour to Queen Claude, wife of King François I of France. Diane and her husband often entertained the King and Queen

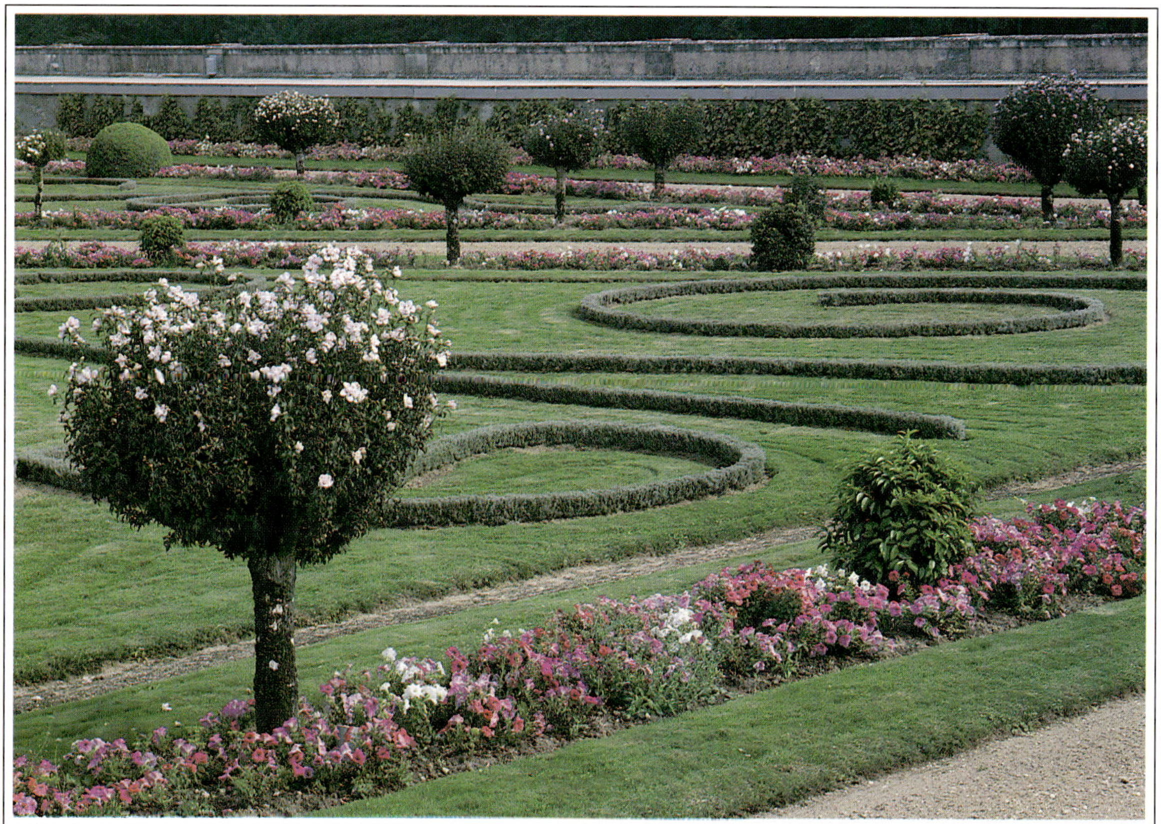

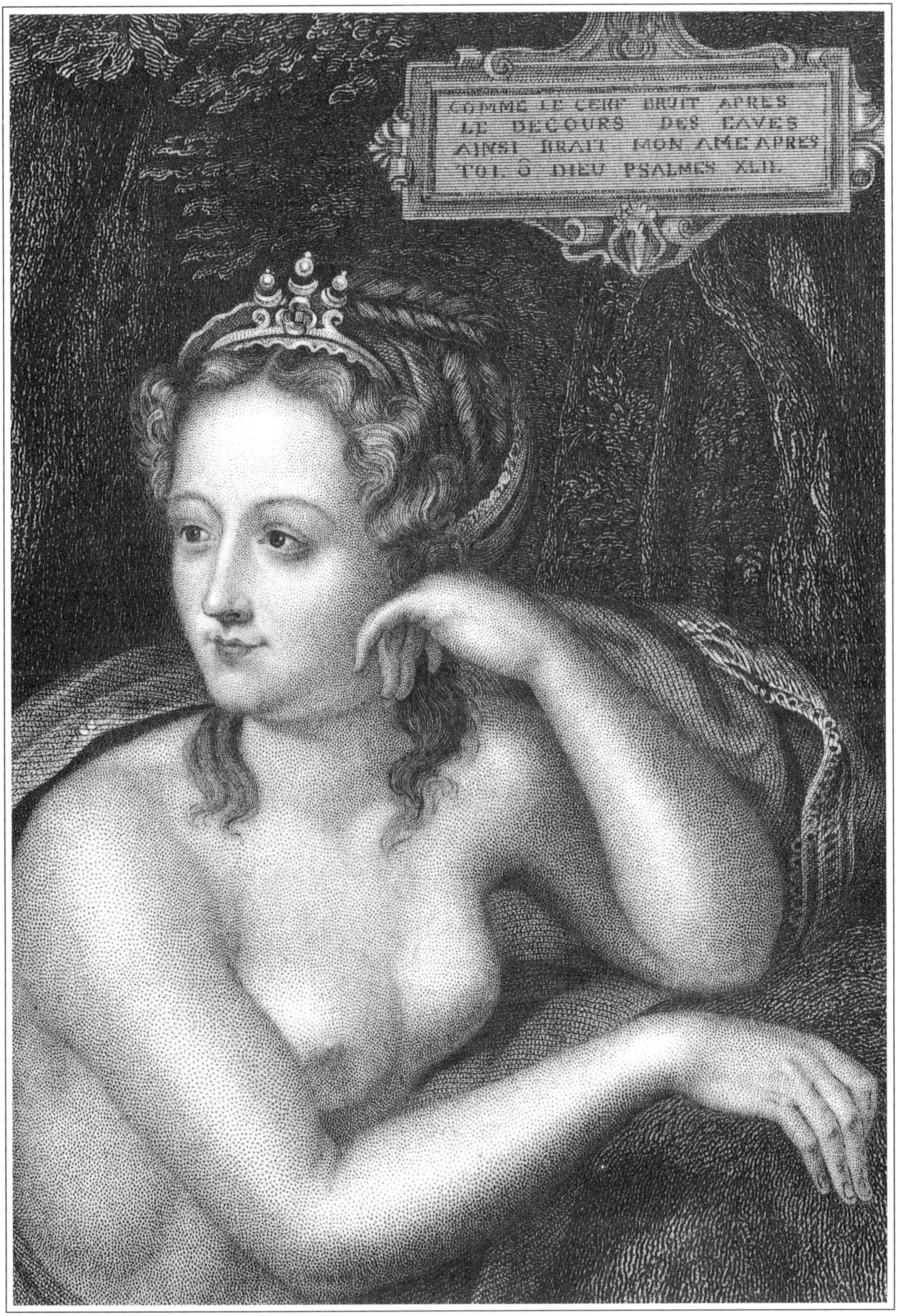
COMME LE CERF BRUIT APRES
LE DECOURS DES EAVES
AINSI BRAIT MON AME APRES
TOI Ô DIEU PSALMES XLII

and their entourage at d'Anet, a favourite hunting area surrounded by forests. She shared her husband's love for the hunt, and achieved a reputation herself for being skilled at the sport. During these eventful years Diane bore two daughters to Louis de Brézé. When Louis died in 1531, Diane mourned him sincerely, giving him a grand funeral and a splendid memorial in Rouen Cathedral. From that time on she wore only black and white;

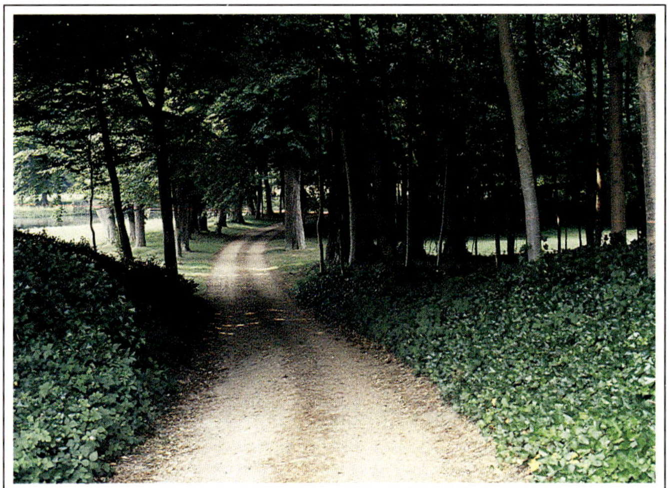

ABOVE: *Château d'Anet.*

the elegant combination of black and white in rich silks of fashionable design reportedly suited her to perfection, enhancing her loveliness and slim figure.

Legend has it that each day, throughout all her life, in summer and in winter, she bathed in cold spring water, and also rode her horse for several hours whatever the weather. As well as being peerlessly lovely, Diane was said to be highly intelligent, witty, and generous of nature.

Diane de Poitiers was depicted by famous painters and sculptors as the mythological huntress-goddess of the moon, Diana, and some of these works can still be seen in museums and art galleries.

Diane was at court when the second son of François I, Prince Henri (later King Henri II) was born. The Prince's childhood was marred by four years of captivity in Spain, which possibly contributed to his reputation for being reserved and moody. He formed a strong attachment to Diane at an early age and, as he grew older his love became more intense, despite her being nearly twenty years his senior. Eventually, Diane became Henri's mistress, and he remained her ardent lover for the rest of his life, adopting the same black and white apparel. The death of his elder brother, the Dauphin, in 1536 ensured Henri's succession to the throne when his father King François I died in 1547.

Fourteen years earlier, in 1533, the court arranged a political marriage between Henri and Catherine de Medici. Catherine, unattractive and by all accounts a rather unpleasant woman, bitterly resented Henri's love for Diane, although it was Diane who encouraged Henri to father the children Catherine bore him after eleven years of childlessness.

King Henri II gave his beloved mistress many priceless gifts as proof of his undying love for her, including the romantic Chenonceaux Castle, or Château. Catherine was reportedly furious, and waited for the time when she could seek revenge as she coveted Chenonceaux for herself. Henri also gave Diane the money to completely rebuild her manor-house at Anet and to landscape the grounds. She did both with magnificent results. Diane chose the cleverest craftsmen of the day to remake her establishment, recognising the talents of some who were as yet unknown. The architect Philibert de l'Orme created, within a wide gallery, a large garden divided into twenty-four squares containing aromatic plants and flowers. On each side stood two beautiful white marble fountains by Jean Goujon; some of the aromatic, favourite plants of the time were violets, jasmine, rosemary, lavender and pinks.

De l'Orme drained the marshlands close to the house, and created an upper level for his new buildings, and a lower level for part of the garden. The main body of the Château contained apartments for Diane and for the King. There were reception halls, and one vast wing was devoted solely to the 'Galerie de Diane'. In an area bordering the orangerie was a sculpture of Diane and a stag, now in the Louvre. When completed the princely ménage comprised an imposing portal and a chapel.

Beyond the principal building a splendid crescent-shaped double staircase led down to the large enclosed Renaissance garden; behind it was a lake, and a park divided into a number of compartments, some planted as miniature wildflower meadows watered by streams, others with ornamental trees clipped into shapes. Tame deer wandered in wooded enclosures and the whole wonderfully designed estate and the chateau, when finished, became known as 'A jewel of the French Renaissance'.

King Henri II met with a fatal accident on the jousting field in 1559, and Diane's life changed immediately. Queen Catherine promptly took the Château Chenonceaux from Diane in exchange for the Château Chaumont, which had a sinister reputation. Château d'Anet remained Diane's property until she died aged 66, seven years after Henri's untimely death. The Lordship of Anet was inherited by Diane's second daughter, Louise, who in turn gave it to her son, Charles de Lorraine, Duc d'Aumale. From then on, Anet passed to various owners (some of whom were connected to Diane) until the French Revolution in 1789, when it became vacant and subsequently neglected. Eventually, the Château d'Anet was bequeathed to the present owner by her grandmother and restoration work began. Madame, with her husband, continue the restoration of this exceptional Château.

It was another day of sunshine when we journeyed to the Château d'Anet. We felt stirred at seeing the majestic home which had once belonged to such a fascinating woman of French history as Diane de Poitiers. We lingered for a while in a secluded green dell and imagined the shades of Diane and Henri, close together, gliding past unaware of the present-day and of us.

A commemoration of our visit is an elegant silk scarf bought from the charming boutique at Château d'Anet. It is especially significant when one examines the intricate symbolic designs which celebrate the love story of Henri and Diane. Designed by Chalmette of Paris, the cream-white surface has a graceful all-over pattern of stylised fleur-de-lis — the ancient motif of the royal houses of France. The stalks merge into delicately trailing delineated straps and buckles, representing a bridle. In the centre of the scarf are the words 'Diane de Poitiers', and beneath is her personal emblem of three interlocked crescent moons, which are repeated. The border has a design of swirling foliage and lily or iris blooms, either one thought to be the origin of the heraldic flower. The well-known interfaced initials of H and D are clearly seen, which the couple used frequently on their possessions and gifts to each other.

BELOW: *The intricate and symbolic designs on this scarf celebrate the love story of Henri and Diane.*

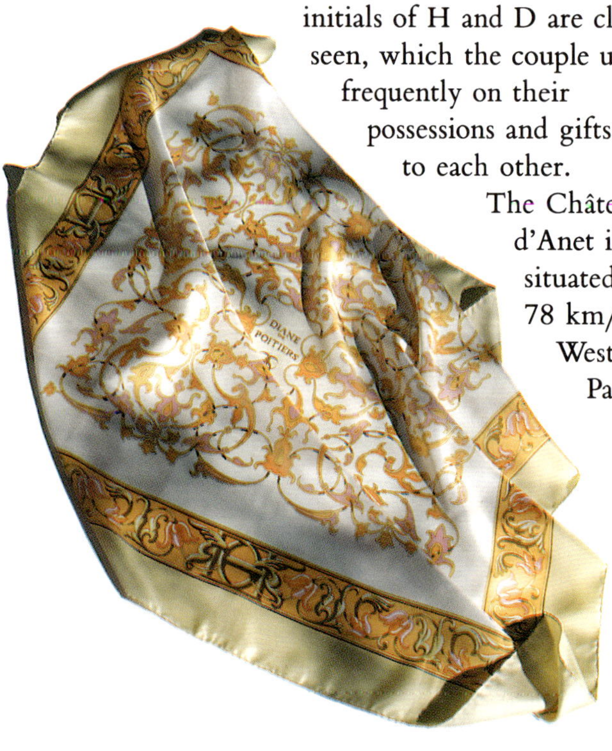

The Château d'Anet is situated 78 km/48 m West of Paris and 16 km/10 m from Dreux. Take the Autoroute A13 (towards Rouen), leave it at Mantes Sud, then follow the D 928 (towards Dreux), where you will also find that there are many good restaurants available in and around Anet.

The Chateau d'Anet is a member of 'La Demeure Historique', 57 Quai de la Tournelle, 75005 Paris, Telephone 43.29.02.86. 'La Demeure Historique' is a non-profit organisation with a membership of 1 500 privately owned historic monuments, mostly opened to the public. Under the aegis of 'La Demeure Historique', the owners of these chateaux have achieved a vast program of restoration and furtherance of public awareness and cultural renaissance.

For further information, please apply to:
Château d'Anet, 28260 ANET
Eure-et-Loir, France.
Telephone 37.41.90.07.

The château is open to the public between 1 November and 31 March, Saturdays from 2 p.m. to 5 p.m., Sundays and holidays from 10 a.m. to 11.30 a.m., and from 2 p.m. to 5 p.m. Between 1 April and 31 October it is open every afternoon except Tuesday, from 2.30 p.m. to 6.30 p.m., and on Sundays and holidays from 2.30 p.m. to 6.30 p.m. The château is also available for groups, on demand, in the morning. The Funerary Chapel has the same opening hours.

Château de Chenonceaux, Loire Valley, France

The fairy-tale Château de Chenonceaux (often referred to as a 'Castle') was one of the superb gifts King Henri II of France gave to his idolised royal mistress Diane de Poitiers. However, after Henri's death in 1559, the dowager Queen Catherine de Medici seized the long-desired castle for herself in exchange for the Château of Chaumont.

Chenonceaux was originally built in 1513 on the foundations of a fortified mill for Thomas Bohier, Controller of the Royal Treasury under Francois I. The tower, known as the *Tour des Marques*, is seen as you reach the castle, and still bears the name of the family who owned the mill in the thirteenth century. After the death of Thomas Bohier in 1535, his son Antoine relinquished the castle to the crown in settlement of debts contracted by his father.

A long avenue of plane trees forms an imposing entrance to the castle. The scene then opens out on to an imaginative building with clustered turrets and tall arches across the River Cher. It looks not only grand but breathtaking. Set in acres of ground there are straight avenues of trees and formal parterres are outlined in clipped santolina (cotton lavender) or in flowering lavender (*Lavandula augustifolia*). Intersecting pathways are marked at their junctions by topiary pruned into pyramids and there is now a 'Diane Garden' and

BELOW: *Château de Chenonceaux, a site of passion and jealousy.*

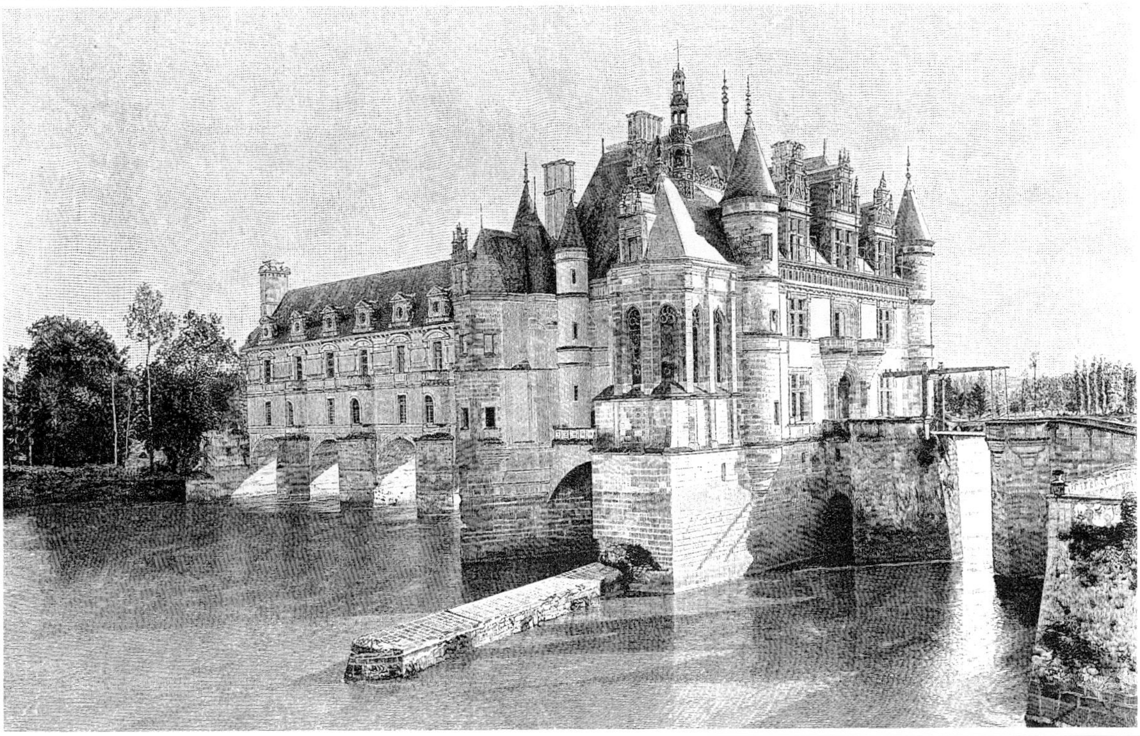

a 'Catherine's Garden'. The earlier gardens are said to have been ordered and laid out by Diane.

The interior of Chenonceaux is charming and majestic, commanding both awe and respect. It bears the mark of Diane de Poitiers, who made many improvements to the Château and who had commissioned Philibert de l'Orme to build the bridge connecting the castle to the garden. There is a Diane de Poitier's Room, which was used by Diane when she stayed here — the fireplace is by Jean Goujon, the Henri II armchairs are upholstered in Cordoba leather and the Flemish tapestries date from the sixteenth century.

The presence of Catherine de Medici is also felt strongly. She came frequently to Chenonceaux when she was regent, and made her own additions and alterations to the mansion. You can see her Green Study and the library. The superb gallery, which she had constructed, is 59 metres/65 yards long and spans the River Cher. It is thought that the gallery had already been planned by Diane and her architect de l'Orme. There is a grand drawing room, the room of the Five Queens, a chapel, a room of Catherine de Medici, and many other significant rooms. Not to be missed is the Waxworks Museum, filled with richly dressed regal figures of the men and women of the past who had close links with Chenonceaux.

The Menier family, who have owned Chenonceaux since 1913, have carried out considerable restoration work with a view to keeping the original appearance of the facade. Visitors will appreciate, as we did, the tea and the fascinating shop where a treasure chest of inexpensive memorabilia of Chenonceaux and its bygone glories may be bought.

Château de Villandry

Journeying from one garden to another in France, we often stopped for picnic lunches on the way. One day we sat on a grassy bank beside the River Eure while enjoying *déjeuner* and looked at the remains of a twelfth century wooden bridge, while at one end an ancient half-timbered house straddled the water, possibly once a busy toll-house. In villages where we had spent the previous night, there were small shops and open-air fruit stalls. We bought *baguettes*, still warm from the baker's oven, fresh cheeses, fruit — mostly a punnet of fragrant, velvety raspberries — and wine.

It was exciting to arrive at the Château Villandry, renowned for its unique gardens. Seen first at the entrance is the enormous château, a gracious and imposing building begun in 1533 by Jean le Breton, Secretary of State to François I of France. The estate changed hands several times during the following centuries, until Dr Joachim Carvallo bought the château and its land in 1906. The grounds were run-down and the beauty of the original building had been marred by architecturally out-of-character additions. Dr Carvallo began the long task of restoring the chateau to its former style, methodically re-planning the extensive gardens. Villandry covers 7 hectares (17 acres), including the buildings and courtyards. It is believed that Dr Carvallo was inspired by mediaeval engravings to devise the kitchen garden in the semblance of cloistered garths where monks tended herbs, vegetables and flowers. Dr Carvallo's concepts for the gardens today are carried on brilliantly by his grandson and his grandson's wife Monsieur and Madame Carvallo.

It is said that Villandry is the most French of all the gardens in France, having remained untouched by prevailing fashions over several hundred years since the Renaissance, fashions such as Le Notre's vistas and the English romantic style. It has also been described as the 'ultimate kitchen garden'.

The far-sighted design of this amazing estate is to be marvelled at, especially when you consider the year-round planning that results in the displays that make Villandry so famous. One admires the patterns of neat box potagers encompassing superb vegetables — just as pleasing to the eye as beautiful flowers — and the extent of espaliered apple and pear trees trained along rustic trellises. There are also impeccable topiary yews, avenues of pleached limes, paths of pale sand, arbours, standard red roses, a vast herb garden with all kinds of named herbs growing within tidy beds separated by fine gravel paths, and semi-circular rose-covered arbours

BELOW: *Representations of tragic love at Chateau de Villandry: this* jardin d'amour *combines shapes of blades and daggers, while red flowers bleed red blood onto its stark lines.*

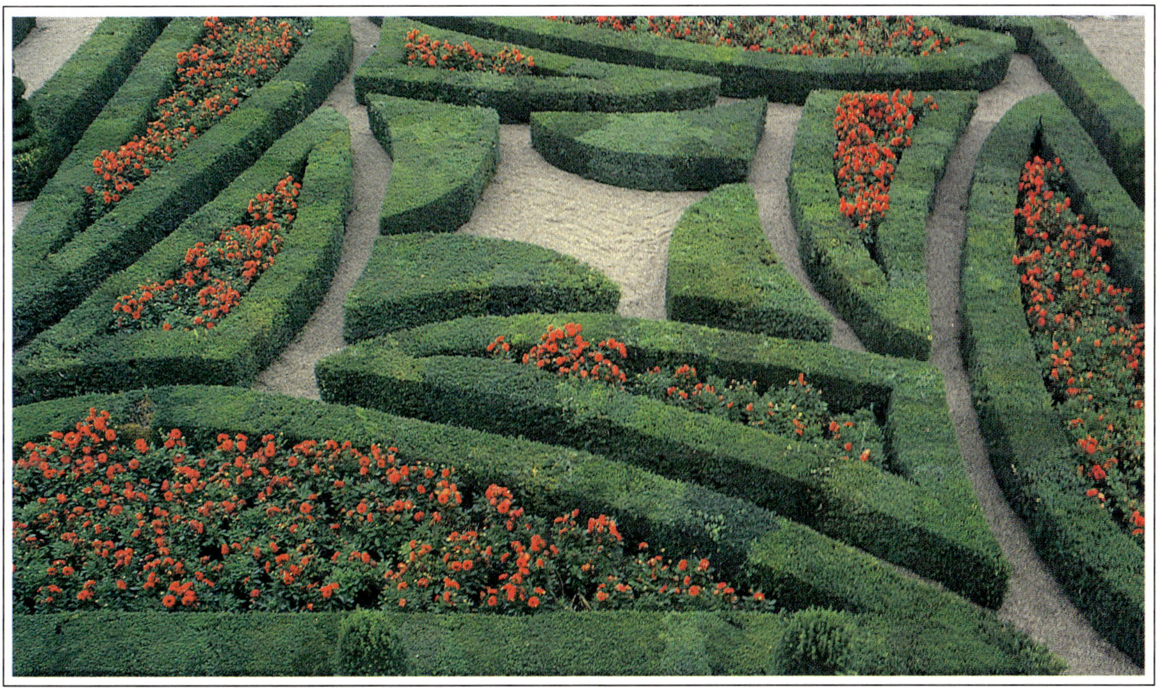

placed at intersections where one may sit and absorb the surroundings, and remember them long afterwards.

The secret of Villandry's popularity is that everyone — garden enthusiasts or not — can relate to vegetables, fruit and herbs, however unusual. The manner of planting within intricately shaped potagers and the fashioning of disciplined trees is complex, but not too much for the mind to grasp. Every plant that grows is thriving and healthy, repaying the constant care lavished on them, while the whole garden gives the same feeling of pleasure one has when entering a well-kept house where the floors are clean, the furniture shines and the copper gleams, and all is in order.

A booklet that enumerates the twelve month gardening program explains that the terraced gardens are on three levels: the kitchen garden is at the lowest level; the ornamental gardens, which extend into the herb gardens, are at the middle level; and the water gardens are at the highest level. The kitchen garden consists of nine vegetable patches all identical in size and enclosed in box, but different in design. Two plans have to be prepared each year, and all the gardeners take part under the direction of Mme Carvallo. After the first crop has been picked different vegetables are planted for rotation. At the same time composting, weeding, pruning, trimming, watering and many other tasks are consistently performed.

It is revealing to learn that Villandry is almost self-sufficient. It has its own source of water, three heated greenhouses, a tunnel, 'forcing' or cold frames, and propagates more than 90 per cent of the flower and vegetable plants. The box are trimmed with electric clippers, taking four men three weeks to neaten the low box hedges in the kitchen garden, and one month for the high box in the ornamental gardens: this is done twice a year. Nothing is wasted at Villandry; the vegetables go to the

OPPOSITE: *Form, colour and style combine and contrast at Villandry: here, you can see pumpkins, standard roses and begonias in a potager, together producing a vibrant garden.*

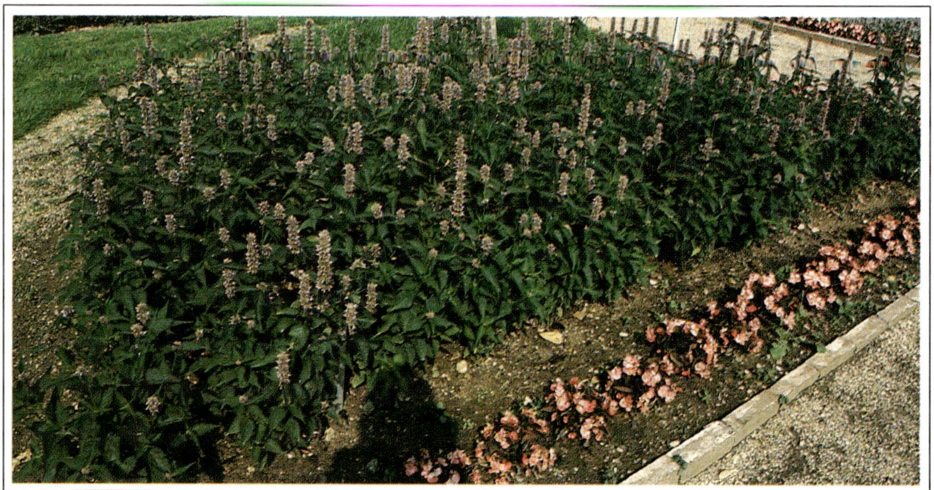

RIGHT: *The secret of Villandry's popularity is that everyone — garden enthusiast or not — can relate to vegetables, fruit and herbs.*

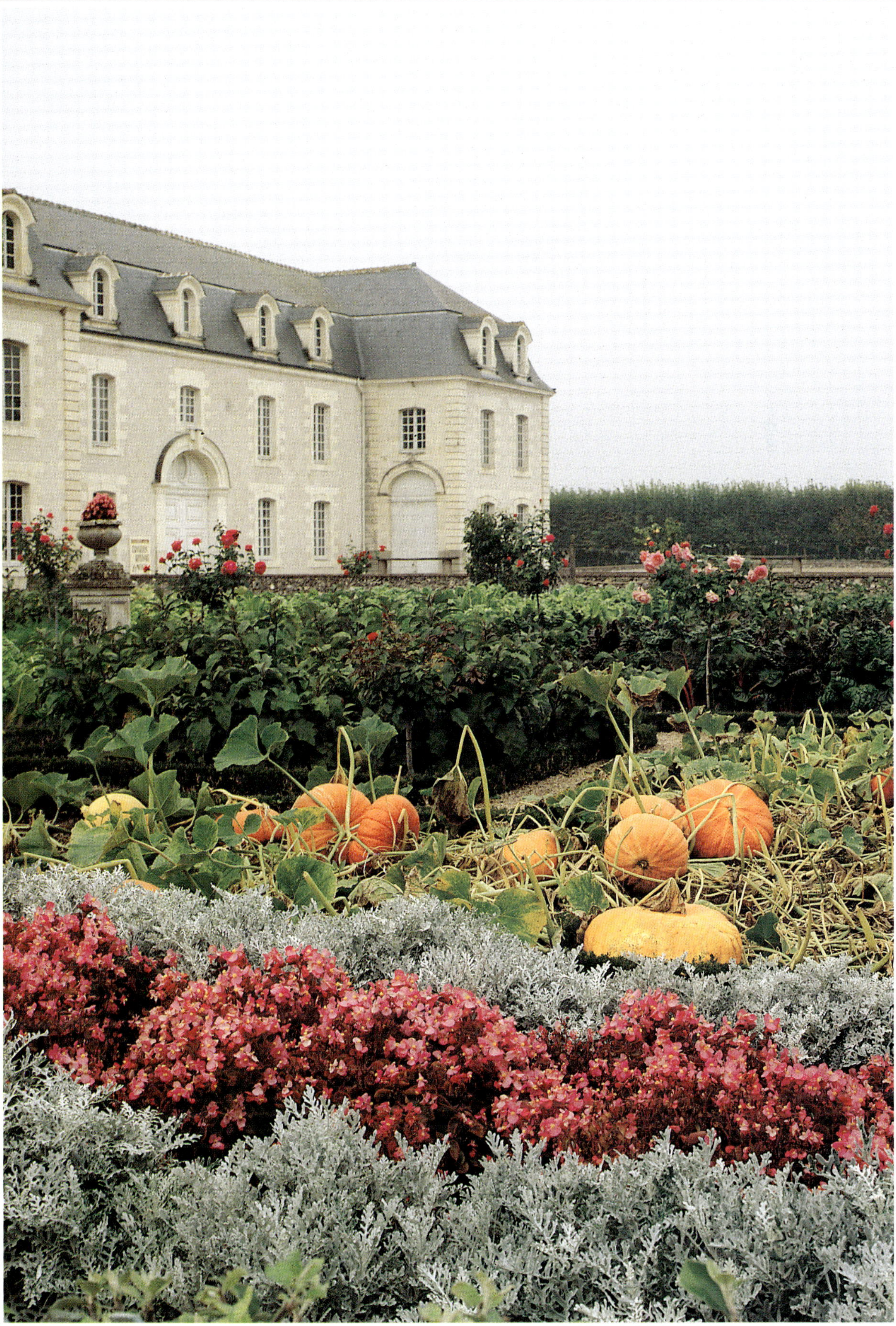

owner's family and the people that work at the château. What is not used goes into a compost, which will eventually return to the garden as mulch.

Before we left Villandry we were taken inside the splendid château and viewed the gardens from above — a dazzling sight. A guide gave an explanatory talk while showing us slides of the garden taken during the four seasons. The vegetables in the box-hedge potagers are changed in spring, summer and autumn; in winter there was an enchanting picture of powdery snow sparkling on green box.

Claude Monet's Garden at Giverny near Vernon

Monet often said that nothing in the world interested him but his painting and his flowers.

We were indeed fortunate to realise our dream of visiting the famous garden which had once belonged to Claude Monet, the illustrious French Impressionist painter, born in 1840. Thanks to the Institut de France (or the Académie des Beaux-Arts), Monet's beloved house and garden are finally in perfect condition. The artist died in 1926. Fresh paint and repairs to the house are kept up and plantings and colour schemes for the garden are carried out just as Monet planned and planted them during his lifetime. The changing seasons bring different flowers as others finish; colours complement the time of year and, except in mid-winter, the garden overflows with blossoms. In spring, for instance, my cousin Elizabeth saw a multitude of tulips in different shades from luminous white streaked with amethyst to pale shell-pink, carmine and claret, their smooth lantern-blooms gleaming gently. Textures, as well as hues, were of utmost importance to Monet, the tulip beds being closely underplanted with delicately shaggy magenta-coloured English daisies (*Bellis perennis*) or tufts of sky-blue forget-me-nots. Friends told us they once saw the garden in autumn when it was all gold, copper and bronze.

It was mid-summer when we arrived, and stepping into the garden the senses were immediately stimulated by the impact of colour — dazzling, original, yet harmonious. First, rising upwards and making a statement was the solid two-storey house with its crushed-brick-pink facade and white trim. Then came a vision of bright leaf-green wooden shutters at every window. A stairway led from the green front door to the garden, with white standard daisies in full bloom on either side. In front of the house was a long, green metal frame with arched supports densely wrapped in roses, cream-buff and coral-pink. The special shade of green paint used at Giverny was the impressionist colour Monet wanted so that it blended with the garden foliage.

The garden, covering

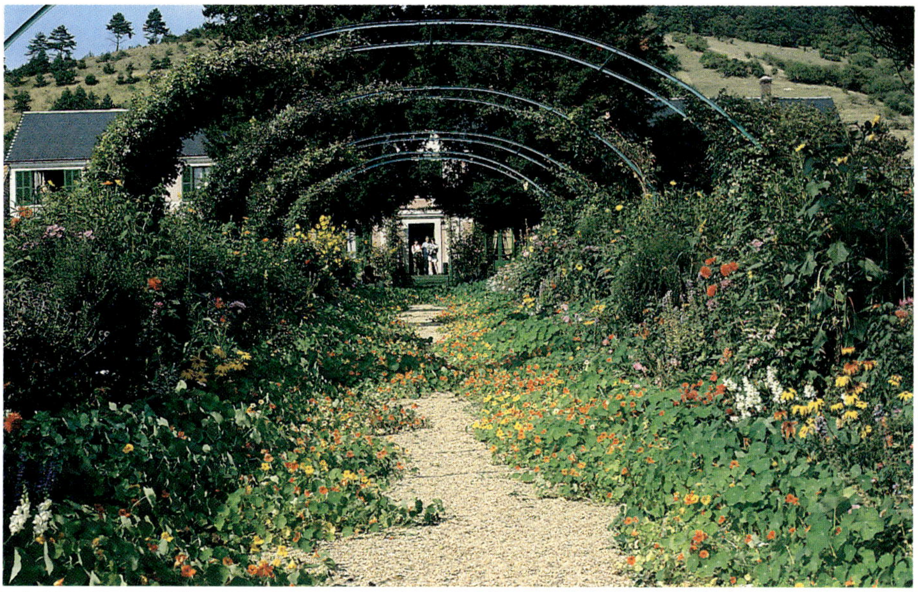

LEFT: *Monet often said that nothing in the world interested him but his painting and his flowers.*

approximately 1 hectare/2.5 acres, is divided into rooms, all quite different, each with its own character and glistening colour, a mirror-image of Monet's own paintings. He disliked formality in his garden, and designed it packed with a brilliant display of flowers. On our visit the earlier tulips had been replaced in front of the pink house by an immense bed of vermillion geraniums, the adjacent garden brimmed with pink geraniums and above them were ranks of standard roses in the same tone.

In another section a wide herbaceous border was planted against a grey stone wall, with many kinds of lilies in variations of yellow, apricot and orange. Among them were delphiniums, peonies, lupins, poppies, wallflowers, Canterbury bells and cornflowers — explosions of pink, purple, amber, gold, blue and white, all in accord. Roses in a variety of colours and shapes bloomed everywhere: sturdy shrub roses, standard roses trained on metal rings, roses clambering up poles or trees, and still more wreathed around metal hoops, forming tunnels of scented tapestry. Walking further on there were jewel-bright nasturtiums joyously tumbling onto the pale-gold gravel path.

In his later more prosperous years Monet was able to enjoy good food. 'For the benefit of his table . . . Monet would grow herbs, spices, and other kitchen plants from the Midi, all of which [he] adored . . .'

Probably the best known feature at Giverny is the Water Garden. An underground walkway runs under a busy road that now divides this part of the garden from the rest. Monet had been inspired to make a water garden after visiting Paris and an exhibition of Japanese prints depicting exotic plants, still water

OPPOSITE TOP: *Descendants of Monet's waterlilies.*

OPPOSITE BOTTOM: *Red geraniums provide a splash of colour at Giverny.*

and bridges. He was eventually given permission to divert part of the River Eure to renew the water in the proposed pools so that he could grow his aquatic plants successfully. As one enters into this completely new world the atmosphere transmutes to the secluded quiet of screening trees and gently moving water with its changing reflections of sky and plants. On the ground and banks are willows, masses of heather, ferns, azaleas and rhododendrons. Winding paths lead one past clumps of bamboo, irises, tamarisks and roses, to the waterlilies of every known variety sown in the pond, their flat pads supporting white, rose, mauve and green flowers. You cross the green Japanese bridge hung with wisteria to the other side, and to another bend in the path where the stream bends too, and there are more waterlilies, more reflections, more trees and more flowers guarding this hidden, secret region.

Claude Monet is one of the few great innovative painters who achieved recognition in his lifetime, and gained the means not only to buy his house and garden at Giverny, but to make the improvements he envisaged, and to maintain the property.

However, fame did not come quickly. Monet persevered with his unconventional style, which was original and against the traditional manner, even though he was ridiculed and laughed at whenever he exhibited his work. He and his first wife Camille and their elder son suffered poverty and near-starvation for at least ten years. Camille died not long after the birth of their second son, and before Claude received acknowledgment for his work. His family begged him many times to return to a comfortable and secure life at Le Havre and their wholesale grocery business, however, Monet was obsessed with his painting. As a boy, he showed talent as an artist and made pocket money by drawing comic caricatures of the people at Le Havre. Then Eugène Boudin (1824–1898), a struggling artist of great promise, with a new approach to painting, saw Monet's parodies in a shop window, and discerned the gift beneath the clever sketches. Boudin met Claude, and together they went to the countryside to paint. Monet said later that 'It was as if a veil was torn from my eyes; I understood what painting could be.'

Claude Monet became known as the father of Impressionism. His one desire was to paint his impression of a subject at a particular moment of the day; to capture the light, the air, and the very vibration of the fleeting second. With his technique of tiny brush strokes in colours as he perceived them through the sharpness of his eye and his extraordinary sense of light he succeeded in painting on canvas subtle colours of the ever-changing atmosphere, so ephemeral that it could never be the same again. This is why Monet painted one subject many times, for example, his haystacks, Rouen Cathedral, and most famous of all, his waterlily series.

Monet spent many happy years at Giverny, marrying his second wife Alice Hoschedé, a widow and an old family friend, in 1892. One of Alice's daughters, Blanche, married Monet's son Jean, so with the children from both marriages and their spouses and children too, the house at Giverny was filled with family and friends.

Sadly, Alice Monet died in 1911, and Jean Monet in 1914. Blanche stayed on with Claude and was a great comfort to him, especially as his eyesight was failing from cataracts. He still painted in a large new studio, which was built on to the house, urged by his friend Georges Clemenceau. Monet now worked mainly from memory, and began his waterlily series, *Les Décorations des Nymphéas*, described as 'great abstract masterpieces'.

When Claude Monet died, Clemenceau hurried to attend his friend's funeral. On finding his coffin draped in black, he exclaimed 'No black for Monet' and replaced the cloth with a 'bright multi-coloured shawl'.

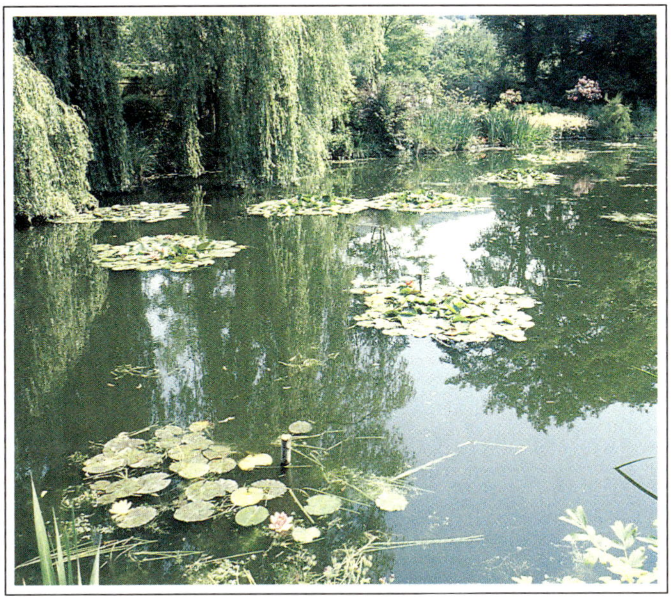

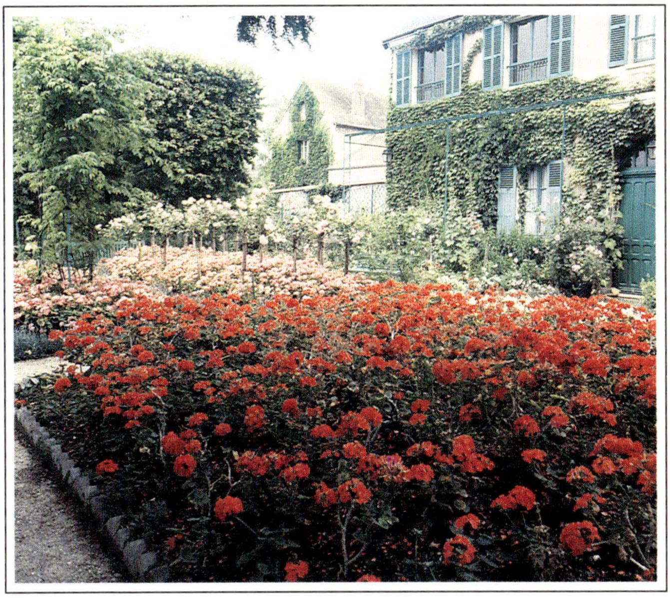

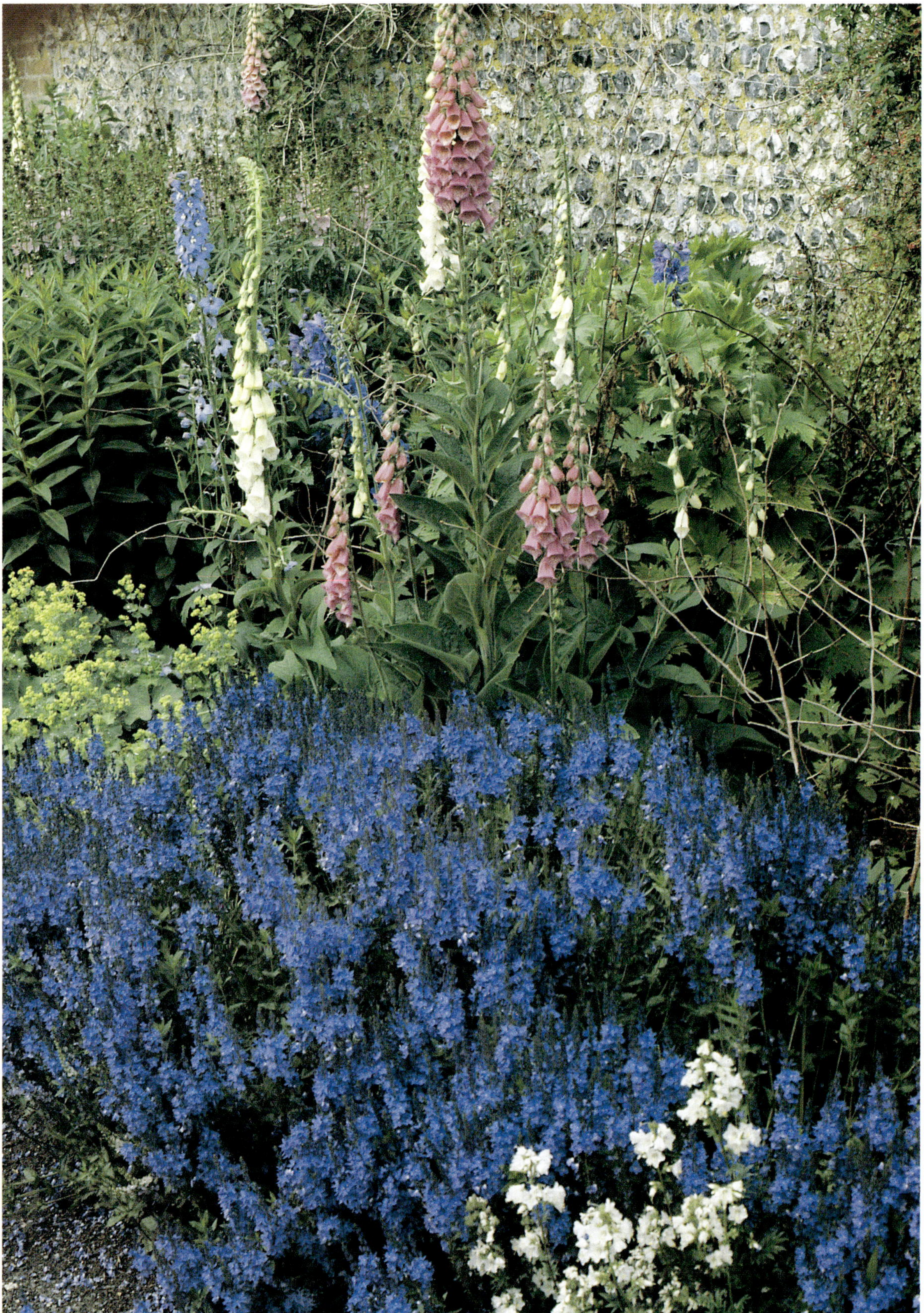

ABOVE: *Tintinhull Manor.*

BIBLIOGRAPHY

This list is not intended to be comprehensive but, rather, highlights some of the many books we found useful. For gardening information, and detailed discussion of the uses of herbs and ways of growing them—in gardens or in containers—see our *Hemphill's Book of Herbs*, Kevin Weldon & Associates, 1990.

We hope you enjoy further investigations of the themes of *The Fragrant Garden*, as explored in this list:

Apicius *De Re Coquinaria*, trans Joseph Dommers Vehling as *Cookery and Dining in Imperial Rome*, Dover, 1977

Bayard, Tania *Sweet Herbs and Sundry Flowers*, The Metropolitan Museum of Art, New York, David R. Godine Publisher, Boston, 1985

Betjamin, Jon *John Masefield—Selected Poems*, Heinemann, 1978

Bradley, Marion *The Mists of Avalon*, Sphere Books, London, 1984

Cooper, Guy & Clive Boursnell & Gordon Taylor *English Herb Gardens*, Weidenfeld and Nicolson, London, 1986

Fox, Levi *The Shakespearian Garden*, [Issued on behalf of the Shakespeare Birthplace Trust], Norwich, England, 1954

Fox, Robin Lane *An Illustrated Garden Book*, Michael Joseph, 1986

Glendinning, Victoria *Vita: The Life of V. Sackville-West*, Weldenfeld and Nicolson, London, 1983

Hemphill, John & Rosemary *Hemphill's Book of Herbs*, Kevin Weldon & Associates Pty Ltd, Sydney, 1990

Jekyll, Gertrude *A Gardener's Testament*, Papermac, 1984

Gardens for Small Country Houses, Country Life Library, London, 1912

Jellicoe, Jeffrey & Susan Jeffrey & Patrick Goode & Michael Lancaster *The Oxford Companion to Gardens*, Oxford University Press, Oxford and New York, 1986

Leyel, C. F. *Diet and Commonsense*, Chatto and Windus, London, 1936

Elixirs of Life, Faber and Faber, London, 1948

Magic of Herbs, Cope, London, 1932

Compassionate Herbs, Faber and Faber, London, 1947

Culpeper's English Physician and Complete Herbal, Lane Cove, 1971

Macoboy, Stirling *Perennials for Bed and Border*, Sydney, Lansdowne, 1983

Mare, Walter de la *Collected Poems*, Faber and Faber, London, 1979

Masefield, John *Chaucer*, Cambridge University Press, 1931

Collected Poems, London, Heinemann, 1936

Rohde, Eleanour Sinclair *Gardens of Delight*, The Medici Society Ltd London, 1974

Old English Gardening Books, Chiswick Press, London, 1974

The Scented Garden, London, 1931

Shakespeare's Wild Flowers, Fairy Folklore, Gardens, Herb Gatherers of Simples and Bee Lore, London, 1935

Scott-James, Anne *Sissinghurst: The Making of a Garden*, London, Michael Joseph, 1975

Tennyson, Alfred (Lord) *Poems*, Collins, London and Glasgow, 1954

Watson, Sara Ruth *V. Sackville-West*, Twayne, New York, 1972

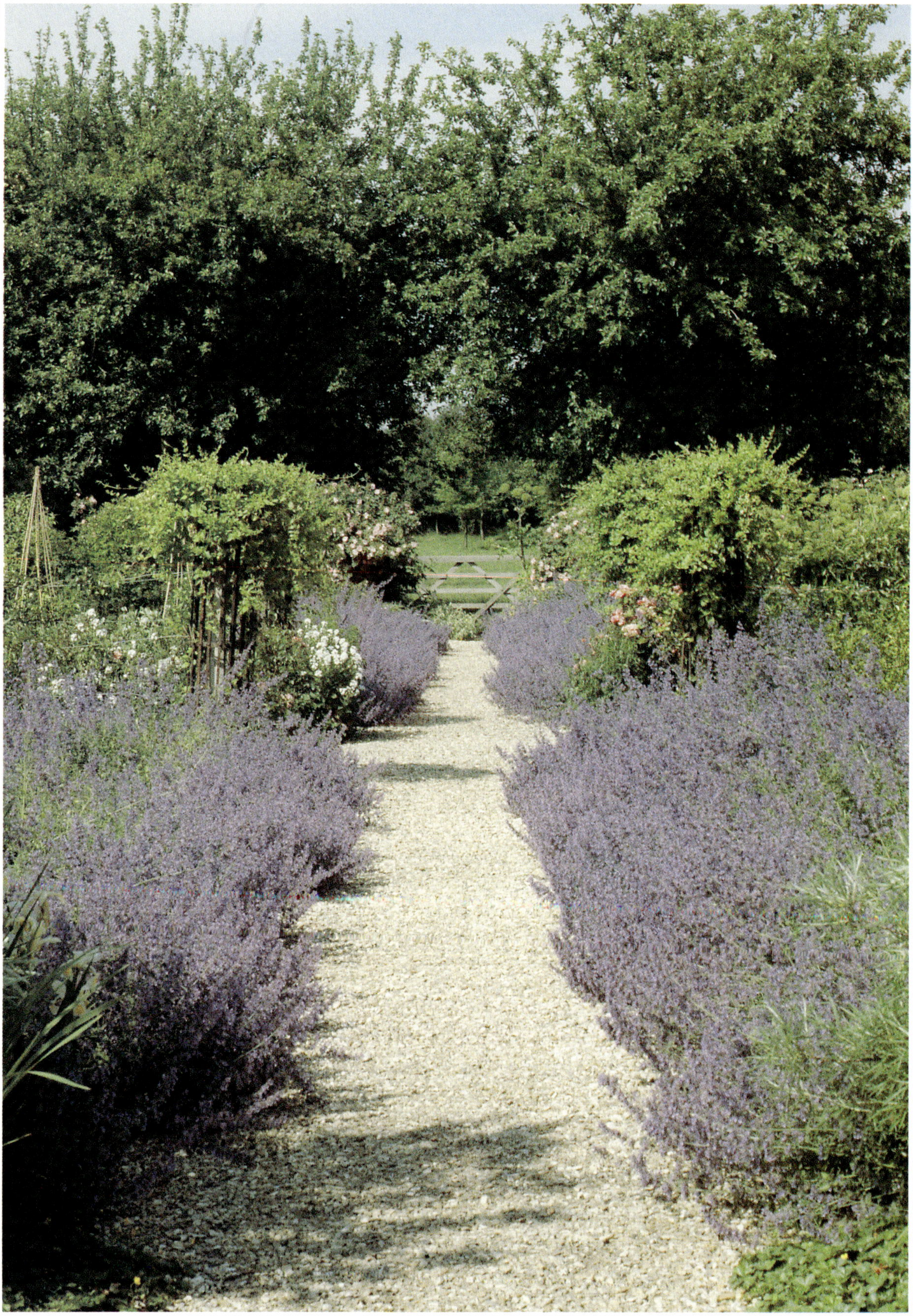

ABOVE: *Lavender and foxgloves.*

PICTORIAL SOURCES

The photographs in *The Fragrant Garden* were taken by John Hemphill, with the following exceptions:

Frontispiece ~ Château de Villandry c Tony Mott

Dedication ~ Collection of herbs in pots c Harry Smith Collection

PAGES

x–1 ~ Wisley RHS Garden, Surrey c Andy Williams

3 ~ Druids c Mary Evans Picture Library

4–5 ~ Sissinghurst Castle Gardens c Pamela Harper

8 ~ Pompeii, Casa del Frutteto c Scala, Venice

10 ~ Witches c Fortean Picture Library

11 ~ Knebworth House c Heather Angel

12 ~ Sixteenth century gypsies c Mary Evans Picture Library

14 ~ Arthur and Guinevere c Mary Evans Picture Library

15 ~ Arthur in Avalon c Mary Evans Picture Library

18–19 ~ Fossanova Abbey c Tony Mott

20 ~ Jenkyn Palace, Hampshire c Heather Angel

21 ~ With thanks to the State Library of New South Wales

23 ~ With thanks to the State Library of New South Wales

25 ~ c Scala, Venice

28–29 ~ Palazzo Piccolomini, Pienza, Italy c Heather Angel

30 ~ c Lauros-Giraudon

31 ~ Sixteenth century German herb garden c Mary Evans/Fawcett Library

32–33 ~ New Place, Stratford c Andrew Lawson

36 ~ With thanks to the State Library of New South Wales

37 ~ Sixteenth century druggist c Mary Evans Picture Library

39 ~ Herb wheel c Harry Smith

40 ~ *Digitalis pupurea* by Ligozzi Jacopo c Scala, Venice

41 ~ John Tradescant, Junior and Senior c Mary Evans Picture Library

42–43 ~ Drummond Castle, Perthshire c Heather Angel

44 ~ Sissinghurst c Pamela Harper

46–47 ~ Sissinghurst c Andy Williams

49 ~ c Mary Evans Picture Library

50–51 ~ Barnsley House c George Wright

51 ~ Mosely Old Hall, Wolverhampton c Heather Angel

54–55 ~ North Spain c Heather Angel

56 ~ c Heather Angel

58–59 ~ Villa Gamberaia c George Wright

61 ~ Chenies Manor Hosue, Herts c Heather Angel

62 ~ Topiary Elephant c Ian Hemphill

64 ~ Bramdean House, Glos. c Heather Angel

67 ~ Cranborne Manor, Dorset c Heather Angel

69 ~ Garzoni, Collodi, Italy c Heather Angel

70 ~ Villa Celsa c George Wright

71 ~ Doddington Hall c George Wright

73 ~ Balneath Manor, Chailey c Harry Smith

74–75 ~ Kew Palace, London c Harry Smith Collection

76 ~ Château de Villandry c Heather Angel

77 ~ Cranborne Manor c George Wright

79 ~ Scotney Castle c Harry Smith

80–81 ~ Hatfield Herbs c George Wright

84 ~ Horsted Palace Gardens c Heather Angel

86 ~ Rousham Palace Gardens, Oxford c Heather Angel

87 ~ Villa Celsa c George Wright

88–89 ~ Elvaston Castle Country Park c Heather Angel

90 ~ Packam Park Herb Garden c Harry Smith

91 ~ Castello Balduino c Tony Mott

93 ~ Barnsley House c George Wright

94–95 ~ Barnsley House c George Wright

98–99 ~ Great Dixter c Lorna Rose

101 ~ Wrest Park House and Gardens c English Heritage

102–103 ~ Leeds Castle c Andy Williams

106–107 ~ Leeds Castle c Andy Williams

109 ~ Sissinghurst c Lorna Rose

111 ~ Sissinghurst c Andy Williams

112–113 ~ Sissinghurst c Andy Williams

114 ~ Sissinghurst c Tony Mott

116 ~ Chelsea Physic Garden c Tony Mott

117 ~ Sixteenth Century Physic Garden c Mary Evans Picture Library

120 ~ Ligozzi Jacopo *Angelica arcangelica* c Scala, Venice

123 ~ Château de Villandry c Tony Mott

126 ~ Château de Chenonceaux c Heather Angel

127 ~ Diane de Poitiers c Mary Evans Picture Library

130 ~ c Melanie Fedderson

131 ~ Château de Chenonceaux c Mary Evans

133 ~ Château de Villandry c Heather Angel

135 ~ Château de Villandry c Heather Angel

137 ~ Giverny c Tony Mott

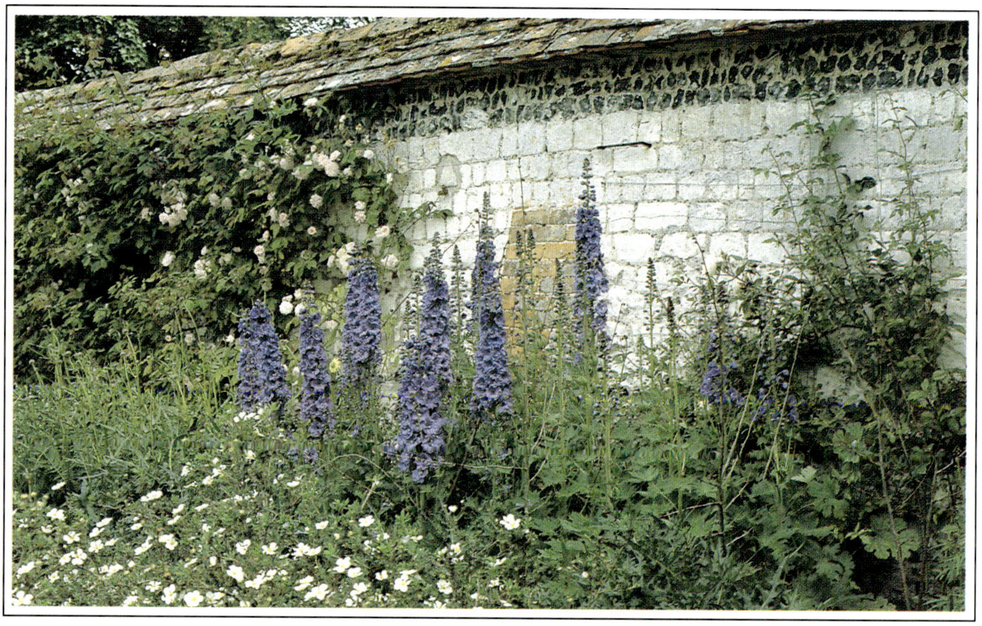

ABOVE: *Foxgloves complement an old stone wall.*

INDEX

Entries in **bold** *refer to photographs.*

N